When I first spotted Pat Legako in a deliverance seminar, I knew she was a *winner.* She soaked up the teaching and I could see wheels turning in her head. Things were making sense to her and I knew she was going to be using what she was learning. I also spotted her in seminars run by colleagues from other ministries and I knew she was out to learn all that she could on the broadest spectrum of topics within the field of deliverance. And learn she did.

In the past, Pat has been able to come along to some of our Global Harvest Ministries' deliverance seminars to assist the ministry team as they pray for people needing hands on, immediate, help. On one such occasion, a woman along with a young teen son approached me for prayer and I immediately went to Pat to see if she'd be willing to work with this distraught woman whose son was schizophrenic. Pat realized that it would take time and special work so she arranged to see these people back in Oklahoma for an extended couple of days of prayer. She learned all she could about the mental disorder and prayed in the light of the scientific evidence that she and her husband uncovered – with dramatic results. A barely functional individual turned into a teen having the ability to concentrate and study and drastically improve his behavior in social settings. What a joy to hear of this breakthrough!

Pat is a no-nonsense nurse, married to a no-nonsense medical doctor in the family practice field. They thoroughly understand physical healing both as a science and in the spiritual sense. They understand and are used to seeing the miraculous. They delve into ways to blend the two when it comes to ministry and they are uniquely qualified to do this.

Doris M. Wagner, Doctor of Practical Ministry
Global Harvest Ministry
Colorado Springs, Colorado
May 2006

DELIVERANCE

PAT LEGAKO & CYNDI GRIBBLE

DELIVERANCE
RESCUING GOD'S PEOPLE

DEVELOPING AND OPERATING THE MINISTRY

TATE PUBLISHING & *Enterprises*

TATE PUBLISHING
& Enterprises

Tate Publishing is committed to excellence in the publishing industry. Our staff of highly trained professionals, including editors, graphic designers, and marketing personnel, work together to produce the very finest books available. The company reflects the philosophy established by the founders, based on Psalms 68:11,

"THE LORD GAVE THE WORD AND GREAT WAS THE COMPANY OF THOSE WHO PUBLISHED IT."

If you would like further information, please contact us:
1.888.361.9473 | www.tatepublishing.com
TATE PUBLISHING *& Enterprises*, LLC | 127 E. Trade Center Terrace
Mustang, Oklahoma 73064 USA

TABLE OF CONTENTS

FOREWORD 9

INTRODUCTION 11

PART ONE - THE SCRIPTURAL BASIS FOR DELIVERANCE

1 – HOLLYWOOD OR HOLY WORK? 14

2 – IN THE SHADOW OF THE CROSS 21

3 – HOODWINKED 27

PART TWO - THE BASICS OF STARTING A DELIVERANCE MINISTRY

4 – ASSEMBLING THE DELIVERANCE TEAM. 34

5 – DEALING WITH DEMONS. 41

6 – DISMANTLING DEMONIC STRUCTURES 50

PART THREE - SPECIFIC DELIVERANCE ISSUES

7 – THE MINISTRY OF FORGIVENESS 66

8 – THE ROOT OF REJECTION 76

9 – BREAKING GENERATIONAL CURSES. 86

10 – THE DANGERS OF FREEMASONRY 92

11 – SOUL TIES 97

PART FOUR - THE SPIRITUAL STRONGMEN

12 – THE STRONGMAN OF PRIDE. 106

13 – WHOREDOMS AND BONDAGE. 112

14 – SPIRIT OF DIVINATION 118

15 – FAMILIAR SPIRITS 128

16 –JEALOUSY, HEAVINESS, SORROW AND GRIEF. 133

17 – SPIRIT OF FEAR. 138

18 – LYING, SEDUCING, ERROR AND ANTICHRIST. 143

19 – DEAF AND DUMB, INFIRMITY AND DEATH. 148

20 – SPIRIT OF PERVERSION 152

PART FIVE - OTHER DEMONIC SPIRITS AND ISSUES

21 – GUILT, SHAME, LAWLESSNESS AND CRITICAL SPIRITS 160

22 – RELIGIOUS, NATIVE AMERICAN, WARRING SPIRITS, WORD CURSES AND NAMES 166

23 – ACCIDENTS AND TRAUMA 173

PART SIX - THE DELIVERANCE SESSION: STEP BY STEP

24 – UNDERSTANDING THE QUESTIONNAIRE 182

25 – PREPARING FOR DELIVERANCE 203

26 – THE PERSONAL DELIVERANCE SESSION 209

27 – TEEN DELIVERANCE 223

28 – CHILDREN'S DELIVERANCE 229

29 – AFTER CARE 236

PART SEVEN - APPENDICES

APPENDIX A

SECTION 1: THE ADULT KEY 250

SECTION 2: THE ADOLESCENT KEY 282

SECTION 3: THE CHILD'S KEY 318

SECTION 4: BATTLE PLAN TEMPLATE 346

SECTION 5: EXAMPLE BATTLE PLAN 348

APPENDIX B

SECTION 1: PRAYERS FOR SPECIFIC PURPOSES 353

SECTION 2: FREEDOM SCRIPTURES 376

APPENDIX C

SECTION 1: INSTRUCTION LETTER & SCRIPT FOR TAPE 389

SECTION 2: FORMS AND WAIVERS 401

SECTION 3: SUGGESTED READING AND TAPE LISTS 406

INDEX 409

FOREWORD

I was totally delighted when I discovered that this book was soon to be published. It is based upon a wealth of experience and borne out of one of the most outstanding local church deliverance ministries that we have in the US today.

Pat Legako and Cyndi Gribble started a deliverance ministry in their own church and were soon out and about the state of Oklahoma training others. Church on the Rock, Oklahoma City, is what I consider to be the key church leading prayer and spiritual warfare in that state. They are literally out to see all of Oklahoma saved. They sing songs about it! They pull together the statewide Oklahoma Apostolic Prayer Network, and John Benefiel does a masterful job of leading that effort. Among many other things, they work extensively to correct injustices among the White and Red People in their state and are influential to bringing this cause to the forefront on the national level as well.

So, as a church, spiritual warfare is an understood topic. It was a perfect incubator for initiating a local church deliverance ministry. I am convinced that is why God raised up Pat and Cyndi to work under John's covering in this effort.

You hold in your hands a carefully crafted textbook and manual. Its simplicity and step-by-step teaching are unusually clear. Explanations cannot be misinterpreted and I am so pleased to see this Holy Spirit led book available to the Body of Christ. It is my prayer that it becomes a major textbook for training in educational institutions and churches alike. This is a detailed, well organized, and thorough piece of work with many tools such as questionnaires, forms, sample prayers, and other instructions that have been formulated after years of experience dealing with hundreds and hundreds of people.

Beginners in deliverance ministry will be walked through step-by-step outlines and many possible cause and effect scenarios are discussed. Those that have been in deliverance ministry for years will also benefit from some of the deep insights articulated here.

Hats off to Pat and Cyndi for doing the Body of Christ this enormous service. Great will be your reward, ladies, as you see thousands helped through lives salvaged and changed and snatched from the grip of the enemy!

Doris M. Wagner, Doctor of Practical Ministry
Global Harvest Ministry
Colorado Springs, Colorado
May 2006

INTRODUCTION

Jesus is returning for a bride without spot or blemish, yet every Sunday congregations are filled with Christians with addictions to alcohol, drugs and tobacco. A recent survey suggests that the fastest growing market for pornography in America is among Christians. Christians' lives are being torn apart by divorce, abuse, and incest. Churches full of good Christian people find the fulfillment of their vision jeopardized by congregations infected by gossip, conflict, division, even sexual immorality.

We pray, study the Bible, attend services and seek God for guidance, but still these and other problems persist. What are good-intentioned, God-loving Christians, church leaders and pastors overlooking?

The accuser of the brethren, Satan, is actively pursuing the people of God and fully intends to kill, steal and destroy. The message that many Christians are missing is that self-discipline alone is not enough to stop Satan from his onslaught against the Church. Jesus told us to cast out demons in His name, but for the most part we have neglected to follow His instructions.

This book provides a basic, scripture-supported teaching on what the Bible says about Satan and demons, both before and after Calvary, and the scriptural foundation for ministry to cast out demons, or "Deliverance Ministry." *Deliverance: Rescuing God's People* also walks the reader through demonic structures, how demons gain entry and power in the lives of Christians and how to recognize them and their influence. Questions are addressed regarding how demons behave and whether we can expect furniture to levitate and heads to spin in circles. More importantly, it teaches Christians how to control demons and keep them in check.

This book presents a step-by-step, beginner's guide to establishing and operating a Deliverance Ministry in the local church. This book equips the reader to assemble the ministry team, prepare for deliverance and offers user-friendly instructions on how to handle a personal deliverance session in an orderly and controlled manner. New revelations on the role of forgiveness in deliverance and specific methods for conducting deliverance that prevent recurrence of the problem make this book unlike other texts or teachings on this subject.

Included are forms for legal waivers, questionnaires to assist in evaluating deliverance needs, descriptions of traits and tricks of specific demons, sample prayers for specific situations and instructions on After Care. The Appendix also contains training tools including the "key" to the questionnaire, exercises and sample written strategies for the session. We believe this book, along with the leading of the Holy Spirit and the Bible, will equip the reader to develop a turn-key ministry in deliverance in a church of any size.

Deliverance: Rescuing God's People was a joint effort of the two authors and the contributions of each are intertwined throughout the book in content, examples and testimonies. Because *Deliverance* is about this important instruction to the Church and not about the authors or their life stories, we felt that attempting to attribute specific passages to the specific author would create confusion and would not add value for the reader. Therefore, the book is written with one voice without distinction between the authors.

It is our prayer and belief that the Holy Spirit will provide revelation and wisdom to the reader to enable the message in this book to bear fruit in your life and ministry.

For copies of the Appendices plus the questionnaires, please log onto our website at www.DeliveranceRescuingGodsPeople.com, and follow the directions for free downloads for owners of this book.

PART ONE

THE SCRIPTURAL BASIS FOR DELIVERANCE

1 - HOLLYWOOD OR HOLY WORK?

Satan knows that he is headed to hell and his strategy is to take as many people with him as possible. But, does Satan—the personification of evil—really exist?

If so, are demons real? Are they active and present in this world? Or are they nothing more than a marketing gimmick for box-office success dreamed up by the moguls of Hollywood?

These are fair questions. And ones the world looks to the Church to answer.

In 1973, *The Exorcist* hit the big screen with never-to-be-forgotten scenes of a little girl possessed by a demon. In an effort to set her free, a Catholic priest fought against supernatural powers that threatened to overwhelm him. The world watched in horror as the child's bed levitated, her head twisted to impossible positions, she spoke chillingly in a demonic voice and vomited thick green gunk. That movie, perhaps more than any other, forced the world, and more importantly the church, to ask these questions that still echo today.

As Christians, our primary source of information must be the Holy Bible. So let's begin with whether this evil entity exists, or if he's no more than a myth passed down through the generations to scare bad little boys and girls (and adults) into some semblance of good behavior.

In the King James Version of the Bible, the name Satan is mentioned 54 times. The term devil or devils is mentioned 115 times. As we will see later, some of the names ascribed to this evil force are Lucifer, Satan,

Devil, Accuser, Tempter, the king of Tyre, the Prince of Light and Beelzebub. Clearly, the Bible has a lot to say on the subject.

IN THE BEGINNING

We get a glimpse into Satan's beginnings from the Prophet Ezekiel who refers to him as the king of Tyre. According to Ezekiel, Satan began life as an angel, created by God as an Anointed Cherub, perfect in beauty and full of wisdom. At that time, before the earth was formed, this creature appeared to be a musician and a musical instrument all in one. The Bible says he was covered with beautiful stones. A timbrel (small drum or tambourine) and pipe (a type of wind instrument) were built into him. Ezekiel also says that this angelic being was cast out of the mountain of God, because he became corrupted by his own beauty. After falling to earth, he was present in the Garden of Eden.

The account is found in Ezekiel 28:12–19 (NKJV):

> Son of man, take up a lamentation for the king of Tyre, and say to him, "Thus says the Lord God: 'You were the seal of perfection, full of wisdom and perfect in beauty. You were in Eden, the garden of God; every precious stone was your covering: the sardius, topaz, and diamond, beryl, onyx, and jasper, sapphire, turquoise, and emerald with gold. The workmanship of your timbrels and pipes was prepared for you on the day you were created. You were the anointed cherub who covers; I established you; you were on the holy mountain of God; you walked back and forth in the midst of fiery stones.

> You were perfect in your ways from the day you were created, till iniquity was found in you. By the abundance of your trading you became filled with violence within, and you sinned; therefore I cast you as a profane thing out of the mountain of God; and I destroyed you, O covering cherub, from the midst of the fiery stones. Your heart was lifted up because of your beauty; you corrupted your wisdom for the

sake of your splendor; I cast you to the ground, I laid you before kings, that they might gaze at you.

You defiled your sanctuaries by the multitude of your iniquities, by the iniquity of your trading; therefore I brought fire from your midst; it devoured you, and I turned you to ashes upon the earth in the sight of all who saw you. All who knew you among the peoples are astonished at you; you have become a horror, and shall be no more forever.'"

FALLING STAR

The prophet Isaiah revealed that Satan's original name had been Lucifer, which means "brilliant star" or "bringing light." After his fall from heaven, Lucifer was called Satan, which means, "contrary, adversary, enemy or accuser." According to Isaiah, the sin that cost Lucifer everything was pride. Isaiah's account is as follows:

How art thou fallen from heaven, O Lucifer, son of the morning! how art thou cut down to the ground, which didst weaken the nations! For thou hast said in thine heart, I will ascend into heaven, I will exalt my throne above the stars of God: I will sit also upon the mount of the congregation, in the sides of the north: I will ascend above the heights of the clouds; I will be like the most High. Yet thou shalt be brought down to hell, to the sides of the pit. (Isaiah 14:12–16, KJV)

According to the Bible, long before Jesus came to earth in the form of a man, He saw Satan fall from heaven. In Luke 10:18 (KJV), Jesus told his disciples, "I beheld Satan as lightning fall from heaven."

After his fall from heaven, Satan—now referred to as a serpent in the Garden of Eden—played a key role in enticing Adam and Eve to sin. Their sin caused them to be driven from the Garden and forced to live under a curse (Genesis 3:1–24). It's clear that all the inhabitants of the world are still living to some degree under the curse brought on by the sin of our ultimate ancestors, Adam and Eve. From a world view, Satan created havoc that is still present today.

The book of Revelation describes four names ascribed to the fallen angel. Revelation 12:9–11 refers to him as an old Serpent, the Devil, Satan and the Accuser of the Brethren. It also gives us two important keys: One key is how he spends his time. It says that he accuses the brethren (us!) before the Lord day and night. The second key is how we can overcome him—by the blood of Jesus and our words.

THE ACCUSER

Having established that Satan exists, let's take a glimpse at how he appeared in the Old Testament. In Zechariah 3:1 (KJV), the Lord showed Zechariah how Satan resisted Joshua the High Priest: "And he shewed me Joshua the high priest standing before the angel of the Lord, and Satan standing at his right hand to resist him."

In Job we read, "Now there was a day when the sons of God came to present themselves before the Lord, and Satan came also among them. And the Lord said unto Satan, Whence comest thou? Then Satan answered the Lord, and said, from going to and fro in the earth, and from walking up and down in it" (Job 1:6–8, KJV). The book of Job paints a picture of how Satan's accusations brought indescribable anguish upon a righteous man. However, Job persevered in trusting God and the Lord restored to him twice as much as he lost.

The Old Testament also reveals how Satan, along with the angels that fell from heaven with him, attempts to stop God's purposes on the earth. We see Michael the Archangel contending with the Devil in a dispute over Moses' body (Jude 1:9–10, NKJV).

SATAN STALLS ANSWERED PRAYER

Another Old Testament incident worth noting occurred when Daniel began to pray and fast before God for certain revelation. Three weeks into his fast, an angel of the Lord appeared before him and said that God had answered his prayer from the first day he prayed! However, as angels were bringing his answer, their way was blocked by a demonic entity called the prince of the kingdom of Persia, which refers to a territorial spirit that kept Persia under Satan's control. To break the stalemate, God dispatched Michael the Archangel to defeat the prince of Persia, allowing the angel to break through with the answer to Daniel's prayer (Daniel 10:2–14).

A GODLY KING

An Old Testament hero of faith was King David. The Bible describes him as a man after God's own heart. Yet he committed a great sin when he disobeyed God and took a census of all the people of Israel. This sin brought judgment not just on King David, but on the entire nation of Israel. Thousands died of the resulting plague. What caused this godly king to commit such a crime? The Bible recorded it like this, "And Satan stood up against Israel, and provoked David to number Israel" (First Chronicles 21:1, KJV). This scripture demonstrates that Satan was behind David's transgression.

These few examples show us clearly that Satan not only hindered the prayers of the faithful, but he also provoked the righteous to sin. But that's the Old Testament. Jesus is our Lord, Savior and the Author and Finisher of our faith. Let's take a look at what Jesus did, and said, about the devil.

JESUS VS. SATAN

Amazing as it might seem, the Bible says the reason that Jesus came to earth and sacrificed His life on the cross was because of Satan. Had Satan not enticed Adam and Eve to sin in the Garden of Eden, there would have been no need for the redemption of mankind. However, Jesus' purpose in coming to earth was to destroy the works of the devil. First John 3:8 tells us that, "He that committeth sin is of the devil; for the devil sinneth from the beginning. For this purpose the Son of God was manifested, that he might destroy the works of the devil" (KJV).

So we see that Jesus' purpose on earth was to correct the great damage that Satan had done to the world and its inhabitants. The redemption of mankind on the cross was the final blow to all of Satan's plans and allowed Jesus to take back all authority on the earth. But let's look at other ways that Jesus set the people free from Satan's control.

Mary Magdalene was a key personality in the early Church because she anointed Jesus with precious oils and washed His feet with her tears before the crucifixion. After His resurrection, Mary was the first person to whom Jesus appeared. Yet, according to the Bible, Jesus had cast seven demonic spirits out of her. Mark 16:9 tells us, "Now when Jesus was risen early the first day of the week, he appeared first to Mary Magdalene, out of whom he had cast seven devils" (KJV).

Jesus described the devil's role on earth in the Parable of the Tares found in Matthew 13:37–39. In this passage Jesus explained, "He that soweth the good seed is the Son of man; the field is the world; the good seed are the children of the kingdom; but the tares are the children of the wicked one; the enemy that sowed them is the devil; the harvest is the end of the world; and the reapers are the angels" (KJV).

SETTING THE CAPTIVES FREE

The Bible also makes it clear that Jesus ministered deliverance to multitudes of people. In Matthew 8:16, the Bible records, "When the even was come, they brought unto him many that were possessed with devils: and he cast out the spirits with his word, and healed all that were sick" (KJV).

In Mark 1:32 (KJV) we find, "And at even, when the sun did set, they brought unto him all that were diseased, and them that were possessed with devils. And all the city was gathered at the door. And he healed many that were sick of divers diseases, and cast out many devils; and suffered not the devils to speak, because they knew him."

Again, in Luke 4:41 (KJV) we read, "And devils also came out of many, crying out, and saying, Thou are Christ the Son of God. And he rebuking them suffered them not to speak: for they knew that he was Christ."

In Acts 10:38 (KJV), we are told, "How God anointed Jesus of Nazareth with the Holy Ghost and power; who went about doing good, and healing all that were oppressed of the devil; for God was with him."

Unmistakably, a great deal of Jesus' ministry was casting out demonic spirits and setting people free. But even though Jesus had authority over them, He was fully man and was tempted by Satan. In fact, prior to His public ministry, Jesus was tempted by the devil for 40 days (Matthew 4:1–10).

It is important to note that Jesus did not rebuke Satan or accuse him of lying when he offered Him all the kingdoms of the world. Obviously, Satan had gained authority over the earth when Adam and Eve sinned in the Garden. That's why we are still dealing with his temptations today.

The Bible also records that hell, the everlasting fire, was prepared for the devil and his fallen angels. We find this in Matthew 25:41 (KJV), "Then shall he say also unto them on the left hand, Depart from me, ye cursed, into everlasting fire, prepared for the devil and his angels . . ."

That just about sums up the Parable of the Tares: Satan knows that he is headed to hell and his strategy is to take as many people with him as possible. This is the battle of the ages, and no Hollywood mogul dreamed it up.

This is one of those cases where fact is truly stranger than fiction.

Defeating the enemy of God is no plot from Hollywood—it is a most holy work.

2 - IN THE SHADOW OF THE CROSS

Thank God that we live in the shadow of the cross, for it was on Calvary that Jesus paid the full price for the redemption of the world. When He uttered the words, "It is finished!" the veil of the temple ripped apart, forever opening the way for mankind to enter into the Holy of Holies. Calvary was the ultimate defeat of Satan and all his demonic hosts. That leaves us with a question which begs to be answered. When Jesus uttered the words, "It is finished!" did He mean that the world—and all of us who live in it—no longer have to deal with Satan and his evil cohorts?

If you look at worldwide terrorism, natural disasters like the tsunami that redefined parts of the world, the AIDS epidemic, famines, plagues, child abuse and drive-by shootings, it would seem that is not the case. However, we must never base our beliefs on what we see; but rather, the Word of God must be our final answer. So what does the Bible have to say about Satan and demons, in the shadow of the cross?

The tenth chapter of Hebrews gives us an interesting glimpse into this question. It says, "But this man, after he had offered one sacrifice for sins for ever, sat down on the right hand of God; from henceforth expecting till his enemies be made his footstool" (Hebrews 10:12–13, KJV).

This scripture doesn't say that Jesus sat at the right hand of the Father with His enemies as a footstool under His feet. It says that He is seated at the right hand of God *expecting* His enemies to be made His footstool!

Clearly, Jesus' enemies are Satan and his demonic forces, and Jesus is expecting someone to make them His footstool. Who might He be expecting to do that except His body on earth—the Church?

AFTER THE CROSS

Let's begin by looking at what the Bible says about Satan and Christians *after* the cross. In the book of Acts we find two members of the early Church, Ananias, and his wife, Sapphira. This couple, on their own accord, sold a piece of land and kept part of the money while donating part of it to the Church. It was their money to keep or give, but they made a fatal mistake when they lied to the apostles by telling them that the amount they got from the sale was the amount they donated. In the confrontation that followed, Peter said that Satan had filled Ananias' heart.

> But Peter said, "Ananias, Satan has filled your heart. When you claimed this was the full price, you were lying to the Holy Spirit. The property was yours to sell or not, as you wished. And after selling it, it was yours to decide how much to give. How could you do a thing like this? You weren't lying to us, but to God." As soon as Ananias heard these words, he fell to the floor, dead! Everyone was terrified, and the younger men covered him with a sheet and took him out and buried him. (Acts 5:3–6, TLB)

A while later, Sapphira showed up with the same story and she also died instantly. As far as we know, these were born again believers, but the Bible says that Satan filled their hearts. If that's the case, obviously, Christians could be oppressed of the devil after the cross. But perhaps they hadn't truly been born again. That point is unclear. So let's look at someone who was unquestionably born again—the Apostle Paul.

When Paul was arrested for preaching the gospel and taken before King Agrippa, he told the king about his conversion on the road to Damascus. When God spoke to him in a blinding light, Paul was commissioned by God to take the gospel to the Gentiles. Part of that commission is listed in Acts 26:18 (KJV), "To open their eyes, and to turn them from darkness to light, and from the power of Satan unto God . . ." This means that Paul's commission, which occurred *after* Calvary, was to deliver people out of Satan's power.

Paul also wrote a letter to the church in Thessalonica and said, "Wherefore we would have come unto you, even I Paul, once and again; but Satan hindered us," (First Thessalonians 2:18, NKJV).

This scripture is of particular significance because it shows us that Paul, one of the greatest apostles that ever lived, was hindered by Satan. This occurred after the cross, so Jesus must *not* have meant that our dealings with the devil were over when He said, "It is finished."

Another scripture that reveals that the Church wasn't finished with Satan at Calvary is found in Romans 16:20. Paul wrote, "And the God of peace shall bruise Satan under your feet shortly" (KJV). Notice that Paul did not say that Satan was already bruised under our feet, but that it would happen shortly.

JESUS GIVES AUTHORITY OVER DEMONS

Having seen that the battle between the Church and Satan is not yet finished, we must take a close look at the model Jesus gave for dealing with Satan and his demons. The Bible tells us in Mark 3:14–15, that Jesus " . . . ordained the twelve, that they should be with him, and that he might send them forth to preach, and to have power to heal sickness, and to cast out devils" (KJV).

In Matthew 10:5–8, we see that Jesus sent twelve disciples out to minister. Jesus was very specific, telling them they were not sent to the Gentiles or the Samaritans, but rather to the Israelites. He instructed them to preach, heal the sick, raise the dead and cast out devils.

Later, seventy disciples returned to Jesus, and were excited because "even the devils are subject unto us through thy name" (Luke 10:17, KJV). Jesus answered and said, "Behold I give unto you power to tread on serpents and scorpions, and over all the power of the enemy: and nothing shall by any means hurt you. Notwithstanding in this rejoice not, that the spirits are subject to you; but rather rejoice, because your names are written in heaven."

Now let's take a close look at the last thing Jesus said before He returned to heaven and took His place at the right hand of the Father. We call this passage of scripture The Great Commission. It is considered to be the commissioning, not only of the early Church, but the Church today and until Jesus returns again.

> And he said unto them, Go ye into all the world, and preach the gospel to every creature. He that believeth and is baptized shall be saved; but he that believeth not shall be damned. And these signs shall follow them that believe; In my name shall they cast out devils; they shall speak with new tongues; They shall take up serpents; and if they drink any deadly thing, it shall not hurt them; they shall lay hands on the sick, and they shall recover. So then after the Lord had spoken unto them, he was received up into heaven, and sat on the right hand of God. (Mark 16:15–19, KJV)

Notice first of all that Jesus commissioned the Church to go into the entire world to preach. He follows with a list of signs that will follow those who believe. The first sign listed is in His name shall they cast out devils. This took place in the shadow of the cross! It was the last piece of business Jesus assigned to His followers before He returned to heaven. Might these be the things we are required to do in order to make Jesus' enemies become His footstool?

It is impossible to take this text in its entirety and separate preaching the gospel from casting out demons, speaking in tongues or healing the sick. If The Great Commission is fulfilled, all these signs will also be fulfilled—and Jesus' enemies will become His footstool.

ENEMY AT THE GATES

This chapter would not be complete without pausing to take a look at the advice the Bible gives Christians about Satan. First and foremost, the

Bible makes it clear that there is an enemy at our gates. First Peter 5:8 tells us, "Be sober, be vigilant; because your adversary the devil, as a roaring lion, walketh about, seeking whom he may devour" (KJV).

That is a solemn warning from God, and one we should not overlook. Another piece of advice is found in First Corinthians 10:20–21, " . . . I would not that ye should have fellowship with devils. Ye cannot drink the cup of the Lord, and the cup of devils: ye cannot be partakers of the Lord's table, and of the table of devils" (KJV).

We are warned not to be ignorant of the devil's devices (Second Corinthians 2:11). We are instructed to resist the devil (James 4:7–8). We are admonished not to give place to the devil (Ephesians 4:27). We are cautioned to watch out for false apostles who attempt to transform themselves into apostles of Christ (Second Corinthians 11:13–15, KJV). And we are told to recover ourselves out of the snare of the devil (Second Timothy 2:26, KJV).

And just in case we're still not sure who our enemy is, the Bible spells it out in Ephesians 6:11–12: "Put on the whole armor of God, that ye may be able to stand against the wiles of the devil. For we wrestle not against flesh and blood, but against principalities, against powers, against the rulers of the darkness of this world, against spiritual wickedness in high places" (KJV).

CAN CHRISTIANS BE AFFLICTED BY DEMONS?

In spite of the above scriptures, many people still believe that a Christian cannot be oppressed or afflicted by the devil. They believe that deliverance is for the unsaved, not the children of God. Keeping in mind that Israel was the original child of God, Matthew 15:22–29 tells us the story of a woman from Canaan who begged Jesus to deliver her daughter from the grasp of a demon. This woman was not an Israelite.

Jesus' response to this Gentile is very important, because it deals with deliverance. He said, "It is not meet to take the children's bread, and to cast it to the dogs" (KJV). The Living Bible translates the verse this way, "It doesn't seem right to take bread from the children and throw it to the dogs."

Jesus calls deliverance from demons "the children's bread." Are you a born again child of God? If so, deliverance from the devil is your birthright.

The woman in this story did not have the birthright to ask for her daughter to be delivered. But her answer brought a miracle long before God sent Paul to the Gentiles. She said, "Truth, Lord, yet the dogs eat of the crumbs which fall from their master's table" (KJV). Jesus responded to her faith by delivering the woman's daughter from the demon.

Is there still a question in your mind that deliverance is not for Christians? Have you been taught that deliverance is for the lost, but a Christian doesn't need deliverance? Then we must look at one other thing that Jesus said:

> This evil nation is like a man possessed by a demon. For if the demon leaves, it goes into the deserts for a while, seeking rest but finding none. Then it says, "I will return to the man I came from." So it returns and finds the man's heart clean but empty! Then the demon finds seven other spirits more evil than itself, and all enter the man and live in him. And so he is worse off than before. (Matthew 12:43–45, KJV)

This passage of scripture gives a picture of what would happen if someone who had not been born again were to go through deliverance. Because his heart was empty (without Jesus!) the demons would return with fresh recruits and the man would be worse than before. Clearly, only those who have invited Jesus into their hearts are candidates for deliverance. That's why Jesus gave us our instructions in order. First, preach the Gospel and win the lost, *then* cast out demons.

The time is growing short and our work is not finished.

We must make Jesus' enemies to be His footstool.

3 - HOODWINKED

Our flight to England was uneventful and my husband and I landed with the usual mixture of jetlag and excitement. We wandered through castles, visited Stratford-on-Avon and watched the Changing of the Guard. During one of our wanderings, we stumbled into a demonstration of falconry. The falcon is a powerful bird of prey with keen eyesight, a wide wingspan and a beak that can rip apart a man's arm. His handler controlled him by putting a hood over his head and eyes. The falcon, like Samson of old, had lost his ability to see. While he sat tethered to his perch with the hood over his head, we could pet him without causing him to stir at all.

The truth is that most Christians have been as hoodwinked as that falcon. The Church, to whom Jesus left all authority, has lost the ability to see her enemy. Instead of a powerful fighting force, we've sat hooded in our church pews while the devil and his demons wreck havoc in both the world around us and in our own lives.

Deliverance removes the hood that covers our spiritual vision.

If you look up the word "deliver" in *Strong's Exhaustive Concordance of the Bible,* you will find that it means "to rescue." When the devil is messing in your life, you're in danger of death to your body, death to your joy, death to the call of God upon your life and death to your mortal soul. Jesus said that Satan comes to steal, kill and destroy. If the devil can't kill you, he'll try to torture you while you're on this earth.

The *World Book Dictionary* defines deliver as, "to set free, to rescue, to save, to liberate and to release." One example is to deliver an animal from a trap. That's a good example of what happens to us. The devil has booby-trapped all kinds of things along our path and we have unwittingly stepped right into them. Now we need someone to help free us.

WHAT DO YOU POSSESS?

As Derek Prince explains in his book, *They Shall Expel Demons,* there's been a lot of confusion about the term "possession" as it relates to the devil. You may wonder how a Christian could be possessed by the devil when we are possessed by God. Let's settle that issue once and for all time. A demon cannot possess you if you're born again. We get confused by the King James translation of the word *daimonizomai,* which is translated, "to be possessed with devils." There are twelve times in the New Testament when that word is translated "to be possessed by a devil or devils." This has caused confusion because it implies ownership by the demon. The actual meaning of the word is "to be vexed, or subject to demonic influence."

The truth is that a demon doesn't possess you; it subjects you.

We've actually had it backwards when we talk about being possessed by a demon. When I did a word study, I found that the actual meaning of the word implies that you own the demon. That's a critical thing to know, because what you own, you can disown.

Another source of confusion is the myth that demons attach to the spirit. Demons do not attach to your spirit. They attach to your soul—mind, will and emotions—and to your body.

THE STATE OF BEING SAVED

One other common objection we hear about Christians going through deliverance is that they were delivered when they were born again. That is correct; many people get a measure of deliverance at conversion. But let's look at salvation. You were born again, which the King James Bible translated the word as "saved."

When I received Jesus as my personal savior, I believed I had been saved. I didn't really know everything it meant, but I thought it was wonderful. Then I started hearing about healing. I didn't know that healing was connected to salvation, but the Greek word for salvation is *soteria,* which means to "rescue, bring to safety, deliver, health, salvation, save, saving." When I was born again, I didn't have any idea that deliverance or healing was mine as well.

If, like me, all you appropriated from your salvation was eternal life, that's what will manifest in your life. You appropriated salvation from the list because someone taught you that you could. If you want the other things offered there, you have to appropriate them the same way. You won't automatically get safety and protection because you don't know it's yours. Likewise, if you need deliverance (and we all do), then you'll need to appropriate it.

REDEEMED FROM THE CURSE

I am thankful that Jesus has delivered me from all the curse of the law, because He was made a curse for me. That's something to shout about! If you aren't familiar with that promise, you'll find it in Galatians 3:13 (KJV), "Christ hath redeemed us from the curse of the law, being made a curse for us: for it is written, Cursed is every one that hangeth on a tree."

Have you ever read the curses listed in Deuteronomy? Sickness, disease, miscarriages, barrenness, poverty, mold and mildew are a few of the curses listed there. We've been redeemed from them!

So why, you might wonder, do Christians get sick, miscarry, are barren and plagued with poverty? Again, we each have to learn what provisions Jesus bought for us on the cross, and then we have to appropriate them. James 4:2 (NKJV) says, " . . . you do not have because you do not ask." Many times we don't ask God for what we need. Even when we ask, we must receive and put into effect in our lives what He gives us. The bottom line—God sent His only Son to pay the ultimate price for our deliverance from all curses and from all the hand of the enemy. Let us determine to take full advantage of those blessings.

There are many ways to receive deliverance; let's review some of them here:

1. *Conversion.* The first time that deliverance can occur in the life of a believer is at the time of conversion. The Bible says, "But he that is joined unto the Lord is one spirit" (First Corinthians 6:17, KJV). When you become one spirit with the Lord God Almighty, something has to make way. Some people change dramatically when they are born again. I've heard people say, "Everything changed the moment I was saved. I was immediately delivered from an addiction." It is not uncommon for new converts to be instantly delivered from addictions to nicotine, alcohol or drugs.

Other people are born again without any outward change in their lives. That doesn't mean that they didn't get a measure of deliverance at the moment of conversion. It only means that it wasn't outwardly evident.

2. *Water Baptism.* Water baptism is a prophetic act representing a deep spiritual truth—that we died and were buried in Christ Jesus and we have risen to new life in Him. This isn't just symbolic; it is a divine exchange that often results in deliverance.

3. *Baptism of the Holy Spirit.* Deliverance also takes place when a person receives the baptism of the Holy Spirit. Because this involves a greater degree of yielding to the Holy Spirit, the Lord can take over more territory in our mind, will, emotions or body.

4. *Times of Repentance.* You will see as you read through this book that sin is an open door to the demonic. God and all the forces of heaven are ready and waiting to enforce your deliverance, but that spiritual door cannot be shut except through genuine repentance. That's why repentance is one of the greatest methods of deliverance.

5. *Mass Deliverance.* Mass deliverance can occur two different ways. One way this happens is when a group of people are attending a deliverance conference or at a church service where the leader prays for mass deliverance for everyone in attendance. Many people have been miracu-

lously set free in these meetings. A second way mass deliverance occurs is by a supernatural move of God. In one such instance, angels appeared on one side of a congregation. Everyone in that section was supernaturally healed and delivered from demonic oppression.

6. *Anointed Teaching and Preaching.* You may have heard pastors pray that no one would leave a service unchanged. That is not just wishful thinking on their part; it is the will of God. Anointed preaching and teaching brings about the greatest miracle of all time—the miracle of the new birth. But it doesn't stop there. Just sitting under anointed teaching and preaching can bring about deliverance. For instance, you may get a revelation of something in your life that is holding you back from God's best, and you say, "Okay, I'm putting that down." That revelation leads to change which can bring deliverance from demonic oppression. Other times you won't even realize there's been a change in your life until the next time you're confronted with a situation that usually trips you up. You'll suddenly realize that you don't react the same way. That is a powerful example of deliverance.

7. *Praise and Worship.* Think about the time King Saul became tormented by demonic spirits. What drove them away so that he could have peace? It was young David, the shepherd boy, playing his harp. Praise and worship is one of the most powerful weapons of warfare in our arsenal. Perhaps because it represents Lucifer's original call, demons cannot tolerate the sound of praise and worship. Playing it in your home day and night can drive back the powers of darkness.

8. *Breaking Generational Curses.* Many times generational curses have been passed down through a family line. The Bible says that a curse will not light without cause, so we must ask the Holy Spirit to reveal the open door that caused the curse. For instance, I know of one family who discovered that for several generations past, the men had been part of the Ku Klux Klan. They had sinned against God through their rejection and cruelty to other people. When this hidden sin came to light, the family repented for the sin and iniquity of their forefathers and the generational curse was broken.

9. *Personal Deliverance Sessions.* I've heard this called "whole personality deliverance," which is a good description. This is the type of deliverance with which we will deal in this book. It is a very thorough and methodical way of recognizing open doors in an individual's life and delivering him from demonic oppression.

A HANDY DANDY THING TO KNOW

Much of what I know about deliverance I learned from Doris Wagner, author of *How to Cast Out Demons, A Beginner's Guide.* I was attending a deliverance workshop by Doris when she said, "You know, deliverance is just a handy dandy thing to know." I thought, you know, that's right. It isn't some big, hairy deal. Don't get me wrong, you can't just jump out there without knowing what you're doing. But the fact is that deliverance should be nothing more than an everyday fact of life for the Christian.

Doris Wagner has some other truisms that are worth remembering. She has done an amazing number of deliverances in her lifetime and has bumped up against all kinds of objections. For instance, people occasionally say to her, "You see a demon behind every bush." To that Doris answers, "Not so, but if there is one behind that bush, I want to make sure it leaves."

Other people have said, "You are using the name of Jesus as though it were Christian magic. We need to be careful about that." Doris answers, "I sure would hate to face a demon without the name of Jesus."

And lastly, people occasionally tell Doris, "I don't believe in demons."

To which Doris answers, "Do you want to follow me around for a week?" These quotes are from *How to Cast Out Demons, A Beginner's Guide* by Doris Wagner.

PART TWO

THE BASICS OF STARTING A DELIVERANCE MINISTRY

4 – ASSEMBLING THE DELIVERANCE TEAM

There is no biblical example of specialized deliverance teams whose only form of ministry is deliverance. Jesus trained and sent out teams of people who preached the gospel, led the lost to eternal salvation, healed the sick and cast out demons. Our deliverance team is made up of a diverse group of people who pastor home groups, serve in church leadership, flow in the prophetic, teach in the children's ministry, function in the ministry of helps and minister in music. However, they are set apart to also minister in deliverance because they have been through deliverance themselves, have been approved by leadership for this ministry and have been trained.

When assembling a deliverance team, the first and most important role is that of the pastor. By its very nature, deliverance is a front lines ministry; therefore, it must always be properly submitted to spiritual authority. The pastor must have the vision for deliverance in your church, because he is the person to whom God gives the overall plan for your congregation. The pastor must also have or get knowledge about deliverance ministry, have faith for deliverance and be willing to act on it. Once the pastor has confirmation from the Lord to proceed, he should be willing to lead prayer and fasting for the ministry itself, for the team and all those to whom the team will minister.

The role of the pastor includes determining how to structure the deliverance ministry, approving the questionnaire or other tools used, leading and guiding in choosing team members and helping to train and direct them as needed.

When we began our deliverance ministry, our senior pastor, Dr. John Benefiel, appointed me to head the team. At that time, he told me that I could choose members for the team from anyone already in church leadership positions. Anyone outside of church leadership positions would have to be approved by him on an individual basis. Many times when someone outside of church leadership expressed an interest in deliverance, and I submitted his name to Dr. Benefiel, he immediately approved him. On other occasions he just said, "No." I didn't press for an explanation. That simply meant that he was privy to something in the person's life that I didn't know about, and those things are none of my business. Occasionally he would say, "I see a spirit of control in that person," or "She has a tendency to gossip, let's wait and watch for a while."

Everyone has to go through deliverance before they can be considered for deliverance ministry in our church. Sometimes there is a time lapse from the time of personal deliverance until you see the manifestation of that freedom. Dr. Benefiel was wise enough to allow that to occur before thrusting the person into an adversarial position with the enemy.

TRAITS OF A SUCCESSFUL DELIVERANCE MINISTER

In order to have a successful deliverance ministry, it must be consecrated and totally yielded to God. The motives of everyone involved are crucial. This is no place for those trying to make a name for themselves or those who want attention. The following are the traits of a successful deliverance minister.

Under Authority

Perhaps one of the most important traits of a deliverance minister is that he be a person under authority. It is only through rightly appropriating God's authority that deliverance occurs. Therefore, the deliverance minister must be submitted to God's authority, submitted to pastoral authority, submitted to church leadership and to the authority of the deliverance team leader. He must also be open minded about the method of deliverance; he can't be controlling.

We have no problem with this in our church, because our pastor set things in order. He is fully in charge, and we are under his authority. He has given us freedom to run the ministry within the boundaries and guidelines he has set, but he stays involved. He regularly preaches deliverance from the pulpit and it has become a badge of honor in our church to have gone through deliverance. He is now requesting that everyone going into church leadership go through deliverance first and he requires deliverance for any couple before he marries them. By his example deliverance is very important in the lives of our church family and is very well accepted.

A Holy Life

It's important for deliverance ministers to live a holy life. First John 3:9 tells us, "Whosoever is born of God doth not commit sin; for his seed remaineth in him: and he cannot sin, because he is born of God" (KJV).

The Living Bible puts it this way, "The person who has been born into God's family does not make a practice of sinning, because now God's life is in him; so he can't keep on sinning, for this new life has been born into him and controls him—he has been born again."

The deliverance minister doesn't have to be perfect, but if you're operating in sin while trying to cast out demons, you're going to get in trouble. For instance, someone who is committing sexual sin and tries to cast that spirit out of another person will not be successful. The demons can see what spirits are attached to the deliverance team member and they will simply laugh. Deliverance is not going to happen. It simply isn't wise to get into a confrontational situation with the enemy if you have an open door to the demonic in your own life.

Full of Faith and Confidence in God's Word

The deliverance minister must be full of faith and confidence in God's Word. A lack of faith in one of the members praying for deliverance can block the whole process. He should have a solid knowledge and understanding of the Bible and be able to stand in faith on the scriptures.

This really harkens back to authority, because the deliverance minister must be submitted to the written Word of God, and be able to wield the Sword of the Spirit (the Word of God) in spiritual warfare.

Humble Before God and Man

The deliverance minister must be humble before God and man. Jesus warned, "Notwithstanding in this rejoice not, that the spirits are subject unto you; but rather rejoice, because your names are written in heaven" (Luke 10:20, KJV). Team members should not be show-offs, fascinated with the demonic or looking for status.

Reliable

Reliability is an important trait for the deliverance minister. If you've scheduled a deliverance and the person has spent a lot of time preparing for it, then you cancel the session, it can be devastating to the person. He may assume that you've looked at his questionnaire, seen all the unsavory things that have happened in his life and decided you don't want to pray with him. These people have opened their hearts, souls and minds to you. They've revealed their deepest, darkest secrets. It took trust and humility on their part to prepare, and you must take that gift seriously. We've had a lot of people who arrived for deliverance and had to drive around the block several times before they got the nerve to come inside. So although this isn't a big deal for you, it's a very big deal to them and they deserve to be treated with respect.

Confidential and Forgetful

The deliverance minister must have the integrity to keep everything that was said and done in the deliverance session in strictest confidence. Breaking confidentiality is the worst kind of integrity breach in this ministry. This is no place for people with a tendency toward gossip. Our pastor has told us repeatedly that if he ever hears of anything in a deliverance session being discussed outside the session, the people involved will be permanently removed from the team.

The person going through deliverance may come up to you at church and say, "I'm excited about my deliverance!" Or he may say something to you about the session once it's over, and that's all right. But no deliverance minister should ever initiate any form of conversation with that person, in public, about an upcoming or completed deliverance. Don't even say, "I'm looking forward to your session tomorrow." You should guard his confidence in every possible way, even the fact that he has scheduled a deliverance session.

Another godly trait of a deliverance minister is forgetfulness. I'm not talking about someone with a bad memory. I'm talking about those people who will allow God to simply remove the details of the deliverance from their memory banks once the session is over. This is God's grace. Usually, the minute a deliverance session is finished, we forget what we prayed. I've had people come up to me in church and say, "Do you remember when you prayed for me and . . ." They are usually surprised to learn that I don't remember a thing about it. In my personal prayer time, I often ask God to make me forget the details.

Exceptions to Confidentiality

There are exceptions to the confidentiality issue which we make public in our literature and on the instruction sheet to the person coming for deliverance. Some of these exceptions are people at risk for suicide, pedophilia and other crimes against elders and children. When our deliverance ministers pray with someone with these issues, they tell me and I report it to the pastor. In the case of someone battling pedophilia, the pastor needs to know so he can make sure that the individual does not work in the children's ministry at church. Likewise, the pastor should be told immediately if anyone is in danger of suicide.

These situations can create legal issues as well. For instance, in Oklahoma, if we learn the identity of a victim of pedophilia, we are obligated to report it to the law enforcement authorities. To fail to report this would be illegal and could put the church or ministry at risk. I know of a situation involving another ministry in which a man battling pedophilia told his ministry team member that he had already reported his crime to authorities. In fact, he had not, and this created great problems for the ministry involved. When we are dealing with these crimes, we make sure the individual knows that there is certain information that we must report by law. It is also illegal in many jurisdictions to know that a person is in danger of taking his or her life without reporting it to the authorities. These issues should be researched in your local jurisdiction.

Maturity and Wisdom

The deliverance minister needs the maturity and wisdom to know how to separate the demon from the person. You will hear about all the horrible things that the person did—the secret, hidden things that no one knows—and you must be able to hate the demons that led him into that situation while loving the person unconditionally. There will be times when you hear something about a personal friend of yours or about your pastor, a hurt that has occurred because of one of these people. You must be willing to hear it and deal with the hurt in the person with whom you are praying without becoming offended by him or with the person who hurt him.

TRAINING THE TEAM

When new members have been approved for the deliverance team, they are given a list of required reading, which includes our training manual. In addition, they listen to tapes from deliverance conferences that we've taught. We require every team member to read, *How to Cast Out Demons, A Beginners Guide* by Doris Wagner, and we have other books available that deal with children's deliverance, teen deliverance and other subjects. A suggested study list is included at the end of this book.

Once they've read and listened to the training materials, the rest of their training is through an apprenticeship. A regular two-person team is assigned to do the actual deliverance, but at times we've had as many as five or six apprentices with us to train. A new minister usually apprentices with us for least four deliverance sessions. By the third time he will lead part of the session. Finally, he will lead almost an entire session before we give him questionnaire packets and send him out with another minister to do deliverances.

INTERCESSORS

Another important part of the deliverance team is intercessors. While they may or may not minister deliverance themselves, intercessors are crucial to the success of the team. They will be given the briefest information regarding an upcoming deliverance, such as the date and time, the name of the person to receive deliverance and the names of the team as well as any trainees, but no other details. The intercessor should cover that session with prayer, depending on the Holy Spirit to give specifics about what to pray. They may be led by the Lord to fast for the person.

Details of how the team operates and prepares for the deliverance session will be covered in Chapters 24 through 26.

5 – DEALING WITH DEMONS

While *The Exorcist* brought the whole concept of deliverance to the forefront in 1973, it also created a good deal of unwarranted fear. Don't get me wrong, I wouldn't want to be an unbeliever and have a confrontation with demons, but born again Christians who understand their God-given authority have nothing to fear.

Still, the biggest question on everyone's mind is: How do demons behave when confronted? Will they cause the furniture to levitate? Will the person's head spin around in circles? Will they vomit thick, green gunk like the child in *The Exorcist?*

Those are valid questions and ones that both members of the deliverance team and people going through deliverance have a right to know. After *The Exorcist* hit the big screen in the 1970s, it spawned renewed interest in deliverance and many Christians began deliverance ministries with very little teaching or training. I was part of that movement, and it almost caused me to shun deliverance forever. I saw people thrown against walls as they cackled in demonic voices.

Let me assure you, that isn't how we operate our deliverance ministry today. In the intervening years we've learned a great deal about our spiritual authority and how to use it. If a demon tries to take over the deliverance by manifesting in scary, theatrical ways, or if it attempts to harm the person, we use our authority to stop it immediately. We generally don't even let demons speak.

You may find this hard to believe, but overall, deliverance is usually pleasant. That doesn't mean we don't take the situation seriously, but it does mean that we're not afraid of demons, we know our authority, and we refuse to take *ourselves* too seriously.

To minister deliverance, you absolutely must understand what your authority is and where it comes from. Demons are not the least bit afraid of you. If you try to go up against a demon by yourself, you'll fail miserably and it can be dangerous for everyone involved. It is Jesus' blood, His name and His authority—along with forgiveness—that gives you the power to cast out demons. You must know who you are in Christ, and be unwavering in your faith and authority. Don't leave home without Him.

HOW DEMONS LEAVE

So now to the answer you've been waiting to hear. What happens when demons are confronted? When I first agreed to be a part of our deliverance ministry, I read a lot of books and listened to tapes on the subject. These resources talked a lot about the significance of things like yawning or coughing. So I got into the Word of God to do my own research. I went through the concordance and looked up every instance in the King James Bible where the word "spirit" was used. That began the teachings on spirits that you will see later in the book.

In the process, I discovered an interesting thing. One of the actual definitions of the word spirit is "an expulsion of air." I thought back to when the Holy Spirit fell on the day of Pentecost—they heard a sound like a "rushing wind." It made sense that if the Holy Spirit is like a rushing wind, unclean spirits are no more than an expulsion of air.

After years in this ministry, we've found that the most common way demons leave is through yawning, coughing or clearing the throat—expulsions of air! One gentleman came for deliverance and started coughing when he got to the front door. Before he'd even sat down, he was coughing and sputtering. It was as though the demons knew they had to go and didn't want to wait around to hear the name of Jesus.

It's not uncommon for people to belch when demons leave them. We were praying for one very proper lady who gave a little burp. She covered her mouth, apologized and was obviously very embarrassed. I said, "If you need to belch, just do it. There's no need to apologize." The next time we cast something out, she rattled the rafters. As this continued to happen all three of us got so tickled that we laughed all the way through her deliverance.

Demons can also leave by way of the stomach. It's not unusual for the person to feel some nausea as you pray. We keep a lined trash can nearby because occasionally someone coughs up phlegm or even vomits. Once, we had to stand in the bathroom and lay hands on a man as he hung his head over the toilet. We're rarely exposed to anything too unpleasant. However, I get so happy when demons leave that I just don't care.

I'll never forget the first time I was praying for a woman when I suddenly felt short of breath. I thought that was odd, so I asked the woman if she felt anything unusual. "Yes," she said, "my lungs feel tight and I'm short of breath." I realized that the Holy Spirit was showing me that a demon was hiding out in her lungs. When we got rid of it, she said, "I can breathe deeply now!" So could I! Since then, I've learned that the Lord will often show us in our own bodies what is going on in someone else's body so we'll know how to proceed. For some reason the spirit of rejection is often attached to the lungs and it often leaves when the person exhales.

Strange as it might seem, we've also seen demons leave through the eyes. The spirit of witchcraft often shows up in the eyes, and it's helpful to have one minister watching the person closely while the other prays. On one occasion, we were casting a spirit of witchcraft out of a woman when the whites of her eyes turned a blood red. As soon as we got rid of that spirit her eyes returned to normal. I've also seen them leave through tears. That's why, if someone starts to cry, I don't try to stop them. Let them cry.

Sometimes demons also leave through the ears. We were praying against a spirit of error on one occasion when the woman said, "My ears are suddenly plugged up. I can barely hear what you're saying." As soon as we cast that spirit out, her ears popped open.

Along with understanding how demons leave, the other thing most people want to know is how they manifest physically. Truthfully, demons would probably put on a dog-and-pony show that would make *The Exorcist* look mild if you let them. We simply don't allow it.

If they manifest and try to hurt someone, command them to stop immediately in the name of Jesus. You might say something like, "In Jesus' name I command you to stop trying to harm this person!"

If you let them, the demons will take over the session. Under no circumstances should you allow that to happen. Command the demons to be subject to you in the name of Jesus.

There is a couple in our church who, years ago, were fighting to save their daughter's life after she married a very demonized, abusive man. Like most of us, at that time they had no knowledge about deliverance. The mother, who we will call Mary, was frantic to get help for her daughter. She finally found one couple in the area who was doing deliverances. Mary went through her own deliverance, and after they rescued their daughter from almost certain death, the daughter, too, was mightily delivered.

Mary's husband, who we'll call Keith, couldn't deny that deliverance had made a big difference in his daughter's life, but he was convinced that for the most part it was foolishness, and there was certainly no need for *him* to go through deliverance.

Mary, however, begged him until he finally relented and set up a time for a personal deliverance session. "The couple came to our house for the deliverance," Keith recalls. "I still thought it was foolishness, but I wanted to get my wife off my back. We'd hardly gotten started when suddenly my eyes slammed shut—I couldn't open them! My mouth opened, and I was horrified to hear the most hideous laughter rise out of my innermost being. I've never heard anything like that mocking laughter, and I hope to never hear it again.

The woman minister said, 'It's manifesting.' She grabbed the anointing oil and the male minister grabbed the Bible. He started to pray; he was binding up and casting out demons as fast as he could. The woman got the anointing oil open and anointed my forehead with oil. Instantly my neck started swelling. It swelled from the bottom half of my ears to half way over my shoulders. The pain was excruciating, but I couldn't stop the obscene laughter. And I still couldn't open my eyes. The woman touched me with the oil again, and this time it felt like someone stuck a burning cigarette on my forehead.

The male minister began reading scripture aloud, and the woman poured what felt like half a bottle of oil over my head. The minute she did that—it lifted. The swelling disappeared, the laughter stopped, and I opened my eyes. I kept thinking, 'This is nonsense and hooey,' but I just sat there too stunned to move. I think the couple doing the deliverance needed a minute to regroup, too. After a few minutes, we went through the rest of the deliverance and then they left.

I wanted to believe that there was a logical explanation for what happened and that deliverance was bogus. But when I walked into the bathroom and glanced in the mirror, there was a red mark, almost like a burn, in the form of a cross where the woman had anointed me with oil on my forehead. It didn't fade for several days.

To be honest, I was devastated. I realized that somewhere along the line I'd been sold a bill of goods where the devil was concerned. After several days of feeling deceived and stupid, I decided to research the scriptures and find out what was going on. I also started devouring the books I'd laughed at my wife for reading. As soon as I finished one, I started another.

My wife and I have been active in deliverance ministry for many years now, and I've never seen a manifestation like the one I experienced. The primary spirits that had to be cast out of me were a spirit of pride and a spirit of anger, both of which were generational in my family."

WHEN DEMONS SPEAK

Sometimes a demon will try to engage you in conversation. Basically, we just say, "I don't want to hear from you. Be quiet in Jesus' name." It is a mistake to ask demons information such as their names or how they entered the person's life. You can count on the demons to lie and conversing with them simply becomes a distraction which is what they are after. We take instructions from Jesus' example in Luke 4:35. When a demon tried to start a conversation, Jesus refused to be drawn in. He sternly told it to be quiet and come out. No yelling or screaming; just a no-nonsense command and an absolute expectation that the demon would obey.

The rule of thumb is that whatever demons say, you tell them the exact opposite. For instance, if they say, "We'll never come out," I would answer, "Oh yes; you'll come out now, in Jesus' name." Remind them that they are to be silent in Jesus' name.

Sometimes demons will try to discourage the person for whom you're praying. They might say, "This isn't working." My response would be, "In the name of Jesus it *is* working. That's why you're so nervous. Now be silent and get out, in the name of Jesus."

WILL YOU "SEE" A DEMON?

Depending on your personal discernment of spirits, you may or may not actually "see" a demon during the deliverance session. It's not unusual for one member of the deliverance team to see a demon and the others not to see it. If a demon appears visually, it isn't a cause for concern. More often, you will see the effects of the demon's activity in the person such as red blotches on the skin, redness of the eyes, facial expression and similar displays.

Sometimes the Holy Spirit will allow you to see the spirit because it may help you in some way to cast it out. If you have the feeling the spirit is showing itself in an attempt to frighten you, command it in the name of Jesus to be silent, tell it that it has no power here and you will not allow it to be disruptive. Remind it that it is bound, muzzled and gagged and the only thing you will allow it to do is leave when it is told to do so. It has been our experience that the person for whom you are praying doesn't see the demon, but if he does, help him to understand that the blood of Jesus is our protection and that the demon has no power to harm him.

Sometimes the deliverance session is going well, but suddenly you get stuck. When that happens, there is no need to feel embarrassed or to panic. Take your time. Just say, "Wait just a moment, I think we need to pray."

Occasionally the demon will do something to try and scare you. This happened once when we were doing a deliverance that started late one evening. Around one a.m., the demon began roaring like a lion! This caught us by surprise and it took us a moment to digest what was happening and we told it to stop. A few minutes later it started roaring again. We said, "You're just trying to scare us, but we're not afraid. Now come out in the mighty name of Jesus!" When the demon realized we were not afraid and its tactic was not working, it gave up.

One thing you need to understand is that you can learn as much as possible, you can go as far as your natural knowledge will take you, but if God doesn't show up you might as well go home and plug in a video. Because you will not be successful if the Holy Spirit doesn't take over for you. The good news is that He can and He will. God is still vitally interested in setting the captives free and deliverance sessions are a high priority on His agenda.

So when you feel stuck, just pray and let the Holy Spirit lead you. Sometimes I take a short break. It's amazing what revelation you can get from God if you just spend a few minutes alone with Him.

BLOCKAGES TO DELIVERANCE

There are a few things that you may bump up against that will block the deliverance. The most common is unwillingness on the part of the person receiving prayer to forgive. Everything may be going fine, but suddenly you reach a point where the person has to forgive a certain individual. If he balks even after you do what you can to help him, don't go on with the deliverance, because it isn't going to work. If he wants to complete the deliverance process, he can reschedule when he's able to forgive.

Being unrepentant over sin will also block deliverance. For instance, we had a man who admitted to having sex before marriage, but he refused to repent and acknowledge it as sin. "We were consenting adults," he explained. At that point, he had no conviction in his heart that he'd committed sin. We had to help him recognize it as sin and repent for it, so that he could receive his deliverance.

On another occasion, we prayed for a woman who'd had an abortion before she became a Christian. To her, an abortion was no more than getting rid of a few cells, and she did not acknowledge it as sin. In these situations, you should explain God's view of the situation without being hard or judgmental. If they aren't at the point where they are willing to acknowledge their sin, don't proceed, because their lack of repentance will block the deliverance.

The unwillingness to give up old habits can also block deliverance. On one occasion, a man asked if he could take a break and go smoke a cigarette. We said, "Well, no." It became readily clear that we couldn't cast out a spirit of bondage, because he wasn't willing to give up his old habits. We gently advised him to go home and pray about it. We prayed with him to bind the spirit of bondage, but didn't cast it out. Six weeks later, he returned and finished his deliverance.

Many people who've been hurt over the years have built up inner walls to protect themselves. Those walls will block deliverance. If they aren't willing to take down the walls, you can't go any further.

Fear is another huge blockage to deliverance. They may be afraid of the process, afraid of demons, afraid of change, afraid of not knowing what their life will be like after deliverance. We have even encountered people who were afraid that without the spirit of lust their sex life and marriage would fall apart. They may be most afraid that they will do something to let the demons back in and end up seven times worse. (Luke 11:26). In these cases, you have to take the time to find out what they're afraid of and deal with each fear. For instance, sometimes it helps to simply explain that the Holy Spirit is a lot more powerful than a demon, and we will pray that the Holy Spirit will fill all the places vacated by a demon.

There are some cases when you may need to ask God to reveal a point at which a demon entered while a person was in the womb. In one such instance, members of our team were praying for a young woman who'd been adopted as an infant. The team member asked the Lord to reveal any entry points from the womb. The young woman, who'd never met her birth mother and knew nothing about her, was suddenly overwhelmed by the smell of alcohol. She heard a woman's voice (that she believed to be her birth mother) repeating over and over in a panicked voice, "I can't take it anymore! I just can't take it!"

Interestingly, this young woman had been diagnosed as a teenager with an anxiety disorder associated with panic attacks for which she was on medication. Following her deliverance, she went home and told her adoptive parents about the experience. They were stunned, and said, "There's no way for you to know this, but from the age of two through six, you were plagued by sleepwalking. We put locks high on all the doors, because we were concerned that you might wander off in the middle of the night. We would find you running through the house, sound asleep but with your eyes open wide in terror. You would be sweating profusely, and you'd often say over and over, "I can't take it anymore! I just can't take it!"

The interesting thing about this case was that the young woman's only contact with her birth mother was in the womb. According to the adoption attorney, after she was born, her birth mother never even held her.

Following the deliverance, the young woman's panic attacks decreased gradually until she was able to get off of her medication. I doubt that any deliverance that did not involve praying over her in the womb would have delivered her from the panic which was passed down from her birth mother.

6 – DISMANTLING DEMONIC STRUCTURES

The Bible explains that Satan's kingdom is organized into a hierarchy of structures called principalities, powers, rulers of the darkness of this age and spiritual wickedness in heavenly places (Ephesians 6:12). In addition to the demons who hold individuals in captivity (ground level), there is a hierarchy of spirits whose function is to hold cities, territories and nations in bondage (strategic level).

Leaders of the Oklahoma Apostolic Prayer Network, (formerly the Oklahoma Concert of Prayer) are dealing with three strategic demonic structures over our state, some of which were established long ago when the ancient Egyptian god, Baal, was worshipped in Oklahoma as evidenced by ancient etchings in local caves. The carvings in those caves, assumed for years to be some ancient form of Native American language, have in recent years been identified as Egyptian. Roughly translated, the writings say, "We claim this land for Baal."

To be honest, I was delighted that the church leaders dealt with the strategic level of warfare. I was happy to do the ground level warfare: dealing with one person and one demon at a time. In November of 1999, about four months after we'd begun our deliverance ministry, internationally recognized prophet Chuck Pierce spoke at one of our meetings of the Oklahoma Concert of Prayer. He explained that the demonic structure over a territory extends all the way from the second heaven, down through the individuals and straight into the land. He went on to explain that when we strike a blow at the ground level, we weaken those strategic level structures in the heavenlies. In other words, the demonic structures affecting the individual are linked to those over cities, territories and nations. You can't strike a blow to one part of that structure without affecting the whole. That was the moment I understood that our ground level warfare is a crucial step to freeing an entire territory.

KNOW YOUR ENEMY

The term "unclean spirits" is found in the New Testament about twenty times, and the term "evil spirit" is used six times. The word devil is actually *diabolos,* which is a title for Satan himself. Some people think that to get delivered, you have to deal with Satan.

While Satan is the head of his hierarchy, it's very doubtful that he will show up personally in a deliverance session. For ground level warfare, you'll be dealing with demons, and there are some things that are important to understand about them. Demons have distinct personalities and assignments against God's people, making them individually recognizable. They are organized under leaders (Strongmen) with Satan as the head. They have varying degrees of wickedness as we see in Luke 11:26, "Then he goes and takes with him seven other spirits more wicked than himself, and they enter and dwell there; and the last state of that man is worse than the first" (NKJV). We will discuss the individual Strongmen in Chapters 12–20.

All demons intend to do evil; no demon intends to do anything good. They are also masters of deception and will try to trick you. Their purpose is to inflict as much misery as possible in this life and in the next. Many times, however, they gain a foothold in an individual's life by pretending to be a friend. In children, they may become an imaginary playmate.

I know one woman whose family was torn apart when she was a toddler. She and the other siblings were sent to live in a children's home. Through that emotional trauma, a demon began ministering to her, and convinced her that it was her friend. Through her childhood and into adulthood, that spirit was the one never-changing force in her life. When she was raped, she allowed that spirit to comfort her, never imagining that the spirit itself was setting up the horrors that she experienced. Giving up this false friend was a frightening and emotional dilemma, but today she is very instrumental in setting captives free.

THEY ARE VULNERABLE TO THE BLOOD OF JESUS AND TO THE HOLY SPIRIT

Demons do have supernatural or super-human abilities which they use to execute their plans against people. They are craftier than we are—until we allow the Holy Spirit to show us what's going on. The thing to remember is that no matter how tough they think they are, the Holy Spirit has always got them out-gunned. The reason that deliverance works is that demons are vulnerable to the blood of Jesus and to the Holy Spirit. Demons are super-human but not super-God.

STRONGHOLDS

You may have heard a lot about demonic strongholds. A stronghold is a center of demonic control. These centers of control might be in your mind and in your thought patterns. Demonic strongholds can be in your emotions. An example of this might be when someone always reacts in anger, even though that's not how he wants to react. Demonic control centers can also have a stronghold in your body. Others, such as strife, might be a demonic stronghold in your home, your family or your church.

These fortresses are created and perpetuated in darkness and deception. I've prayed for a few people who were involved in witchcraft who had actually invited demons into their lives. But 99 times out of 100, people stumble into demonic traps through deception. Rarely does anyone say, "I think I want a demon today."

According to the Bible, demons are rulers of darkness. They like to hide in dark places in our lives, our homes and in our families. They thrive in the dark things that happen behind closed doors, those things that are hidden from light. Deliverance sheds the light of the Holy Spirit into those dark places, giving demons no place to hide.

A lot of people going into a deliverance ministry are concerned about how they will know what demon they're dealing with. A great deal of what you know will be from things you've read, like this book. You'll know a lot by your understanding of scripture, and what you learn at conferences you may attend. But at some point, you'll reach the end of your knowledge, and the Holy Spirit will fill the gap. Don't fall into the intellectual trap of thinking you can figure this out, because deliverance deals with the realm of the spirit.

It is not important that you memorize a long list of "proper" names of demons. Deliverance can take place without knowing the names man has given them. In fact, I feel certain different people and different ministries call the same demon by different names. Don't get legalistic and rigid about what you call the demons. Rely on the Holy Spirit to give you the information you need. Studying the Strongmen later in this book will be helpful because the Strongmen are at the top of the demonic hierarchy. If you have any doubt about what specific spirit you are encountering, you can always address the Strongman that encompasses the type of problem you are dealing with and command it to go and take all the spirits associated with it.

1. *Proper Names*

One way to identify demons is by their proper names. The proper names are names given to them by men. It is not necessary to know their proper name to cast them out, however, it can be a valuable tool. For example, Rabshakeh was a man mentioned in the eighteenth chapter of Second Kings. God had told Israel to defeat a particular enemy. Rabshekeh countered the Lord's will by telling the people, "That enemy is too strong, I don't think you can defeat them." Some deliverance ministers address a demon as a spirit of Rabshekeh when they see someone who is discouraged and doesn't believe in God's power for his life. The demon has been around for ages, long before Rabshekeh was born, so obviously its not actually "named" Rabshekeh. But that same spirit is at work in the world today and calling it by the name of Rabshekeh is simply a convenient way to address it. Jezebel and Absalom are other examples of names spirits are often called based on the behavior they manifest.

2. Functional Names

Perhaps one of the easiest ways to identify a demon is by its functional name. In other words, you identify it by what it is doing in the person's life. If the individual is very fearful, you're dealing with a spirit of fear. A spirit of lust will cause lust to manifest in the person's life. The good news is that you don't have to memorize a whole list of names. I've heard that for every classification of sin in the Bible there is a corresponding demon, and that's probably true. Some people have tried just praying, "I cast out every demon." That won't be a complete deliverance, because it is more effective to identify and cast them out individually.

3. Names of Animals

Another way to identify demons is by certain animals. In both the Old and New Testaments, the Bible refers to a serpent spirit, which shouldn't be a surprise because the serpent is a symbol for Satan. I've prayed for people who began hissing and manifesting like a serpent. I recognized it and cast it out. Likewise, Leviathan is sometimes identified as a serpent or a crocodile spirit (Isaiah 21:1). The book of Revelation describes unclean spirits like frogs (Revelation 16:13), although, as yet, I haven't run into this one.

4. By Location

Demons can also be identified by their location in an individual's body. As mentioned previously, we often see witchcraft manifest in a person's eyes. In addition, sometimes when you're praying against witchcraft, the person's hands may start twitching. That's an interesting manifestation since the Bible says, "I will cut witchcraft out of your hands" (Micah 5:12, ASV). Clearly, there is a link between witchcraft and the hands. Similarly, it's not unusual to see a spirit of pride manifest in the neck, as we saw in Keith's situation.

5. By Entry Point

By far, one of the most common ways to identify demons is by their point of entry. When it has been identified what event, activity, curse or action allowed the demon to enter; the demon can be addressed in that way and cast out. An example would be "In the name of Jesus, the spirit that entered when she was in the car wreck . . ." If you have identified the type of spirit or the type of behavior that resulted, the statement can be expanded to "In the name of Jesus, the spirit of fear that entered when she was in the car wreck . . ."

OPEN DOORS

A man brought his son to Jesus for deliverance, and immediately the boy fell to the ground in what sounds like a seizure (Mark 9:21). Jesus asked the boy's father, "How long has he been like this?" The father answered, "From childhood."

In this brief exchange, Jesus was finding out when the door had been opened that allowed the demon into the boy's life. Either it had been opened in childhood or he had inherited it. Today we also have the task of determining where and when a door opened to demons in the life of those for whom we pray.

To understand open doors, picture your life as a long hall or corridor with doors along each side, many of which are standing open. These doors are opened by things we've done, things that have been done to us and things we have inherited. An open door gives demons a legal right to enter your life. It's not "breaking and entering" if the door is standing wide open. One door may be opened to a spirit of fear because you were terrified when you rode your first roller coaster when you were five years old. Another door may be opened because a spirit of alcohol or bondage was passed down your family line, or it may have been opened by your own drinking.

With the door standing open, demons can come in and out and move freely in your life. Once we know what opened the doors, we can do what's necessary to cast the demon out and close the door behind it. We often use the corridor illustration with people with whom we are praying as we find deliverance is easier and more effective when the individual has a good understanding of the process. Once he understands the concept of the entry points and open doors, he will often be able to begin identifying entry points on his own. This understanding also helps the individual keep the doors closed after his deliverance. We will discuss how to close them in a later chapter.

When the doors are properly closed and the demons cast out, the demons are on the outside of the doors. As long as we keep the doors closed and locked, there is nothing the demons can do to reopen them and reenter our lives. What many people experience after this door-slamming deliverance is that when confronted with the same situations as in the past, their reactions are no longer automatic, knee-jerk or out of their control. They now have an opportunity to make a decision about how they will react. It is their responsibility to make the right decision.

A man with whom we prayed to cast out a spirit of anger told us he had problems at work with a certain individual. His reaction to this person was often immediate, uncontrollable anger. After his deliverance, he reported to us that the individual at work had confronted him and he felt himself beginning to react in the usual way. He realized what was happening and stopped himself. He physically took a step backward. He said when he stepped back, he discerned that the spirit of anger stayed where it had been. Once he'd distanced himself from the anger, he was able to stay in control and make the decision to react differently.

The demons can't reopen the doors, but *we* can. We can reopen a door by returning to the sin that opened it in the first place, by moving away from God and letting our faith get "cold," by allowing unforgiveness back into our lives and similar missteps.

Just because we have closed the doors, the evicted demon won't forget about us. It will try to get back in. It will knock on the door, even beat on the door. Sometimes its attempts are incessant and constant. Eventually, if it continues to experience complete failure, it will usually back off. You can still expect an occasional assault on the door, and it will try to catch you in an unguarded moment when you might be tempted to crack the door open just enough for it to push its way back in your life.

For example, if you have been delivered from a spirit of addiction such as alcoholism or drug addiction, that spirit may try to catch you in a weak moment when you are emotionally vulnerable, such as after an argument with your spouse or after being fired from your job. It may knock on that closed door and try to talk you into having a few drinks to dull the hurt. If you give in, you've opened the door and let it back into your life. This explains why there is such a high recurrence rate among addicts who have been rehabilitated without deliverance.

With God, there is always good news, though. If you make a mistake and reopen a door, you can close it, cast the demon out again and start all over. We find it is important to educate the individuals for whom we pray about this as well. Some people seem to have the idea that they only get one chance at deliverance and if they lose it afterward, there is no more help for them. It is important that they understand that they mustn't take their deliverance lightly and they must take the necessary steps to "keep" their deliverance after our session. (See the chapter on After Care.) However, these people are more relaxed and prepared for deliverance once they understand that it's not a life sentence if they compromise their deliverance afterward. Our ministry offers what we call "brush up sessions" for people in this situation.

Identifying how the demon came into a person's life can be critical to making it leave. Most of the time, when the event occurred the person was unaware that a demon moved in. Commonly, the connection between the effects of the demonic influence and the originating event is not clear and often the connection is never discovered. They hide in the hidden places of the past and this is what allows the demons to run rampant in our lives. As an illustration, think of a mosquito bite. At the time a mosquito actually bites you, there is a stinging sensation that you'll probably notice but you quickly forget about it. But a few minutes or a few hours later, you notice a welt on your skin that itches. The "bite" is long since over, but you are now feeling the effects. If you didn't know something about bites and mosquitoes, you wouldn't know that the sting you felt earlier had anything to do with the itch. As you read the examples of demonic entry points below, you will notice that few people would recognize the events as the entrance of evil spirits.

EIGHT WAYS DEMONS CAN ENTER

The following is a list of some of the ways demons can get a foothold in an individual's life: A good deal of this information is adapted from Derek Prince's book, *They Shall Expel Demons*.

1. *Inherited through the family line*
According to the Bible, the sins of the fathers are passed down to later generations. In these instances, the individuals inherited the situation at birth. This will be covered in detail later in the chapter.

2. *Negative parental influences*
This could be something as simple as a mother who is terrified of snakes and she teaches her child to be fearful. Another example might be a promiscuous parent whose actions throw open doors for demons in the lives of the family members.

3. *Pressures in early childhood*
One example of this would be a child thrown into an adult role of trying to "parent" siblings. A young girl whose father has abandoned her may receive a spirit that causes her to mistrust men. A child exposed to overly rigid teachers or parents may be vulnerable to a spirit of fear of authority.

4. *Emotional shock or sustained emotional pressure*
Children in abusive homes live every day in fearful circumstances, which creates great emotional stress. Financial fears, such as the fear of being evicted, can cause sustained emotional pressure and open the door to demons. Children and adults alike can open doors to spirits of anger and rage when continually confronted with circumstances that make them feel helpless and abused.

5. Sinful acts or habits

This is the easiest way to open the door to demonic control. A person who commits adultery has opened the door to a spirit of lust. A child who plays with a Ouija board can open the door to familiar spirits and the spirit of divination.

6. False religion

Practice of any false religion opens the door to the devil, but this may not always be straightforward. For instance, we prayed for a lady and were puzzled that a demon was actually running up and down her arm—from shoulder to wrist—as we prayed. It was very stubborn and wouldn't leave. Thankfully, the Lord helped us ask the questions that got to the root of the problem. As a teenager she'd broken her wrist, and her parents took her to a faith healer who laid his hands on her arm and healed her. As we questioned her, she recalled that he did not preach or pray in the name of Jesus, but under his own authority. Once she repented and renounced false religion, the demon left and didn't return.

7. Idle words and word curses

In Chapter 26 we will discuss more fully the fact that words have the power of life and death and how to recognize word curses. Too often Christians have been lulled into complacency about what they say, and what they allow others to say, even jokingly, about them.

8. Being a victim of something beyond your control

Even innocent victims of abuse, rape, molestation or rejection can have spirits imparted to them. Suffering injustice often allows spirits of bitterness and anger to enter.

Many people, even after completing the questionnaire and being interviewed, have difficulty accepting that evil spirits could enter their lives by way of some activities such as playing with a Ouija board, holding séances with their friends as children or dressing in costumes and participating in Halloween. They may also fail to recognize the impact of actions such as committing adultery, especially if it was only one time. As the deliverance minister, you will need to be alert for clues to events that the person for whom you are praying may omit or dismiss as inconsequential.

CLUES TO THE PRESENCE OF DEMONS

1. *Behaviors the Individual Can't Control*

The most common clue to the presence of demons is a behavior that the individual can't control. He'll say things like, "I don't want to do that, but I just can't help myself." When someone feels helpless over something in his life, he is probably dealing with a demon. You might hear someone who has struggled with alcoholism say, "It's just got me; I can't get loose." Men who repeatedly hit their wives or children in a rage, then feel remorseful afterward, are probably being driven by a demonic influence. Studies have shown that domestic abuse generally continues to escalate. Without deliverance, it will not stop.

2. *Extreme Mood Changes*

Another clue to the presence of a demon is a sudden change in mood. One woman couldn't figure out what was happening to her husband. On one occasion, they were driving down the street having a great time, when, inexplicably, he turned violently angry, sped up to dangerous speeds, then slammed on the brakes so he could watch her neck whiplash. On another occasion, they were visiting friends when she saw a sudden change in her husband's mood. She hurried him out of the house. At home he said, "I'm glad we left. I just don't know what happened to me. All of a sudden I had an uncontrollable urge to throw something through the front window."

3. *A Craving for Power*

A third clue to the presence of demons is people who crave power and practice manipulation. Some people hunger for power to such a degree that they invite a spirit of witchcraft or a "spirit guide" to help them get it.

4. Persistent, Uncontrollable Bad Habits

Persistent and uncontrollable bad habits are another symptom of the demonic. Lying is one we see a good deal, but it could involve any number of habits. Not all bad habits are demonically driven, but if the person has sincerely tried and has been unable to control the habit, it may well have a spiritual component.

5. A Pattern of Victimization

Seeing a pattern of being a victim is another clue to the presence of demons. Sometimes you'll listen to a person's life story and think, *Isn't there anyone who hasn't taken advantage of you?* When you see those patterns, you're seeing demonic control.

DISCIPLINING DEMONS

Many people go through their entire lives without receiving deliverance from the spirits that are plaguing them. Demonic influence is apparent in the lives of some people more than others, often because some people have learned to "discipline their demons." Without a clear understanding of demonic control, we commonly produce some other explanation for what's happening. A woman who has been repeatedly abused by men is considered unwise in choosing boyfriends and husbands. Someone who is arrogant and egotistical just thinks he's better than everyone else. People who overeat are judged as having no will power. Someone who commits adultery is deemed to have low morals. A person who has lots of accidents is accident prone.

All of those things may be true. But the behavior may be caused by a demon that is driving the person to behave in a certain way or is causing things to happen to him. Often, what's really happening is a combination of the two. A man who smokes cigarettes may try to quit smoking and fail many times. He has to use his own self-discipline and will power to quit, but if he has a spirit of addiction, quitting will require a much higher level of will power. Therefore, he fails over and over again because his will power doesn't prove to be strong enough to overcome both the habit and the demon.

Some people manage to control the demons pretty well by using their own force of will against what the demon is trying to make them do. Without realizing they are dealing with a demon, they find ways to overcome, at least to some extent, the effects of the demonic control. For example, someone with a spirit of rejection may be able to train himself to speak in front of groups, but the job is much more difficult because of the demonic influence. An alcoholic may be able to stop drinking, but the spirit of addiction continues to fight him every day. This is what we call "disciplining demons." At times demons can be kept under control in these ways, however, it takes a great effort and strength of will. The person is trying to block the open door with his own determination. Frequently, the person will relapse back into the old behavior because the demon comes back through the open door in a moment of weakness.

People will often go into counseling for help with behavior that is driven by demons. A person with a spirit of anger may benefit from counseling, but without deliverance he will continue to fight the demon every day of his life. A person who has a phobia of flying can be helped to learn how to cope with the fear and get on an airplane, but he will probably never be comfortable flying if the spirit of fear is at work in his life. These people are keeping the demons under control, but the control is limited and tenuous. Another example of disciplining a demon is the person who has stopped smoking by will power, but no matter how much time passes without a cigarette, he finds himself having the urge to light up after a meal. He has disciplined the demon and is keeping it under control, but the demon is still there putting thoughts and desires in his mind. Counseling can help with the part of the behavior that is driven by habit and poor choices, but all the counseling in the world can't make the demon leave you alone.

After deliverance, many people experience a complete and immediate freedom from any desire to return to the old behavior. However, others undergo a less dramatic release because they still have old habits, mindsets and thought processes related to the behavior. We have heard people make statements after their deliverance that they don't know how to think. They were so used to the old thought process, they have never learned how to think any other way. Someone who has used manipulation all his life to get what he wants doesn't know how to deal with people any other way. He will need to resist the temptation to return to old habits. A person who used drugs or alcohol to deal with stress or disappointment may not have the skills to cope any other way and may need counseling to assist him in developing those skills. After deliverance, these people will find it much easier to overcome the old habit, but it will be necessary for them to exert an extra effort to resist the temptation. Counseling can be helpful following deliverance in learning new coping skills and developing healthy thinking to replace the old demonic state of mind.

The bottom line—*you can't counsel out a demon and you can't cast out a bad habit.* As the deliverance minister, you will find yourself recommending follow-up counseling to some people for whom you've prayed. Although it's tempting, we try to avoid offering to see the person ourselves on an ongoing basis for counseling or ministry. We find that time to perform deliverance is so limited and valuable that it makes more sense for the person to go to someone else for continuing care. In addition, most of us are not certified biblical counselors. Other ministries may be structured differently or have less demands on their time allowing them to be able to offer counseling. We do offer "aftercare," which will be discussed in a later chapter.

PART THREE

SPECIFIC DELIVERANCE ISSUES

7 – THE MINISTRY OF FORGIVENESS

I'm going to let you in on a little secret. When we first started doing deliverance, we battled demons for hours trying to get them to leave. We knew that we had the authority to cast them out, but for some reason they resisted us. We went back to the Lord in prayer and to the Bible in scripture study to find the answer.

The Lord showed us that forgiveness is the hinge pin upon which the entire deliverance turns. It is what causes demons to leave without a fight. It is what will help the person to walk out his deliverance with freedom.

Without forgiveness, those demons have a legal right to stay, and they know it. That's why we now deal with forgiveness very early, right after the Freemasonry Prayer, soul ties and word curses, and before we deal with any other demons. Because once you've been very thorough about forgiving, the rest is easy. We hardly hear a whimper out of the demons as they leave.

To make sure we're on solid scriptural ground, let's look at a few key scriptures:

> And the king called before him the man he had forgiven and said, 'You evil-hearted wretch! Here I forgave you all that tremendous debt, just because you asked me to—shouldn't you have mercy on others, just as I had mercy on you?' Then the angry king sent the man to the torture chamber until he had

paid every last penny due. So shall my heavenly Father do to you if you refuse to truly forgive your brothers. (Matthew 18:32–35, TLB)

According to this scripture, if we do not forgive, God will not forgive us. So there's not a lot of sense in going on with the deliverance if you haven't been forgiven! For example, God forgave you everything, but you can't forgive your abusive ex-husband. According to the Bible, you'll be turned over to the "tormentors," which is another name for demons! So if you choose not to forgive, the demons have a legal right to stay.

Hebrews 12:15 also says, "Watch out that no bitterness takes root among you, for as it springs up it causes deep trouble, hurting many in their spiritual lives" (TLB). If someone has had unforgiveness in his life for awhile, chances are he also has a root of bitterness. The King James Version of that scripture says, "Looking diligently lest any man fail of the grace of God; lest any root of bitterness springing up trouble you, and thereby many be defiled." The word defiled means, "to be stained with demonic processes." A root of bitterness, by definition, gives demons the right to defile, pollute or contaminate you.

Second Corinthians 2:10–11 explains, "Now whom you forgive anything, I also forgive. For if indeed I have forgiven anything, I have forgiven that one for your sakes in the presence of Christ, lest Satan should take advantage of us; for we are not ignorant of his devices" (NKJV). So unforgiveness can give Satan the ability to take advantage of you. Another translation says that it gives Satan the ability to outwit you.

CLUTTERED CLOSETS

There was an old radio show called Fibber McGee and Molly. When Fibber McGee opened his overstuffed closet, you heard clattering and banging as the jumbled, disorganized contents spilled out. In a spiritual sense, Fibber McGee's closet is the place where we stuff all the things that we should have forgiven. We just push it into the closet, shove the door closed and walk away. The rest of our spiritual house might look pretty good. The living room's picked up, the family room is orderly, and the dining room is all set for dinner; because everything is stuffed in that closet.

Our job at the deliverance table is to get people to open that door and deal with what's inside. In the past, we did a lot of "blanket" forgiveness. Since then we've learned a couple of important things from the Lord about forgiving. First, it must be specific. And secondly, it must come from the heart and not the head. And that's why forgiveness often takes more time than anything else in the deliverance session. Forgiveness may sometimes go fairly quickly, but often it takes hours.

FORGIVENESS ISN'T JUSTIFICATION

In order for them to truly be set free from unforgiveness, people need a lot of teaching on forgiveness. First we explain the two principles in the paragraph above—it must be specific and from the heart. Sometimes people are reluctant to forgive because they feel that it lets the other person "get away with it." Holding the grudge is their often unconscious way of punishing the other person. We explain that forgiving doesn't mean that what the person did was right. It doesn't excuse him or let him off the hook at all. It simply changes your response to it. He will still be held accountable to God for what he did. But that's not your problem. You are responsible before God for what *you* do with the hurt.

Forgiveness is not a feeling. It is an act of our will. You don't have to feel like forgiving the person; you simply have to choose to do it. However, the Lord had me take a hard look at the last part of Matthew 18:35 (NIV), " . . . this is how my Heavenly Father will treat you unless you forgive your brother *from your heart*" (emphasis mine).

Forgiving from the heart throws a whole monkey wrench into "blanket" forgiveness and forgiving by rote. So how do you get to your heart? The Lord told me, "Think of specific things that someone did that hurt you, and forgive him for how each one made you *feel*."

Ouch. The Lord wanted us to go into that jumbled closet and get in touch with how we felt when those things happened! Not only was that time consuming, it didn't sound like much fun. But I learned that getting in touch with the emotions that we stuffed there, instead of staying on the intellectual level, would jump-start the healing process, and healing is what deliverance is all about.

In order for this to happen, you often have to relive the emotions that caused you to stuff the experience in the first place. This was particularly hard for me because before my own deliverance, I used to be a gold medalist when it came to stuffing. When confronted with painful experiences, I had a Scarlet O'Hara type of attitude. *I'll think about that tomorrow.* Except of course, tomorrow never came until I had to choose between dealing with it or living with demons.

In ministering forgiveness *from the heart,* if the person seems to be blocking or denying the emotions he feels or felt about the incident, as the minister, you can help by having him repeat after you. Let your facial expression and voice inflection lead him in the right direction. Use emotive words and phrases such as those below.

- I felt humiliated, ashamed
- I felt worthless
- I felt exposed
- I felt hopeless
- I felt unloved
- I felt alone, abandoned
- I felt unimportant, insignificant
- I wanted to be protected, safe
- I wanted to feel cherished, treasured, valuable
- He never made me feel desirable, worthwhile
- I was never appreciated

THE LINK BETWEEN DENIAL AND FORGIVENESS

There are some sneaky little tricks that the devil uses to keep us from forgiving, and the first one is denial. If the devil can talk you into denying that there is anything to forgive, not even recognizing that you need to forgive someone, then you're trapped. He has outwitted you.

One way that people get into denial is that they don't recognize that there was an offense. I always tell people up front, "Look, I'm not ragging on your parents. I'm not trying to get you mad at your husband. I just don't want you to have anything you haven't forgiven, because the consequences are very serious. We could probably write a book about all the good and wonderful things that your family has done for you. But that's not what we're here to do. Today, we're dealing with ways that you've been hurt. Right now, it's not about them, it's about how *you* felt."

Another way that people fall into denial is that they make excuses for the other person. "Well, he didn't know any better." You know, he probably didn't. But that doesn't change the fact that he hurt you. It's the hurt that we need to deal with.

When you identify a situation or event in the life of the person for whom you are praying, that your common sense or the Holy Spirit tells you would be painful or have a negative effect on his life, assume there is a need for forgiveness. Be aware that the emotions of anger and rage are frequently born out of hurt and pain. Human beings are usually uncomfortable with the feeling of hurt because we don't know how to handle it, but we know how to deal with anger—we yell, hit, scream, slam doors. Many people are also more comfortable admitting they are angry than that they were hurt. So whenever you hear "anger," interpret it as "hurt."

Another form of denial is believing that you weren't angry or hurt about the situation. Clue phrases you may hear are, "I wasn't really mad about it," "I didn't really care," "I got over it and haven't thought about it in years." These may be indicators of inner walls (discussed later) or simply failure to recognize the emotion. For a variety of reasons, some people don't want to admit that they were angry with someone. Some people are just "too nice" to be angry. Others are embarrassed to admit it because it is petty or is an unattractive trait in them. As the deliverance minister, you will help them get past these issues, admit the feelings and speak forgiveness over the situation.

We tell people to ask the Holy Spirit to bring to their remembrance any time when someone hurt them, embarrassed or humiliated them, overlooked them, abandoned them, treated them unjustly, made them cry or made them feel like crying. As a rule of thumb, if they remember it on this day, it needs to be forgiven.

They may also tell you that they've already forgiven the person and that may well be true. However, be alert to their demeanor, facial expression and tone of voice when they say it. If there is any sign of clenched teeth, so to speak, you should explore further. Also, be sure to ask if they have spoken the forgiveness aloud. In the deliverance session, we want the demons to hear the person terminate their legal right to invade the person's life.

Akin to denial is simply not recognizing that there has been a wrong done. A good example is when a loved one dies. The loved one clearly is not guilty of any wrong doing, but their death most certainly caused you pain. It is necessary to forgive them for dying.

THE ADULT UNDERSTANDS: THE CHILD JUST HURTS

Another thing that keeps people in denial is that they're hesitant to go back and look at the situation through the eyes of the child they may have been when it happened. This is where they have to get out of their heads and into their hearts. "Mother had to be gone all night because she worked two jobs to support us. I understand that, and it wasn't her fault."

Of course it wasn't her fault. And, of course, you understand that today. But don't tell me that the five-year-old child understood. Don't tell me that she didn't cry at night because her mother wasn't there to tuck her in. It *hurt,* and the five-year-old child didn't know what to do with that pain except stuff it in that closet. You may have even consciously chosen to forgive your mother, however, you forgave her *as an adult* but you may need to go back and forgive *as the child* who was hurt.

FIREWORKS AND FORGIVENESS

The Lord gave me an example of this in my own life. I grew up in a wonderful family—almost like *Ozzie and Harriet.* My parents were very loving and tried never to say or do anything that would hurt me. One of my favorite things was the fireworks on the Fourth of July. On one such holiday when I was around seven years old, I whined to my mother because dad—who was the fireworks guy in our house—wasn't home yet. Mom suggested that I call and ask when he would be home. Dad said, "I'm sorry, it doesn't look like I'm going to make it home in time."

You have to understand that my dad had a full time job as a systems analyst in the daytime, and in the evening he went to night classes at a local university to finish his degree. On this night he was at a study group preparing for a big test the next day. Bottom line, he wasn't out gallivanting around having fun. He was working double time to make our lives better.

My dad didn't do anything wrong. But as a seven-year-old child, I didn't understand that. I felt sad. I felt unimportant. I felt abandoned. I sat on the curb and cried while the other kids on the block played with their sparklers. As an adult, I had to forgive my dad for the way I felt, as a child, when he wasn't there that night.

PRAYER DOESN'T EXCUSE YOU FROM FORGIVING

Another way the enemy traps Christians into unforgiveness is by prayer. Is there anything wrong with prayer? No, unless you use it as a substitute for forgiveness. It might go something like this, "Don't you need to forgive Jane?"

"Oh no, I pray for her every day."

"Did you forgive her?"

"Every single day I ask God to bless her."

"But did you ever forgive her?"

A lot of people are deceived into thinking that praying for the person who hurt them replaces actually forgiving. Forgive them, *then* pray for them.

INNER WALLS

Another element that will keep people from forgiving is emotional remoteness. I really understand these people, because I used to be the queen of remoteness. My way of dealing with pain was to give it enough space until, eventually, it didn't hurt anymore. In the process, I built emotional walls. You see this with children in abusive homes. They just decide not to cry anymore and not to care what anyone does to them. In an attempt to survive, they wall off the pain. In the deliverance session, you must help them choose to tear down those walls. This can be frightening for them because once the wall is gone, the pain can hurt them again. Forgiveness is the way to truly deal with and be rid of the pain once and for all.

GUILT

Guilt is another thing that will keep Christians from forgiving. They feel guilty saying anything negative about their beloved mother who has gone home to be with the Lord. They feel guilty admitting that someone in the church hurt them, because they love their church. Your job as a deliverance minister is to help them realize that guilt is a trick of the devil to keep them in the bondage of unforgiveness.

KEYS TO MINISTERING FORGIVENESS

The following are some keys to being a minister of forgiveness:

The Holy Spirit must be involved

One of the things I always ask the Holy Spirit to do is allow me to operate in the gift of the Word of Knowledge, which is when God gives you information or knowledge of events or situations past or present that you could not otherwise know (First Corinthians 12:8). This gift makes a huge difference in ministering forgiveness to people. For instance, we were praying for a woman one time who had stuffed all her hurt so deeply that she couldn't even remember it. Through the Word of Knowledge, the Lord showed me that her father had beat her in front of her friends, and he had abandoned her on prom night, and never returned to pick her up. When I mentioned this, her face crumpled and she began to weep. The Lord allowed me to peek into her closet and pull out what was hidden there.

You can't rush it

This is hard, especially sometimes for some men, but you can't just go in with a list and say, "Forgive . . . forgive . . . forgive." And you can't let people get away with just glossing over the situation and saying by rote, "I forgive my mother for divorcing my father and moving away to another state." You have to very quietly, and very gently, explore how that felt. Remember they need to forgive the way it made them *feel*. In the example above, a more effective statement of forgiveness would be, "I forgive my mother for divorcing my father and moving away, which made me feel abandoned and scared and unloved." Keep going until you have assurance that the closet is completely cleaned out. It would be a shame to go through the entire deliverance process and have it be incomplete because you were impatient during forgiveness.

Empathize

Sympathy just means you feel sorry for someone. Empathy means that you put yourself in that person's place. That's a godly thing to do and when you do it, the Holy Spirit usually takes over. We prayed for a lady who as a child had been dropped off to live with some relatives. Her mother probably didn't have any choice in the situation, but only came for a visit once every two or three months. When she did show up, she was so busy she hardly had time to talk to her daughter. The woman had so intellectualized this experience that she wasn't in touch with her emotions. I was able to put myself in her place and help her remember the pain of wanting to scream, *"Mama, don't go! Take me with you!"*

Forgive God

Most people have probably stuffed this one so far they don't even know it's there. But in the midst of painful experiences they may have felt as though God deserted them. Deep down, they may have screamed, *"Where were you, God? Why did you let this happen to me?"* Once they get in touch with that, it's very freeing to say, "I repent for blaming you, God. I know you didn't want anyone beating me. I realize that you were there with me."

Ensuring that forgiveness is fully completed will have a positive effect on the rest of the deliverance session. It is sometimes necessary to let the person talk the situation out at length before asking him to speak forgiveness. If it has been stuffed in the closet, it is likely the person has never examined the event before and acknowledged his pain or the effect it had on his life. He must know it is okay to cry, be angry, even yell and call names if it will help. He may need to go through all the emotions he may have been holding back before he is ready to forgive and remove that item from his closet once and for all.

If the forgiveness hasn't been stuffed in the closet, but instead the person has been actually indulging in hurt or anger, it may be necessary to let him cycle through the emotions one last time. He must understand, though, that once he speaks the forgiveness, he must resist the temptation to pick up the old hurt again.

When you have led the person through an emotional forgiveness issue, test the situation to ensure that he has fully dealt with the emotions. He should be able to talk about the person and the situation now calmly and rationally without the emotions he was previously displaying. He will still recognize that the situation was wrong, but he should be more objective about it. If he is still angry or tearful, it may require more work.

Occasionally, you will lead people to forgive what seems on the surface to be rather unlikely people or entities. They may need to speak forgiveness over the government (the IRS took their house), a movie star (for projecting a false image of perfection and causing feelings of inadequacy in the person), an animal (the dog that bit them or their pet that died). These things may seem peculiar, even silly, but I assure you there are times when they are very important.

8 – THE ROOT OF REJECTION

All you have to do is turn on the evening news to get an idea of how pervasive and how dangerous the spirit of rejection can be. Three words can sum it up: Columbine High School. Teens with a deep-seated spirit of rejection took revenge in a killing spree. While Columbine may be an extreme example, children who have been made to feel like outcasts and "nerds" are increasingly taking up arms against those they perceive to be their tormentors.

Because I've been a counselor for a number of years, when I see these heartbreaking newscasts and also when I encounter many of the problems we see in deliverance, my mind rushes ahead to what counsel they need. I suspect that we all need wise counsel from time to time and there is great deal of good to gain from it. However, I want you to understand that counseling will not do a single thing to get rid of demons. It is impossible to counsel them away. Trust me, if it could be done, I would have done it.

We have studied a number of excellent books by authors Noel and Phyl Gibson, a couple from Australia. They believe that the greatest undiagnosed and, therefore, untreated malady in the body of Christ is rejection. This may be the greatest untreated malady on earth.

DEFINITIONS OF REJECTION

In the *Collegiate Dictionary*, the verb "reject" means to refuse to accept. In the *New Oxford English Dictionary*, the definition of reject is to dismiss as inadequate. Another definition is "inappropriate or not to one's taste," or "refuse to show due affection or concern for."

One definition of the noun "reject" is an item that is sold cheaply because of minor flaws. When the spirit of rejection takes hold of an individual, it can make all of these things true in the person's life, either in his own eyes or in the eyes of others, or both.

SUB-SPIRITS UNDER THE SPIRIT OF REJECTION

There are some sub-spirits under the spirit of rejection. The first of these is self-rejection. In this instance, the individual feels so rejected by others that he rejects himself. This may manifest as low self-esteem and self-hatred. Self-rejection may have started as a defense mechanism to protect against rejection by others; the concept is that I'll reject myself before anyone else can do it. However, it opens the door for a demonic spirit of rejection to enter and take up residence.

The second sub-spirit of rejection is the fear of rejection. This person has such a great fear of rejection that he usually withdraws from other people. Fear of rejection can originate as a conditioned response to repeated instances of actual rejection and again, opens the door for the spirit of rejection to cross the threshold into our lives.

The third sub-spirit of rejection is perceived rejection, which usually results from an imagined slight or snub and could also be called "imagined" rejection. The stronger the feeling of rejection is in a person, the more likely he is to image rejection where it doesn't actually exist.

FOUR TYPES OF REJECTION

Listed below are four types of rejection:

Inherited rejection.
Inherited rejection is passed down through a generational curse. The person was born with it, and had nothing to do with acquiring it. Persons born into ethnic, cultural or racial groups that have historically suffered persecution, discrimination or mistreatment are prime candidates for a spirit of inherited rejection.

Purposeful Rejection.

This type of rejection is easy to identify. It takes root because someone doesn't like you. Someone purposefully failed to invite you to a party. Perhaps you were talking to someone and she purposefully turned her back on you and walked away. A spouse left you for another. A parent abandoned you.

Unintentional Rejection.

This happens when your invitation to the party mistakenly went to the wrong address. Or perhaps someone was so lost in his own thoughts that when he passed you in the hall, he failed to acknowledge you.

Imagined Rejection.

Imagined or "perceived" rejection happens a lot more than you might think. One woman had complained to her husband that he didn't make her feel special on her birthday. To correct the situation, he made a special effort to bring her flowers, a gift and took her to a nice dinner for her birthday. Amazingly, she still felt rejected, because he had neglected to get her a sentimental, romantic card. She experienced a combination of unintentional and imagined rejection. Often people who have suffered a great deal of actual rejection become extremely sensitive to it; the spirit of rejection can make them so sensitive that they imagine they are being snubbed when no such thing has happened.

MANNER AND TIMING OF BIRTH

One open door to rejection is the manner and timing of a baby's birth. For instance, any baby conceived out of wedlock, conceived in anger, conceived through rape, incest or adultery will very likely have an open door to the spirit of rejection.

"That shouldn't matter," you might say, "because a baby doesn't have ears at the time of conception." Babies don't have to have ears to hear; they have a spirit and a soul. And though undeveloped, they have a body and mind to which a demon can attach itself. Don't forget, demons have no sympathy or sense of fair play; innocent babies are prime targets.

The following is a partial list of open doors to rejection at conception or birth:

1. The baby is unwanted by one or both parents.
2. The baby causes a serious strain on finances.
3. The baby is born into a large family whose reaction is, "Oh no, not another one."
4. The baby is born a middle child (not being the oldest or the "baby," the middle child may feel overlooked).
5. The baby is not the sex the parents wanted.
6. One parent rejects the other during the pregnancy.

THE MANNER OF BIRTH

1. Manner of delivery is an emergency, protracted or difficult.
2. The baby is born by C-section.
3. The baby is injured during delivery.
4. The baby is premature.
5. The baby is in an incubator and does not experience being held and cuddled in the first few hours or days after birth.
6. The baby doesn't bond with the mother at birth.
7. The baby isn't given physical tenderness.
8. The baby isn't breast-fed.
9. The baby is adopted.

I've read articles about babies born in Eastern block countries that were kept in cribs with little physical contact and not allowed out of the country for adoption until they were around two years old. Eventually these children were adopted by American couples who were desperate for children, and they were both wanted and loved. But by the time the children were five years old, many of the parents were ready to send them back to the orphanages—and some of them did.

The children appeared to be incorrigibles, but the real problem was that they could not bond with anyone. They had suffered major rejection before they were ever born and the rejection continued until they were adopted. In these extreme cases, the root of rejection was so deep that the children did not appear to have the ability to give or receive love. Child psychologists call this phenomenon "attachment disorder." Deliverance would probably have made a difference.

THE LINK BETWEEN REJECTION AND FORGIVENESS

There is a strong link between rejection and forgiveness. When you go through the deliverance session and have the individual release forgiveness to the people identified through the questionnaire or the interview, you need to keep the list of open doors and pray for each of them again when dealing with the root of rejection. In other words, you pray through everything to do with forgiveness, and then hit the same points when praying for rejection. This sounds tedious; however, we have found that when the forgiveness has been fully accomplished, closing the doors to and casting out the spirit of rejection is fairly straightforward and reasonably quick.

PERCEIVED REJECTION

When you listen to what things caused the individual to feel rejected you might honestly think, *I wouldn't feel rejected by that!* And you'd be right, you probably wouldn't feel rejected in similar circumstances. The difference in how individuals respond to the same stimulus may be explained, at least in part, in the book *The Five Love Languages* by Gary Chapman. I would recommend you read this book, but for a quick review, the following are the five most common ways that different people receive love.

1. Physical touch
2. Words of affirmation
3. Quality time
4. Acts of service
5. Receiving gifts

We generally show love to others in the same language in which we receive love. I'll use myself as an example of how these work and why they make a difference in rejection issues. I grew up in a family with my parents and one sister. Both my sister and I have the same love language. We feel loved from words of affirmation (support, approval), and probably our secondary love language is acts of service (showing love through deeds). That worked out very well, because our father's love language was words of affirmation and our mother's love language was acts of service. These were the ways they showed their love to us. As you can imagine, we both grew up feeling loved and well adjusted. Dad spent lots of time listening and talking to us, and in a classic "act of service," Mom would get up and fry chicken every morning because my sister was a finicky eater and wouldn't eat anything else for lunch.

My mother disciplined us primarily by spanking, which was a relief to me. When I misbehaved, I just wanted to get a spanking and get it over with. But my dad didn't spank. He would sit down and talk about the problem, making sure I understood what I'd done wrong. When he used words to show approval to me I received it as love and acceptance. But because my love language is words of affirmation, for him to use words to correct me was pure agony. I felt so rejected that I wept and cried and wished that he would just spank me.

Because no one in my family had the love language of physical touch, there wasn't much physical contact in our family. I don't remember ever sitting on my parents' laps and I don't remember being hugged. Occasionally, my mother would give us a little peck on the cheek, but that was about as demonstrative as we got.

Someone else would have felt very alone and rejected because of the lack of physical contact, but because it wasn't part of my love language, it didn't bother me. If there had been a third sibling whose love language was physical contact, without a doubt she would have had rejection issues.

I got a real shock when I married into my husband's family, because my mother-in-law would hug a lamppost. When you've never been hugged, you don't know what to do with your arms. I had to learn how to respond to her affection. Because her love language is obviously physical touch, if I hadn't learned to respond to her hugs, she might have felt rejected by me.

So learn to listen to people and find out what hurts them, because a person's perception is his reality.

REJECTION IN THE FAMILY, HOME OR SCHOOL

Another way a door to rejection opens is through the family, home or school environment. The following is a partial list of ways this might happen.

1. Alcoholism in one or both parents
2. Being unable to invite friends over because the child doesn't know who might be drunk or abusive
3. Being spoiled, pampered or overprotected
   This doesn't sound like it would bring rejection, but children need boundaries. If they don't get those boundaries, they feel rejected.
4. Unjust or overly harsh discipline by parents or teachers
5. Being called names, teased or picked on
6. Being embarrassed, criticized or put down
7. Events that caused humiliation
8. Being financially "poor," "needy" or unable to "keep up with the Joneses"
9. Wearing braces or glasses
   This can either be an open door for rejection or a status symbol, depending on the child and the environment.
10. Parents getting a divorce
11. Lack of supervision, being alone a lot or a latch-key kid
12. Poor school performance
13. Learning disabilities
14. Constant criticism

15. Pregnancy outside of marriage

16. Having an abortion

    This causes a woman to reject herself as well as feel rejected by others.

17. An abusive or neglectful spouse

18. Being fired or laid off

19. Being unable to find employment

20. Becoming ill or disabled

21. Feeling as though you don't measure up, for whatever reason

22. Not having a good relationship with your adult children

23. Having children who choose the other spouse over you

24. Not getting to see your children or grandchildren

The following is a list of key words and phrases that, when used to describe how the person felt, should flag to you the presence of a root of rejection: embarrassed, neglected, abused, left out, disappointed, laughed at, peeved, made fun of, overlooked, not wanted, made to feel inadequate, ashamed, no guidance, no boundaries and failure. All of the preceding are simply examples to help you learn to recognize an open door or the effects of the spirit of rejection. Be flexible and sensitive to the leading of the Holy Spirit in recognizing issues needing the attention of the deliverance minister.

SYMPTOMS OF REJECTION

Rejection lets in many of the following symptoms, which can be actual demons or simply emotions driven by the feeling of rejection: inferiority, anxiety, worry, depression, the tendency to blame oneself, low self image, self-condemnation, self-hatred, self-accusation, guilt, shame, fear and feelings of inadequacy. Rejection manifests in a wide variety of symptoms.

Aggressive Reaction—When a person with any type of rejection has an aggressive reaction to it he is likely to reject everyone else before he can be rejected himself. This may manifest as rebellion, fighting, being argumentative, criticism, harshness, hardness, refusing comfort, stubbornness, defiance, racial prejudice, swearing and foul language. When you find someone who swears or uses foul language, you will almost always find a person with a spirit of rejection.

Counter Measures to Rejection–In an effort to counter the symptoms of rejection people use pride, haughtiness, arrogance, envy, jealousy, covetousness, striving or competitiveness, perfectionism, performance and manipulation; in doing so they both overcompensate for the problem and open themselves up for more demonic activity. These "counter measures" aren't deliberate efforts to be obnoxious or overbearing. These individuals usually don't realize what is happening. They are simply unconsciously looking for a way to survive the pain of rejection. Regrettably, most of the techniques employed to deal with rejection cause them to be disagreeable and undesirable which leads people to reject them more and more.

Symptoms Turned Inward–In an effort to protect themselves from further pain, many people with a spirit of rejection turn inward. They rely on withdrawal, isolation, independence, self-protectiveness, self-centeredness, selfishness, self-justification, self-righteousness, self-idolatry and self-pity.

Many of the measures to counter the fear of rejection are associated or "linked" with a spirit of pride. It is not difficult to understand that arrogance, envy and possessiveness are related to pride. However, the connection between pride and the inwardly turned symptoms such as self-pity and self-hatred are less obvious. When an individual feels that he is the ugliest person in the world, or the stupidest, the most unworthy and so unlovable that even God can't love him or that his sins are so bad that God could never forgive them, he is exhibiting another form of pride. The "pride of the worm" (Psalms 22:6) makes a person feel that he is different from everyone else. Even though he feels he is *worse* than anyone else, in effect he is just as self-focused as the person who believes he's *better* than anyone else. The spirit of pride and the spirit of rejection work together to convince the person that he is, in a negative way, more significant than others.

Rejected people also try to protect themselves through inner vows. When you make an inner vow, you build an inner wall around your emotions. Sometimes, in the case of abused children, these are essential for survival, but as an adult they lead to a hardness of the emotions and the inability to adequately give and receive love. During deliverance when you recognize a wall, be very gentle as you discuss it; it can be a very frightening business for the individual. You'll need to lead him to repent for building it and lead him to tear it down. It may not be immediately apparent why he should repent for making the inner vow, and it may require some education to help the individual understand. The Lord wants us to trust in Him for protection and anything we use to protect ourselves that doesn't involve Him is sin. The individual may need plenty of time to deal with inner walls. Examples of inner vows might be:

1. I will never let anyone get close to me again.

2. No one will ever hurt me like that again.

3. I'll never be like my mother.

4. I'll never do that to my children.

5. The words "I will never . . ." or "I will always . . ." identify an inner vow.

For a sample prayer for the casting out of a spirit of rejection, refer to Appendix B, Section 1.

9 – BREAKING GENERATIONAL CURSES

One of the least understood ways of transferring demons is through a generational curse. The Bible admonishes us that "through knowledge the righteous will be delivered" (Proverbs 11:9, KJV). In other words, without knowledge the righteous *won't* be delivered. There is nowhere that this is truer than in dealing with generational curses, because if someone doesn't figure out what legal grounds allowed demons to oppress previous generations, the same demons will continue to harass the future generations.

To begin, we'll start with the word "curse." A curse provides the legal grounds for demons to operate in a person's life. Proverbs 26:2 tells us that "an undeserved curse does not come to rest" (NIV). Something opened the door to every curse that exists. A biblical example of generational curses and the "door opener" is found in Deuteronomy 28:45–46:

> And all these curses shall come upon thee, and shall pursue thee, and overtake thee, till thou be destroyed; because thou hearkenedst not unto the voice of Jehovah thy God, to keep his commandments and his statutes which he commanded thee: and they shall be upon thee for a sign and for a wonder, and upon thy seed forever. (ASV)

In this case their failure to keep the Lord's commandments opened the door for the curse to enter. These curses are passed down from generation to generation. They will continue until somebody draws a blood-line and says, "It stops right here."

According to the Bible, "He that speaketh flattery to his friends, even the eyes of his children shall fail" (Job 17:5, KJV). This verse makes it very clear that when the father sins, the children will pay for it.

Isaiah said, "Prepare slaughter for his children for the iniquity of their fathers" (Isaiah 14:21, KJV). The book of Jeremiah says, "The fathers have eaten a sour, grape, and the children's teeth are set on edge" (Jeremiah 31:29, KJV).

Perhaps one of the more illustrative scriptures is found in Lamentations 5:7 "Our fathers sinned and are no more, but we bear their iniquities" (KJV). That's crystal clear. However, let's look at a couple of scriptures from the New Testament as well.

"His blood be on us and on our children" (Matt 27:25, KJV).

"Just as through one man; sin entered the world and death through sin, and thus death spread to all men because all sinned" (Romans 5:12,13, NASB). So the propensity to sin is a generational curse passed all the way down from Adam and Eve.

An example from Chuck Pierce's book, *Possessing Your Inheritance,* reminds us that just as we might inherit our mother's nose or our father's eyes, we may inherit our mother's legalism or our father's alcoholism. Medical science has confirmed that we can inherit genes that cause baldness and mental disorders such as schizophrenia from our parents or ancestors. These are other examples in which the child did nothing to cause the problem, but still suffers the consequences indefinitely.

"Oh well," you might say, "I had a really good family and we don't have any generational curses." You may have had a wonderful family, but do you really think that no one in previous generations let sin into their lives or allowed the devil to dupe them?

SIN AND INIQUITY

Sin and iniquity are not the same. Sin is an offense against God and is called "missing the mark." An iniquity includes the warped deeds of sinners, but has a broader definition that encompasses an evil bent or crooked direction toward sin. In other words, iniquity is the propensity to sin, while sin is the act.

We've seen people with a strong propensity to a particular sin in their family line, but because the hand of the Lord was on their life, they hadn't committed the sin. They may also have used their own self-discipline to resist committing the sin, thus sidestepping the curse. However, the iniquity is an open door for that individual and his children, so that generational curse should be dealt with in the deliverance session.

IDENTIFICATION REPENTANCE

God punishes the iniquities of the fathers down to the third and fourth generations (Exodus 20:5). If it isn't dealt with, it will leave a spiritual weakness toward that sin in the family line. The solution is identificational repentance. Identificational repentance means that you repent because of the sins that someone else committed. I am not suggesting that you can repent for your deceased grandfather's sin of rejecting Jesus as his savior, and somehow get him a hall pass out of hell. That's not going to happen. But you can repent because of the sin he committed on earth and apply the blood of Jesus to it, so that the effect of the sin can be removed from you and future generations. If the children are already born you need to pray deliverance over them.

SCRIPTURAL BASIS FOR IDENTIFICATIONAL REPENTANCE

The Bible is full of scriptures that explain identificational repentance, but we'll just look at a few of them. "If they shall confess their iniquity *and the iniquity of their fathers . . ."* (Leviticus 26:40, KJV, emphasis mine).

The book of Daniel is an excellent picture of this kind of repentance. Daniel was in Babylonian captivity when he began praying for the nation of Israel. He said, "We have sinned and committed iniquity. We have done wickedly and rebelled . . ." (Daniel 9:5, KJV). The interesting thing about this passage is that Daniel wasn't even born when Israel committed the sin! Yet he repented on behalf of the nation.

Nehemiah said, " . . . confess the sins of the children of Israel, which we have committed against you; both my father's house and I have sinned" (1:6, KJV). Nehemiah also records, "They stood and confessed their sins and the iniquities of their fathers" (9:1–2, KJV).

SYMPTOMS OF A FAMILY CURSE

The following are a few of the symptoms of a generational curse:

1. *Chronic poverty or chronic financial problems*
    When you see chronic financial problems, the individual may need to repent because of the sin of his forefathers not tithing. Obviously, if the individual is not himself a tither, he will need to repent for his own sin as well.

2. *Chronic sickness or disease in a family line*
    You may see heart disease, diabetes, kidney disease or any number of chronic illnesses passed down from generation to generation.

3. *Chronic marital problems or divorce*
    Whenever divorce runs from generation to generation, you're usually dealing with a curse.

4. *Miscarriages, female problems or barrenness*
    Once again, you'll see patterns of this problem from one generation to another.

5. *Mental illness*
    You'll see a propensity toward mental illness in more than one generation.

6. *A wandering or vagabond spirit*
    Sometimes you see families that never stayed in one place. The person may have a history of moving a great deal, bouncing from job to job or state to state. He may never have owned a house.

7. *A pattern of sexual abuse*
    It's not unusual to see a pattern of abuse that includes grandmother, daughter and granddaughter who were all raped. Occasionally they were each raped at the same age. I know of one instance where each woman in three generations was raped at age fourteen.

8. *Word curses*

   Clues here would be statements such as "You're just like your father," "You have a terrible temper, just like your grandfather," or "All the women in our family are dead before age 60."

9. *Rebelliousness*

   Some families have a history of all the men doing whatever they wanted to do, refusing to obey rules or respect authority. Some may even have a family history of criminal activity.

10. *Freemasonry oaths*

    Freemasonry oaths bring many curses upon a family. This will be dealt with in detail later in this book.

Generalized lifestyles and patterns of behavior shared by members of a family can be strong indicators of a generational curse at work. I know of a father and son who are an example. The father developed a problem with alcohol abuse at an early age. Gradually over the years, this weakness became more and more pronounced until eventually alcoholism and drug addiction took over his life. He has spent his entire adult life suffering the effects of this addiction and the lifestyle that goes with it. He also had an explosive, uncontrollable temper, was physically abusive to women and was involved in numerous physical altercations. He was in and out of jail many times.

His son, we will call him Ronnie, had very limited contact with his father growing up and while he was raised in what we would consider a "normal" home environment by his mother, in his teens he, too, became addicted to drugs. He demonstrated an unmanageable temper as a child which worsened as he grew older. As an adult, his lifestyle became startlingly similar to that of his father. He was terribly addicted to drugs and was in and out of jail several times for drug-related charges and domestic violence.

An interesting illustration of generationally shared behavior was revealed one day after Ronnie had reached adulthood. His older brother, we will call him Cliff, was talking to their aunt, their father's older sister, whom he had met only a couple of times growing up. They were telling family stories and Cliff happened to mention that when Ronnie was about three or four years old he sometimes got so angry that he would go out in front of the house and, in a temper tantrum, get down on his hands and knees and bang his forehead against the concrete surface of the driveway. The aunt hesitated a moment, then told Cliff that his father had done *exactly the same thing* when he was that age. To them it seemed like an almost incredible coincidence, but with an understanding of generational curses we can see the spiritual significance of the shared behavior. It comes as no surprise to learn that the father's father, too, was a lifelong alcoholic with a history of physical abuse.

10 - THE DANGERS OF FREEMASONRY

There are whole books written on Freemasonry, which I suggest you read. Three of these books include *A Servant of Two Masters? The Dilemma of the Christian Freemason,* by Selwyn Stevens and Larry Kunk, Jubilee Resources; *Unmasking Freemasonry - Removing the Hoodwink,* by Selwyn Stevens, Jubilee Resources; and *Masonry, Beyond the Light,* by William Schnoebelen, Chick Publications. In this chapter, I'll give some brief highlights on this very dangerous organization. The correct name is The Free and Ancient Order of Masons, but it is commonly called the Masonic Lodge or the Lodge of Freemasonry. It is a secret society and you'll find that there are good reasons why they keep so many secrets. Although it is extremely demonic and connected with an antichrist spirit, there is a strong representation of Masons in churches. No one knows the exact number of members of this society, but some estimates suggest that it's as high as three-and-a-half million in the United States.

Freemasonry's hold on society is strengthened by the fact that many of their members are respected, leading citizens of our communities and many of their enterprises are benevolent and valuable to the public. We must not, however, allow this to cloak the malevolence of Freemasonry and its associated societies.

Just to give you an idea about what is involved, below are a few clues to the presence of demons in Freemasonry.

1. According to the literature, "There is nothing in the requirements of Masonry to prevent a Catholic, a Muslim, a Jew, a Buddhist, a Protestant, a Mormon or any member of any religion from partaking of its illumination, kneeling at its altars and subscribing to its creed." *(Masonry, Beyond the Light)*

2. Freemasonry is a religion, which on the surface claims to be totally compatible with Christianity, however, its central deity is not God.

3. Jesus is despised and is never mentioned by loyal Freemasons.

4. Only upon reaching the 31st Degree—the Grand Inspector Inquisitor Commander—does the Mason learn that the central deity of Freemasonry is the "Grand Architect of the Universe," not God. *(Unmasking Freemasonry - Removing the Hoodwink)*

5. Statistically, only about two thirds of the members of Freemasonry know that fact.

6. Every member takes an oath never to divulge information about Freemasonry.

7. Only in later degrees is the secret name of the Grand Architect revealed to be Jahbulon, which is a compilation of three names. Jah is a shortened name for Jehovah. The middle syllable, Bul, is an abbreviation of the name Baal, which in the Bible is an idol representing Satan. The third syllable is On, an abbreviation for the Egyptian god Osiris, the god of the underworld. According to Freemasonry literature, On is the source of all that is good in nature. *(A Servant of Two Masters? The Dilemma of the Christian Freemason)*

8. The Masonic deity is the Great Observer, which is represented by the all-seeing eye on our dollar bill. It is the eye above the pyramid which represents Horus, who is the Egyptian god of life.

9. Those who hold high degrees in Freemasonry believe that Lucifer alone is god. (Lucifer is Satan.)

10. Albert Pike, who was the Grand Commander from 1859–1891, wrote a book called *Morals and Dogma of the Ancient and Accepted Scottish Rite of Freemasonry.* In this book Pike writes, "If Lucifer were not God, would Adonai, the God of the Christians, whose deeds prove his cruelty, perfidy and hatred of man, barbarism, and revulsion for science, would Adonai and his priests calumniate (slander) him?" (Adonai is our Christian God.)

11. The literature also states, "Lucifer is God; unfortunately Adonai is also god."

12. Masons have a special Masonic bible. Only very few, carefully selected passages from the Holy Bible are used. Masons are never given open access to the Holy Bible.

FREEMASONRY OATHS

In each degree, or level, of Freemasonry, initiates must take oaths that are also acted out prophetically. For instance, the first degree oath involves the hoodwink, which means to mislead, blindfold and deceive. This oath involves a noose around the neck, a blindfold, choking, and a sword against the breast. Symptoms passed down through the generations following the oath include problems with the throat and tongue, fear of the dark, fear of the light, fear of sudden noises, choking or fear of choking, claustrophobia, asthma, hay fever, emphysema, other breathing problems, stabbing pain and fear of heart attack.

The second degree oaths bring curses upon the heart and chest. They result in symptoms of emotional hardness, apathy, indifference, unbelief and diseases of the heart, lung and chest.

The third degree oaths involve curses to the stomach and womb. Enactments include scenes of ritual murder, falling into a coffin and false resurrection. These curses result in symptoms of fear of death, martyrdom, false martyrdom, fear of violent attack, assault and rape. They will also bring disorders of the liver, womb, gallbladder or stomach.

The Holy Royal Arch degree rituals include removing the head from the body, exposure of the brain to the hot sun and false communion. These curses result in disorders of the brain and mind, confusion and mental illness. Other symptoms include mockery, skepticism and unbelief.

The York Rite vows include a death wish and the ritual of placing a head on top of a church spire. They take unholy communion by drinking from a human skull.

The Shriners, which is limited to the United States, are fairly high degree Masons. Their members wear clown suits and drive around in funny little cars in parades and perform charitable services. However, as inoffensive as the Shriners seem, the curses involve the hoodwink, a mock hanging, mock beheading, mock drinking the blood of the victim, the mock dog urinating on the initiate and offering urine as a commemoration. *(Unmasking Freemasonry–Removing the Hoodwink)*

The 33rd degree oath is bondage. The ritual involves a cable tow— like those used on slaves and prisoners—as a noose around the neck. As the members drink wine from a human skull, they make a death wish that if the oath is violated the wine would turn to poison.

The following are a list of other secret societies:

1. Prince Hall Freemasonry

    Freemasons are prideful and very racially prejudiced. African Americans are not allowed to join the cult, but Prince Hall Freemasonry is for them.

2. The Order of Amaranth

3. Buffaloes

4. Forresters

5. Elks

6. Moose Lodges

7. Eagle Lodges

8. The Grange

9. Riders of the Red Robe

10. Mystic Order of the Veiled Prophets of the Enchanted Realm

11. Mormonism (linked with Freemasonry)

12. Odd fellows

13. Druids

14. Orange

15. Ku Klux Klan

16. The Woodmen of the World

17. Knights of Pythius

18. Eastern Star

19. Daughters of the Eastern Star

20. Rainbow

21. The White Shrine of Jerusalem

22. The International Order of Job's Daughters

23. The Order of DeMolay

SETTING THE CAPTIVES FREE

You won't always know if an individual's ancestors took these oaths, but since the curses spoken are invoked for ten generations, we have everyone say the prayer to renounce Freemasonry and the other secret orders.

If the individual has himself been a Freemason, or taken other similar oaths, he should pray, repent and renounce all connections to the demons. In addition, he should write to the lodge where he was a member and ask to have his name removed from everything, including the ritual bible. Then he needs to destroy every scrap of Masonic regalia he owns such as rings, aprons and books. If he has a copy of the Masonic bible, it should be burned. Demons will attempt to hide these objects for generations, in order to keep the family connected.

For a prayer for the release from Freemasonry refer to Appendix B, Section 1.

11 - SOUL TIES

A soul tie is a very powerful type of bonding between two people, resulting from a covenant-type relationship. Some soul ties are good and appropriate, and others are evil and need to be broken. We'll look first at a few examples of godly soul ties. A classic example of appropriate soul ties are those that exist between a husband and wife. According to the Bible, "For this cause shall a man leave his father and mother, and shall be joined unto his wife, and they two shall be one flesh" (Ephesians 5:31, KJV). The word "joined" in this scripture indicates what we commonly call a soul tie. Married couples are in covenant together and this joining is appropriate.

Good friends can also have godly soul ties. We see an example of this in the relationship between David and Jonathan in the Old Testament. "And it came to pass . . . the soul of Jonathan was knit with the soul of David, and Jonathan loved him as his own soul" (First Samuel 18:1, KJV).

It appears that the souls of good friends are appropriately joined together. Proverbs 18:24 says, "A man who has friends must himself be friendly, but there is a friend who sticks closer than a brother" (NKJV). Proverbs 17:17 tells us, "A friend loves at all times" (NKJV).

The Bible also shows us that the souls of parents and their children should be joined together. An example of this is found in the relationship between Jacob and Joseph. One translation says, "His father loved him and his life was closely bound up in the boy's life."

Godly soul ties also join Christians. According to the Bible, Christians are *supposed* to be joined and knit together: " . . . from whom the whole body, joined and knit together by what every joint supplies, according to the effective working by which every part does its share, causes growth of the body for the edifying of itself in love" (Ephesians 4:16, KJV).

DEMONIC SOUL TIES

An ungodly linking between two people exists when they are joined together through sin, which opens the door for demons to pass back and forth between them. In a soul tie, part of you is spiritually tied to the other person and part of that person is tied to you. Even if there has been no physical contact in many years, a part of the two people is continually bound together. Another ungodly linking is found in Hosea 4:17, "Ephraim is joined to idols" (NKVJ). Clearly, any type of idolatry creates ungodly soul ties.

SEXUALLY TRANSMITTED SOUL TIES

One of the most common ways for people to acquire demonic soul ties is through sexual sin. According to the Bible, when a couple has sex they are joined together. In First Corinthians 6:16 we read, "Or do you not know that he who is joined to a harlot is one body with her? For "The two," He says, "shall become one flesh," (NKJV).

To understand how this operates, just take out the word "harlot" in the above scripture and insert the words "anyone you've ever had sex with." In other words, you are "joined" to anyone with whom you have sexual relations. This includes genital contact of any kind, such as oral sex. During deliverance these discussions are not always comfortable. It can be extremely embarrassing for the individual to have to list every sexual partner he's ever had. However, during a deliverance session, we explain to the individual that we're going to poke, pry, badger and be as nosy as we have to in order to make sure he doesn't leave with any demons. It is important to be matter-of-fact about this issue as with all other areas of deliverance so the individual doesn't feel he is being judged and condemned. Most people find it comforting that they are only asked to list the first names of their sexual partners. We don't want any more detail than absolutely necessary to perform the deliverance.

A lot of people don't realize that an ungodly soul tie exists between a husband and wife if they had sex prior to marriage. "Yes, but we're married now!" they might say. That's true, but they weren't married when they committed the sin of fornication, so they still need to repent of it, and sever the ungodly soul tie. Breaking the ungodly soul tie will allow the godly soul tie between husband and wife to thrive and strengthen.

OTHER TYPES OF SOUL TIES

Bad Company. Another open door to demonic soul ties is through the company you keep. The Bible says, "Do not be deceived: 'Evil company corrupts good habits,' (First Corinthians 15:33, NKJV). The demons at work in the life of the "bad company" you keep will tie the two of you together so that they can get at you. If you run with the wrong crowd, their demons will take advantage of you.

Family Relationships. Evil soul ties also develop in perverted family relationships. Under normal circumstances, godly soul ties exist between parents and a child. But when the child becomes an adult, that bond needs to change a bit. For instance, when an adult child marries, the tie between parent and child should adjust. If a meddling mother won't turn loose, she will drive a wedge between her son and his new wife. She may demand the same loyalty and attention that was acceptable when her son was a child. In spite of the fact that he has his own family, home, job and responsibilities, she may demand that he mow her lawn weekly and discuss all of his decisions with her. She may even insist that her son choose her over his wife whenever there is a conflict.

It's not unusual to see ungodly soul ties exist when a child was greatly desired by his parents. For instance, some couples wait for years, hoping and praying for a child. When they *finally* get their child, one or both parents often make the child the center of their universe. The child may be smothered and overprotected. The relationship actually becomes idolatrous, because the child is exalted to a place above everyone else— even God. This demonic joining must be broken.

It's also not unusual to find ungodly soul ties between twins, especially identical twins. If you're not sure if one exists between twins for whom you are praying, you should deal with it, just in case.

The Dearly Deacesed. People can also have ungodly soul ties with the dead. If an individual had an ungodly soul tie with someone before he died, we've found that death does not sever it. Even though the other party is deceased, if an ungodly soul tie existed, it should be broken during deliverance. While it is normal to experience a period of grief when a loved one dies, protracted mourning can open the door for a spirit of grief, which will create an ungodly soul tie between the individual and the deceased.

In Churches. We can see ungodly soul ties within churches in cases in which the congregants almost idolize the pastor, which allows a soul tie to develop. We often see people in the church who are so joined with another believer that they can hardly make a decision without the other person's approval, which is a symptom of a soul tie. We also always break soul ties with anyone who was a part of the shepherding movement or in similar cases in which a spiritual mentor became controlling.

Witchcraft, Blood Brothers, Oaths of Brotherhood. Soul ties always develop if witchcraft is involved. If the individual called a psychic hot line or consulted a fortune teller or medium, demonic soul ties must be broken with the "advisor."

Any blood covenant results in a soul tie as well. A lot of children unwittingly formed blood covenants when they decided to become "blood brothers" following the example of the Lone Ranger and Tonto. The little girl next door and I didn't have a clue what we were doing when we pricked our fingers and mixed our blood. We just wanted to be blood sisters. If blood was involved, always break an ungodly soul tie.

Anyone who has been involved in Freemasonry, fraternities, sororities, cults or gangs must break those soul ties. Always break soul ties if the individual took an oath of brotherhood. Soul ties can also be passed down through the generations, so watch for this as well.

Soul Ties with Animals. Ungodly soul ties can also exist between individuals and their pets. You can recognize this when someone has an inordinate affection for an animal. Although most of us love our pets, some people put their pets above members of their family. In other instances, the pets literally become the person's children. I've known people who still go every month to visit their pet's grave several years after the pet's death which may be an indication they have an excessive affection for the pet resulting from an ungodly soul tie and a spirit of grief.

Demonic soul ties will also form any time there is a sex act between a human and an animal. When casting these spirits out, we generally give them the name of the type of animal with which the individual had sex. For instance, with a dog, we might cast out a canine spirit. For a cow, we might cast out a bovine spirit. On one occasion, we'd gone through so many names that we had trouble thinking of any more. We had been casting out foul spirits all day so finally, after much consideration, we cast a "fowl" spirit out of the person who had sex with a chicken. If you find it difficult to supply the name of the spirit, don't forget the demon is subject to you in the name of Jesus whether you know its name or not. It isn't absolutely necessary to have a name for it. You can cast it out as "the spirit that came in when . . ."

TRAUMA AND BLOOD TRANSFUSIONS

Soul ties are created when a person is involved in a trauma with another person. An example would be a car wreck. If the person has been involved in a serious car accident, break soul ties with the driver and passengers in his car as well as the driver and passengers in the other cars involved. If he hit a deer, break soul ties with the deer.

There are times when a person is distressed driving past a place where the accident occurred. In these cases the person may have developed a tie with the land based in fear. We have the person break a tie with the location in a similar manner to breaking ties with an animal, then deal with the spirit of fear, dread, etc.

Because the Bible tells us, " . . . the life of the flesh is in the blood:" (Lev 17:11, NAS), there is spiritual danger associated with blood transfusions, which is often a life-saving step following severe shock and trauma. The spiritual danger exists both for the one receiving the blood and the one giving it. It is necessary to break soul ties with recipients of your blood and blood donors whose blood you have received. If you have received a blood transfusion, thank God for the life-saving cells, but break any soul tie with the person who donated the blood. Send back to the person any part of himself that is tied to you in bondage. Call all parts of yourself back that are tied to him. Cast out any demon that entered through the soul tie or through the blood.

If you have been a blood donor, bless the person who received your blood, but break any blood ties that were established. Call back any part of yourself that went to that person with the blood.

The same spiritual danger is present for those giving or receiving an organ or tissue transplant.

IDENTIFYING THE SOUL TIE ASSOCIATED WITH CONTROL

Trying to control another person is ungodly behavior and a soul tie is created between the controlling person and the one being controlled. Below is a list of clues to the presence of ungodly soul ties with people who want to control or have tried to control a person. (The subject of control is discussed in depth in chapter 14.)

1. There is a person who insists on approving all the individual's decisions.
2. They can't make a move without the other person.
3. Extreme possessiveness or jealousy (soul tie with the person of whom they are possessive).
4. They idolized another person.
5. They have been idolized by someone else.
6. They are extremely protective of another person.
7. You hear them say things like, "What would I do without him?" or "I just couldn't live without him."
8. Anyone who was verbally, emotionally or physically abused (soul tie with the abuser).

9. If they've been on either side of a controlling relationship (e.g. they have controlled someone or have been controlled by someone).

10. Any prolonged or intense grief (this may indicate a control soul tie with the deceased).

BREAKING A SOUL TIE

To break a soul tie:

1. Have the individual repent of any sin that allowed the ungodly soul tie.

2. Have the individual repent for allowing the soul tie to exist.

3. Have him renounce the soul tie and take back what the enemy stole from him.

4. Command the demons to leave.

5. Pray that God will forgive any sin that he committed, if appropriate.

For a prayer for breaking soul ties refer to Appendix B, Section 1.

PART FOUR

THE SPIRITUAL STRONGMEN

12 – THE STRONGMAN OF PRIDE

Since pride is the sin that got Lucifer cast out of heaven, it may well be the oldest sin on earth, and all you have to do is look at Satan's history to see how deadly it is. Pride is a spiritual strongman and a strongman opens the door for other spirits. For instance, the Bible says, "Pride goeth before destruction and a haughty spirit before a fall" (Proverbs 16:18, KJV). Clearly, pride and haughtiness are linked. According to *Strong's* concordance, "haughty" means arrogance, pride, to exalt or to rise to great height.

Another symptom of pride is smugness; I'm certain we all know someone who is smug. One definition of smug is "too pleased with your own goodness." They can also be too pleased with their own respectability, cleverness or accomplishments. They may be self-satisfied and complacent—basically too pleased with themselves.

IDLENESS

Strange as it may seem, idleness is another trait connected to pride. You may wonder, as I did, how the two are connected. We see an example of this in Ezekiel 16:49, "Behold, this was the iniquity of thy sister Sodom, pride, fullness of bread, and abundance of idleness was in her and in her daughters, neither did she strengthen the hand of the poor and needy" (KJV). This scripture shows how idleness stemmed from pride.

If you think about people you've known who are idle, they usually think they're too good to work like everyone else does. They may be the person who sits on the sofa while everyone else cleans the kitchen after

Thanksgiving dinner or the person in the workplace who finds a way to get others to do his work.

OBSTINACY

Obstinacy is a sin also linked with pride. Nebuchadnezzar is an Old Testament example of this. "But when his heart was lifted up, and his mind hardened in pride, he was deposed from his kingly throne, and they took his glory from him" (Daniel 5:20, KJV). Someone who is obstinate becomes hardened and stiff-necked with pride.

We see this again in Proverbs 29:1, "He, that being often reproved hardeneth his neck, shall suddenly be destroyed, and that without remedy" (KJV). He had becomes stiff-necked from pride. Many times, we see a spirit of pride physically exhibited or manifested in an individual's neck. This happened in the example we gave earlier of Keith, when his neck swelled during deliverance.

MOCKING

The strongman of pride also lets in mocking and scornful spirits. Once again, in Keith's example, while his neck swelled, the demon manifested with mocking laughter. However, when you deal with a mocking spirit, it may have entered through rejection. These are the things you have to ask the Lord to clarify.

We see pride and haughtiness linked with mocking in Proverbs 21:24, "Mockers are proud, haughty and arrogant" (TLB). The New International Version translates that verse, "Mockers delight in their mockery."

STRIFE

Strife can be another symptom of pride. We all know someone who has been labeled as a "know-it-all." People who think they know it all often fall into strife or conflict with others, because they think they're too smart or too clever to need to listen to what anyone else has to say. Their pride makes them angry that anyone would doubt or question what they say.

A very interesting and somewhat unexpected link to pride is self-deception. Once again, you may wonder what that has to do with pride. The answer is found in Jeremiah 49:16, "The terror you inspire and the pride of your heart has deceived you" (NIV). According to this scripture, self-deception is born out of the pride in your heart.

As there are two sides to every coin, there are also two sides to many spirits. In the case of the spirit of self-deception, one side of the coin is self-exaltation. The flip side is just the opposite: "I'm the worst. I'm the most stupid. I'm the ugliest person there is!" That is the pride of the worm, which is a backwards kind of pride. If you'll notice, it's still about me, me and me. Pride points the way to thinking you're the *very* best or the *very* worst.

Other examples of reverse pride revealing itself is through statements such as, "I'm so unworthy no one could ever love me." He may say, "I'm so disgusting that no one could ever want to be around me," "When I look in the mirror I'm just disgusted."

If he thinks he is the ugliest person in the world, you have to wonder how much time he spends in front of the mirror. One type of pride says, "Everything I touch turns to gold." The reverse side of pride says, "Nothing I do turns out right." The connection between this type of pride and rejection is clear.

CONTENTION

We see in Proverbs 13:10 that, "By pride cometh only contention; But with the well-advised is wisdom" (KJV). The word contention means argumentative, quarrelsome or competitive. Often everything is a contest with a person with a spirit of contention or pride because the need to win may be born out of pride.

The *World Book Dictionary* defines contentious as arguing about trifles. We've all known people who will argue about *anything*. That contentiousness stems from a spirit of pride.

SELF-RIGHTEOUSNESS

Self-righteousness is a form of pride that was most visible in the Phari-
sees in Jesus' day. An example of this is found in Luke 18:11–12, "The
Pharisee stood and prayed thus with himself, God, I thank thee, that I
am not as the rest of men, extortioners, unjust, adulterers, or even as this
publican. I fast twice in the week; I give tithes of all that I get" (ASV).

This entire prayer is about how great he is. Another clue to the link
with the spirit of pride is how many times he uses the word "I." He
thanks God that he is not like other people . . . you know, those other
people who are *sinners.* He is totally oblivious to his own sin of pride and
haughtiness and the spirit of self-righteousness.

THE ULTIMATE FORM OF PRIDE

The ultimate form of pride is what cost Satan everything and results in
hell being filled daily with people for whom it was never created. It is
a pride that results in rejection of God. We find an example of this in
Psalm 10:4, "The wicked, through the pride of his countenance, will not
seek after God: God is not in all his thoughts" (KJV).

According to this scripture, there's no room for God even in this
person's thoughts. So the ultimate form of pride, though it may never be
verbalized, is a deep-seated attitude of pride of heart that believes that
he doesn't *really* need God. This person may be an atheist, but that is not
who we deal with in deliverance.

Outwardly, the individual may appear to be a Christian, but God can
see our hearts and He hears our private thoughts. This person may even
believe that Jesus is the son of God and that most people do need Him
in order to get to heaven. But deep down, he believes that even God
realizes that *he* doesn't need Jesus, because God made him so smart, so
charming and so wise . . . in his own eyes. This may well be the person
to whom Jesus was speaking when he said, "Go away, I never knew you."
Ultimately, just like in Satan's case, pride is rebellion against God.

However, if the individual can see the sin of pride in his own heart
and repent, praying humbly, "Lord, forgive me, I'm a sinner," he can be

delivered from the spirit of pride and one day he will hear, "Well done, thou good and faithful servant."

INDEPENDENCE

We Americans have a tendency toward independence that can really go to seed and become a problem. We may love the song, "I Did It My Way," to which the Lord may respond, "Yes, dear, sadly you really did." He would find it sad, because the whole point of Christianity is that we've been bought by the most precious price ever paid—the blood and suffering of Jesus on the cross. Being born again means we don't do things *our way* any longer. It means that we crucify our own plans and agendas in order to fulfill God's plan for our lives.

That's what makes the pride of independence so dangerous. A symptom of prideful independence may be, "I can do anything I set my mind to." On the surface, this may not seem problematic, but it can be if the person is depending on himself instead of on God. In other words, he has made himself the god of his own life. The Bible says, "Not by might, nor by power, but by my spirit, saith the Lord of hosts" (Zechariah 4:6, KJV). Any time someone is depending on his own abilities, his own wisdom or his own strength to do anything, he is operating in pride.

RELIGIOUS PRIDE

Another strutting kind of pride stems from a religious spirit that causes people to believe that their beliefs are the only right ones. They may also believe that their church is the only right one. This closed-mindedness goes beyond resistance to non-scriptural and non-Christian concepts and stems from religious pride. Another way this may be demonstrated is in people who are convinced that they don't really need—despite the fact that God commands it—to go to church. Again, they have exalted themselves above God and the Bible. They think they are so good or smart or "together" that attending church is unnecessary.

This pride may also manifest in the belief that, unlike other people, they don't need to read and obey the Bible, they don't need to study the Word of God, they don't need to read Christian literature and they don't need to attend Christian seminars and workshops. They are operating in pride.

The attitude of spiritual superiority that accompanies a religious spirit may cause them to believe that they don't need deliverance. They may not say it aloud, but they believe that, *"Other people may have demons, but I certainly don't."*

PREJUDICE

Prejudice is an ultimate form of pride. This demon convinces people that they are better because of their race, their color, their nationality, their education, their social status, their intellect or any number of other things. Christians can also fall into this trap if God has called them to certain kinds of ministry. One example might be missionaries who have made sacrifices to serve God in the foreign missionary field. They may be deceived into thinking that Christians who haven't given up everything for God are inferior.

Because of this nation's early roots in slavery, racial prejudice has been passed down through the generations. Many Christians with the spirit of pride operating through prejudice have recognized racial prejudice in themselves, and having recognized it as a sin, decided to no longer be prejudiced. When those racially prejudiced thoughts or attitudes surface, they shove them down and refuse to respond to them. Although that's a good choice, the demon is still there and should be cast out.

TAKING PRIDE IN SIN

Strange as it may seem, you can actually detect pride in certain people when they confess their sins. You recognize this when they explain that their sins are so much worse than other people's sin. These are the people who say they committed fornication more than anyone else. They stole more money from the company than anyone else. They have a kind of pride over just how great a sinner they actually were. They're proud of it.

This kind of reverse pride is still more about them than it is about God and as they confess their sins, you'd like to see some repentance apart from pride.

13 – WHOREDOMS AND BONDAGE

Whoredoms and Bondage are both spiritual strongmen that are often closely linked together. A myriad of related spirits come under their umbrella.

WHOREDOMS

Whoredoms are really idolatry. Hosea 4:12 explains, " . . . for the spirit of whoredoms hath caused them to err, and they have gone a whoring from under their God" (KJV). The New International Version of the Bible translates whoredoms as a "spirit of prostitution." In the Old Testament, the Jewish people were considered the spouse of God, so when they began worshipping other gods, the Lord called it adultery. *Strong's* definition of whoredoms is "to commit adultery."

Whoredoms represent anything that we put ahead of God. It can be as blatant as worshipping other gods, or as subtle as an ungodly devotion to people or things. If you put your spouse or children ahead of God, it is idolatry, or a spirit of whoredoms. This form of idolatry can manifest as anorexia nervosa or can cause unhealthy attachments to food, sex, diversions, hobbies, sports, television, power, pursuit of a career, the love of money, ambition, video games, possessions, religion, loved ones—any relationship or anything that we put ahead of God.

The spirit of whoredoms takes away the person's free choice to decide how much attention he pays to the subject of his obsession and how important it is in his life. The spirit blinds the person to the knowledge that the behavior is excessive or if he does recognize its damaging effects, he is powerless to make himself stop.

PROSTITUTION

The prostitution connected to whoredoms is not limited to the body. It can involve the mind and spirit, as in the case of the children of Israel who worshipped false gods. One of the symptoms of a spirit of whoredoms is chronic dissatisfaction which causes the person to always want more and more of whatever is the target of his desire. This dissatisfaction drives the person to excess and you'll find that a spirit of whoredoms is usually involved when you are dealing with anything that is excessive. It might involve excessive appetite, excessive dieting, excessive exercise or any other obsession. I followed the life of an aging movie star who, after suffering a life-threatening disease, became obsessed with his health. When the disease went into remission, he began spending his entire day exercising and preparing health concoctions. He had a room in his home literally filled with health remedies and nutritional supplements, carefully catalogued and stored in perfect order. That had become his whole life; he didn't do anything else. His experience with disease had plainly opened a door to a spirit of whoredoms that was driving his obsessive behavior.

To make this clearer, let's examine sexual sin. If someone committed fornication, that involves a spirit of perversion. But if his sexual appetite became an obsession over either the sex act or the thrill of the hunt, we are dealing with whoredoms. Accordingly, all obsessive compulsive disorders stem from the spirit of whoredoms. Sexual fetishes can be driven by a spirit of whoredoms.

BONDAGE

Whoredoms and bondage are linked, so it's important to review them together. The spirit of bondage is mentioned in Romans 8:15, "For ye have not received the spirit of bondage again to fear; but ye have received the Spirit of adoption, whereby we cry, Abba, Father" (KJV). The New

International Version calls bondage "the spirit that makes you a slave again to fear." Clearly, bondage includes any kind of addiction.

Strong's definition of bondage is "to serve, to be in bonds or to tie." Bondages might include addictions to drugs, alcohol, cigarettes, food, television, video games, pornography, sex addictions, unnatural sex acts, rock music, physical exercise, bulimia, religious cults, spending money or gambling.

The two keys that let you know these stem from bondage are that they provide false comfort or an escape. You might hear someone say, "I took drugs to dull the pain." They might say, "I couldn't stand the way I felt, so I slept all the time," or "All I did was watch television, because I didn't want to think about how bad I was hurting." As you can see, each of these activities provided false comfort or escapism.

First Corinthians 6:12 says, "All things are lawful unto me, but all things are not expedient: all things are lawful for me, but I will not be brought under the power of any" (KJV). The New International Version says, " . . . I will not be mastered by any." When you are under the influence of a spirit of bondage, it masters you.

When a spirit of bondage is at work, the person afflicted isn't given a choice in how he will behave. The spirit drives his behavior with addiction and compulsion. Even when he knows in his mind and heart that what he is doing is destructive, he seems powerless to stop. Occasionally someone can control an addiction by sheer will power and determination, but he is only "disciplining the demon." He has to go through life with white knuckles just trying to hold on to his resolve to stop the addictive behavior.

Once he is free of the spirit driving the addiction, he will have the option to decide whether he will give in to bad habits or not. After deliverance from a spirit of bondage, counseling is often needed to help the person learn a new way of thinking and dealing with the everyday struggles of life. In the past he had used the addiction to avoid feeling pain, conflict, confusion and other emotions and he may never have learned other, healthier coping skills. Counseling can be of benefit in helping him develop the skills needed to live a normal life.

One of the ways to differentiate between bondage and whoredoms is by asking the question, "Is this addiction or is it idolatry?" To see the difference, I'll give you an example from my own life. Many years ago, I had a three-pack-a-day cigarette habit. I was a Christian, but with very little revelation at the time. My husband made me an offer: He would take me skiing with my old roommate, if I'd quit smoking. I really wanted to make the trip, so I agreed. However, I was still chain smoking as we drove to the airport. Every time I lit another cigarette, my eight-year-old son said, "Mom, we aren't going, are we?" Before we boarded the airplane, I threw away my cigarettes and I've never had one since. I just said aloud, "Cigarettes are very addictive to me and I can't ever play with them again."

I didn't curse myself by saying I would always be addicted to cigarettes, but regrettably I didn't stop there. I said, "Since I can't smoke, I'm going to eat anything I want to eat." Almost immediately, I started gaining weight. It would be years before I realized that I'd unknowingly opened a door to a spirit of whoredoms. I assumed I had traded one form of bondage (cigarettes) for another (food). It wasn't until I went through my own deliverance that I realized that my relationship with food had become a whoredom.

For instance, let's say it was three in the morning and I was reading an interesting book. One of the characters in the book ate scrambled eggs. The next thing I knew, I was obsessing about scrambled eggs. I *had* to have scrambled eggs; nothing else would do. If I were out of eggs, I left home, found an open store and bought them. Before long, I was in the kitchen scrambling eggs. I was acting on an obsession.

Another clue to a spirit of whoredoms occurred when I went out to eat. For instance, I decided to go out to eat with a friend after church. My friend said, "What do you want to eat?" I said, "I want Japanese food." We drove to a Japanese restaurant, but they'd already closed, so we went to another restaurant and had a steak instead.

The next time we were going out to eat, I said, "I want Japanese food." My friend said, "You *still* want Japanese food?" I looked at her sort of funny and said, "Of course, I haven't had it yet."

It finally dawned on me the difference between my friend and me. If she wanted to eat Japanese food, and we had a steak instead, she would be satisfied because her hunger had been satisfied. My wanting Japanese food had nothing to do with hunger. I wanted it—had to have it—because of obsessive thinking. That's when I realized that I wasn't dealing with a spirit of bondage, but a spirit of whoredoms. Whoredoms control your thinking until you satisfy the obsession. The obsession doesn't stay satisfied for long, though, and the cycle starts over again.

WHOREDOMS AND SOFT DRINKS

The spirit of whoredoms can give you an all-or-nothing type of mind-set. Another example from my own life is that before my deliverance, I couldn't drink just one coke. If I didn't buy any cokes, I wouldn't drink any. But if I drank one coke, before the day was over, I would drink twelve. So I had to either drink a pack of cokes a day or not keep any in the house.

When I went through my deliverance, we had to unlink the bondage and the whoredoms in order to get rid of this behavior. Now I can drink a coke and stop there. I can actually drink half a coke, be satisfied and never finish it. That wouldn't have happened if I hadn't unlinked bondage and whoredoms and gotten rid of them both. Now that I have been set free from the spirit of whoredoms, if I eat or drink more than I should, it is because of my own bad habits and not the influence of the demon.

ADDICTIONS AND COMPULSIONS

Bondage is an addiction or compulsion that provides false comfort. Whoredom is obsessive thinking, which is idolatry. Before I got free of these spirits, I had a problem with network marketing. I would get into a network marketing business and become so obsessed that I didn't want to do anything else. I would even skip church to work on the business. It obsessed my thinking so much that I finally learned to pray about every opportunity that crossed my desk. Each time, the Lord said, "No, that's a stumbling block for you." That doesn't mean that network marketing is a stumbling block for everyone, but I couldn't do it without becoming obsessed. Once again, when I went through deliverance, I was set free.

We were praying for a man who had a motorcycle that he loved. However, he admitted to spending too much money on it. He wanted lots of chrome and he just kept buying chrome for his motorcycle; he thought about it all the time. He already recognized that there was a problem and he sincerely wanted to change his behavior. During his deliverance when we discussed his motorcycle, he said, "Well, I guess if I need to, I'll just sell the thing. I want to be free." This illustrated the "all or nothing" mindset that accompanies the obsession or whoredom. The individual controlled by a spirit of whoredoms can only control the obsession by staying entirely away from the subject of the obsession.

We were able to tell him that he wouldn't have to sell his motorcycle—just get rid of a spirit of whoredoms. Recently, he told me that he is enjoying his motorcycle and hasn't bought anything for it since his deliverance.

Prior to his deliverance, this same man sold his gun collection because he kept obsessing about which gun to buy next. Totally eliminating the subject of his obsession by selling his gun collection or motorcycle was his way of disciplining the demon. Since deliverance he can handle a gun collection, because he's no longer controlled by a spirit of whoredoms. Once he was freed from whoredoms, he was able to enjoy these pleasures in his life without loosing balance and becoming obsessed with them. He will still need to discipline himself to maintain that balance, but he will no longer have to discipline the demons.

14 - SPIRIT OF DIVINATION

One of the primary traits of the strongman of divination is using demonic forces to tell the future. We see an example of this in Acts 16:16–18, "And it came to pass, as we went to prayer, a certain damsel possessed with a spirit of divination met us . . ." (KJV). The New International Version translated the spirit of divination as, "a spirit by which she predicted the future." So divination involves trying to determine the future through demons and apart from the wisdom of God.

Obviously, the actual study and/or practice of witchcraft throws the door wide open for the spirit of divination to enter. Witchcraft seeks to use demonic power to control events and people. Satan has managed to make the practice of witchcraft popular and fashionable today with television shows, movies and books. Wicca is a popular religion devoted to the practice of witchcraft and the worship of demons. The devil is subtle. He doesn't walk up to a person and say, "Hi, I'm the devil, and I'd like to control your life and make sure bad things happen." Most people wouldn't be foolish enough to fall for it and say, "Okay by me!" Instead, you can walk into any toy store and see Ouija boards sitting on the shelf right next to Monopoly. How innocent can you get? It's nothing but a child's toy. There's no warning on the box: Beware - This Will Open the Door for Demons to Harass You for the Rest of Your Life. Satan's tactics are sneaky and insidious.

Items as seemingly innocent as a rabbit's foot lucky charm and a toy magic ball that answers your questions about the future are the devil's way of getting us to practice divination without realizing it. As we've discussed before, ignorance of the evil does not protect us from the entry of demons. Spiritual laws are as absolute as physical laws. Ignorance of the law of gravity will not protect you if you step off the roof of a ten-story building.

Another door opener for the spirit of divination is the horoscope. It's one of the innocent little things the devil uses to ensnare people. I would venture to say that few people today, even Christians, don't know their zodiac sign. Reading the morning newspaper, the person may notice what his horoscope says. He doesn't think too much about it, and eventually may pick up a little book on horoscopes at the grocery store. Without even realizing what he is doing, he starts trying to predict his future without God's guidance.

Some other door openers to the spirit of divination are hypnotists, charmers, magicians who do magic from the power of Satan, handwriting analysis, psychics, fortune tellers and numerology. We must note, however, that not all handwriting analysis is demonic. For instance, psychologists note that people who write back-handed have a tendency to have repressed personalities. That information may not be particularly helpful in your life, but it isn't necessarily demonic either. Other forms of handwriting analysis are used to try to determine the future and are open doors to the demonic. The same is true of "magicians." If the magician is simply a performer who uses illusion to entertain, there is no demonic element involved. It is when the magician uses or attempts to use the power of Satan to make things happen that the devil is invited in.

Passive mind states are another open door for the spirit of divination. Drugs may or may not be used, but in this instance, the individual purposefully clears his mind so that he can clearly hear guidance and direction from demons, particularly familiar spirits, which we will discuss in a later chapter. This activity is a type of sorcery.

Water witching is another way the enemy has duped people. For decades it was an accepted practice among farmers. I remember being a little girl and following my grandfather around while he witched for water. He would never spend money to drill a well until he'd used his divining rod—a forked branch of a tree. He never realized that he was using witchcraft to find his water. And I'm sure he never knew that Hosea 4:12 says, "My people consult their wooden idol, and their {diviner's} wand informs them; For a spirit of harlotry has led {them} astray, And they have played the harlot, {departing} from their God" (NASB).

Rebellion is a door opener for the spirit of divination. First Samuel 15:23 says, "For rebellion is as the sin of witchcraft, and stubbornness is as iniquity and idolatry. Because thou hast rejected the word of the Lord ..." (KJV). Whenever you see rebellion, you should always cast out a spirit of divination.

PHYSICAL PROPS

The spirit of divination is linked to a spirit of witchcraft and both of them often involve physical props which the individual should destroy. These might be crystal balls, pyramids, ouija boards, good luck charms, zodiac signs, crystals and ankhs among other things.

When I was growing up, my sister went through a teenage rebel phase and she had an ankh, which is a cross with a circle on top that is directly associated with Egyptian worship of false gods. I never had an ankh or anything like it. But a few years ago I decided to clean out a closet that was overflowing. Inside I found a jewelry box that my grand-mother gave me when I was about 12 years old. It brought back all sorts of pleasant memories and I sat down to look at the mementos that were inside. Imagine the chill that ran down my spine when I opened a drawer and there lay a silver ankh! It must have been my sister's, and to this day I have no idea how it got in my jewelry box. It had been hiding there for more than 30 years.

CASTING OUT WITCHCRAFT

A spirit of divination is linked to witchcraft and witchcraft can be pretty obstinate about leaving. We've found a few things that help make it pack its bags and move on. We have one team member read scriptures aloud that deal with releasing people from witchcraft (scriptures included in Appendix C, Section 2), while another team member speaks to the spirit and commands it to leave. Be sure the person for whom you are praying keeps his eyes open during the casting out process and as the deliverance minister, keep a close watch on his eyes. Witchcraft seems to be an especially hate-filled demon and we often see a look in the person's eyes of unmitigated, passionate hatred when the demon is commanded to leave. Seeing that look fade away is helpful in knowing that the demon is gone.

A while back we had a rash of people who had literally made pacts with the devil. Those are the hardest to cast out, and we've found it helps to have them renounce the spirit several times. They may say, "I invited you in, but now you are uninvited. You cannot stay; I command you to leave."

If there was a blood pact with the devil or a covenant with a witch, you should also anoint the person with oil.

ASTRAL PROJECTION

The spirit of a man is what gives him life. When the spirit leaves, a human body is clinically dead. Under normal circumstances, the body cannot survive long without the spirit.

Dr. Richard Eby, a Christian and chiropractic physician, in his life story, wrote about falling from a two story balcony and landing on his head. He was pronounced dead. Fourteen hours later, his spirit came back into his body, and he lived. Miraculously, Jesus died and was buried for three days before His spirit returned to claim his body. These are examples of the supernatural power of God.

Astral projection is a perversion of those miracles. During astral projection, a person allows demonic powers to cause his spirit to leave his body for demonic purposes. Sometimes astral projection is a tool used to spy or gain illegal information to use against other people. It is also used for supernatural power encounters. During astral projection, the human body doesn't die because demons link the spirit with the body until the spirit returns. Sometimes hallucinogenic drugs are used as doorways to astral projection.

Occasionally demons will hold the spirit out of the body until it dies, then they use the body as a bargaining chip. Wanting to get back to his body, the individual may make a new pact with the devil. Demons can also mimic near-death experiences.

People who have participated in astral projection must repent and renounce and break all pacts with the demons. The spirit of divination must be cast out along with all spirits that came in during the passive mind state.

CONTROLLING SPIRITS

Any time you deal with spirits linked with witchcraft, you should deal with a spirit of control as well. Although the term "spirit of control" is overused, the problem of controlling spirits is very prevalent. For instance, some people say, "He is very controlling," when the person is just bossy. You can have a bossy personality without there being a demonic element to it.

A spirit of control could be defined as an attempt to dominate another person in order to fulfill one's own desires. By definition, anything that violates another person's will is witchcraft, but the individual probably has no idea that he is practicing witchcraft.

A spirit of control will always involve manipulation or intimidation. As with pride, there are two sides of control. One side is when the individual controls other people. The flip side is when he submits to someone controlling him. You will see some people who do both at the same time.

The person with a spirit of control may be obsessed with supervising and controlling other people's behavior—beyond normal bossiness. This control is characterized by manipulation. The controlling spirit can be categorized into two parts: emotional manipulation and spiritual manipulation.

EMOTIONAL MANIPULATION

A person with a spirit of control will do whatever it takes to get his victim under his power. He may over react or under react to things. He may blow up and threaten at the slightest misstep. If he thinks you aren't going to do exactly what he wants you to do, he may react in anger. Or he may just withdraw and give you the silent treatment for days at a time. Both of these reactions are beyond pushy; they are manipulating by playing on the emotions.

Control often presents itself as angry, bossy and threatening, but that's not always the case. The type of control that is often harder to peg is the person who exerts "gentle control." He may use tears and helplessness. He might be very loving and say, "I love you so much! How could you even think about leaving home to go to college?" Some controlling people act very helpless in order to make the victim feel an overwhelming sense of responsibility to them and play on guilt and pity. This can happen in any type of relationship and is very tied to co-dependency. Controlling people may seem sweet, but they expect you to fix their problems.

It's very hard to break free when someone "loves" you so much. This was portrayed very well in a movie called "Only the Lonely" starring John Candy. He played the role of a man in his mid-thirties who had never been married and was devoted to his mother. When he finally went on a date, she called him and complained of chest pains, and he had to end his evening and come running home to take care of his mother. She had no intention of letting him marry and move away from her control.

We prayed for a woman who grew up in an environment very similar to the one in the movie. Her mother was very controlling. On one occasion, her mother took an overdose of medication, but made sure that the family saw her pass out. The manipulation was, "If you don't do what I want, I'll kill myself."

On other occasions, she would faint if she didn't get her way. When she fainted, the whole world stopped and everyone turned their attention to Mom. These are classic forms of manipulations.

Look or listen for things like this:

1. You don't love me anymore.

2. After everything I've done for you.

3. I guess you don't need me anymore.

4. You're the only one I can turn to.

5. Anything that plays on the person's pity or sense of guilt.

ANGER AND THREATS

Another form of emotional manipulation is anger and threats. This is much easier to identify. It often involves word curses, criticism, threats and intimidation. Think of the stereotypical abusive husband. The person's goal is to paralyze his victim with fear or indecision so that she will be easier to control.

Very often this escalates from verbal and emotional abuse to physical abuse.

SPIRITUAL MANIPULATION

A spirit of control operates in the church through spiritual manipulation. These people are led by a spirit of control, not by the Holy Spirit. When praying for them, ask that they would allow the Holy Spirit to lead them. Timothy wrote about this problem in Second Timothy 3:5–6, " . . . having a form of godliness, but denying the power thereof: from such turn away. For of this sort are they which creep into houses, and lead captive silly women laden with sins, led away with divers lusts . . ." (KJV).

Actually this doesn't just happen to weak willed women, it happens to men as well. I like the way the New International Version translates this verse. It says that these people "worm their way in." That is very true. If they came up to you and said, "I'm going to control you for the rest of your life," you wouldn't let them do it. But they're more subtle. They worm their way inside.

Christians who consider themselves to be super-spiritual can be very controlling. They may try to seek to hear God for people in order to control their lives. That's when mentoring switches to control. This person may say, "The pastor isn't teaching what we need to hear." So they organize their own select little group for Bible study. They'll often give false words and visions. If you try to leave the group, they'll be very self-serving and warn you to stay. They will also pray controlling prayers over you, praying for their own human desires for someone else's life, which is nothing more than witchcraft prayers. An example of a witchcraft prayer is a parent praying that his son's marriage will break up because he doesn't like his daughter-in-law or someone praying that a friend or loved one will change churches and come to his church only because he wants him close by. These prayers are selfish and don't take God's will into consideration.

There was a woman who was part of a group I attended at one time, who considered herself to be super-spiritual, but she was actually just super-controlling. She had a grown daughter who was living with her and on one occasion she asked us to pray for her daughter. When she told us what she wanted us to pray, she was asking us to pray witchcraft prayers, which we declined to do. For example, she wanted us to pray that her daughter would be home with her every evening instead of with her friends, and that her daughter would find a job that allowed her to spend more time at home with her mother. These were the mother's desires and didn't take into consideration God's will or what was truly best for her daughter.

TWISTING SCRIPTURES

A person with a spirit of control will twist a scripture in an attempt to control other people. A good example of this is the domineering husband who twists the scripture about women being submissive to their husbands and uses it to make his wife knuckle under and do everything he wants. He may require that she have dinner ready every night promptly at five. She may not be allowed to visit her friends. He may also control and dominate their sex life, forcing her to have sex any time he demands it. He requires all these things in order for his wife to be obedient to the word of God, but in fact, he is imposing his own selfish desires on her.

Controlling or manipulating parents may twist God's commandment to honor your mother and father to control the actions of their children.

SHEPHERDING MOVEMENT

The Shepherding Movement was very popular in the 1970's and probably began as a good idea. Based on the concept of each person having a spiritual mentor, it quickly dissolved into a situation where the mentor took the responsibility to hear from God on behalf of the other person. Instead of encouraging the individual to move toward God, the mentor stood between the person and God. The entire movement became tainted by a spirit of control.

You may run into people who were a part of that movement, and that spirit should be cast out of them. You may also run into controlling pastors, controlling church leaders and individual Christians controlling each other, and each of them needs deliverance from this spirit.

TRAITS OF A CONTROLLING PERSON

The person for whom you are praying often needs some education on the traits of a spirit of control in order to recognize times when they have controlled others or been controlled themselves. The following are a list of traits for which you should look and listen during deliverance. The person for whom you're praying may have done these things to others or had them done to him. Either way, they are clues to the presence of a controlling spirit.

1. He feels important giving orders.

2. He wants the other person to get his approval on all decisions.

3. He makes statements such as, "I can't make it without her."

4. He believes he knows more than anyone else about issues with which the other person is dealing.

5. He undermines the other person's own judgment and opinions.

6. He is very possessive and feels jealous and threatened by the other person's other relationships.

7. He feels he must protect the other person from every experience.

8. He feels if he isn't involved in every decision the other person makes, the person might make a bad choice.

9. He makes plans for the other person, without the other person's permission.

10. The controlling person thinks the victim owes him something and demands it be paid back.

11. He uses guilt to manipulate.

12. He controls through flattery or criticism.

13. He is or has been physically or emotionally abusive or he has been the victim of physical or emotional abuse.

15 – FAMILIAR SPIRITS

Familiar spirits are characterized by communication between a demon and the individual. Familiar spirits attempt to counterfeit the Holy Spirit. In First Samuel 28, Saul sinned against God by seeking advice from familiar spirits, rather than from the Lord. Other examples of familiar spirits are found in Leviticus 20:27 and First Samuel 28:7.

One clue to the presence of familiar spirits is a repeating pattern in someone's life. Someone who goes from one abusive relationship to another probably has a familiar spirit. Someone who is abandoned repeatedly most likely has a familiar spirit of abandonment. He may have a familiar spirit of lust, or a familiar spirit of abuse, each of which promotes the repetitive pattern.

When you look up the word "familiar" you'll find one of the definitions is "father." So you always deal with inherited spirits when a familiar spirit is involved.

OPEN DOORS TO FAMILIAR SPIRITS

The following is a long list of open doors that would allow familiar spirits access:

1. *Necromancy*
Any child or adult, who through purpose or play, got involved in a séance has been involved in necromancy. The purpose of a séance is to call up

the dead, by demonic power. What the séance actually draws is familiar spiritis.

2. *Spirit mediums*
This includes going to a spirit medium who attempts to contact the dead or calling a psychic hotline.

3. *Clairvoyance*
People with this familiar spirit can, among other things, see people or things that are lost. They are occasionally hired by the police to locate missing persons.

4. *Yoga*
Practicing yoga is an open door particularly if the person participated in the meditation or chanted a mantra. Each position of the exercises was created to invoke a demon, therefore, if a person has practiced only the exercise without the meditation, he still needs to repent and renounce it.

5. *Spiritists*
Any time you take mind-altering drugs to get in touch with the "other world," you have participated with spiritists. Also as children, we often attempted to reach the "other world" through the use of the Ouija board or through our own séances.

6. *Passive mind dreamer*
These are trance channelers and false visionaries.

7. *False visions*
Instead of having a word from the Lord, the source is the demonic.

8. *Psychic powers*
If you have ever been to a mind reader or a palm reader, or attempted to do this yourself, even in fun, it opened a door to the demonic.

9. *False prophesies*
Instead of having a vision from the Lord, the source is the demonic.

10. *Transcendental Meditation*

This was extremely popular in the 1980s. The person was taught a mantra. The person was unaware that the word used was the name of a demon and that he was calling on the demon to come and guide him.

11. *Having practiced Extra Sensory Perception (ESP)*
ESP is another way to attempt to gain information apart from God.

12. *Peeping and muttering*
A reference to this is found in Isaiah 8:19, "And when they shall say unto you, Seek unto them that have familiar spirits, and unto wizards that peep, and that mutter: should not a people seek unto their God?" (KJV). Peeping and muttering is a form of false tongues.

13. *Imaginary playmates*
Not all imaginary playmates are dangerous. If the child has an imaginary playmate who gives him direction and tells him what to do or think, it is a demonic spirit guide.

14. *Spirit guides*
People who invite spirit guides are attempting to gain information about their current life or the future. Many times the individual won't realize that this is a sin against God. If he thinks the spirit is sent to him from God, he may be reluctant to part with it.

15. *Psychic lines*
Psychic hot lines are very prevalent today. Their infomercials are on television late at night and draw in many unsuspecting, lonely, frightened people, who are looking for guidance.

16. *Poltergeist activity*
A poltergeist is a spirit, usually mischievous and occasionally malevolent, which manifests its presence by making noises, moving objects, and assaulting people and animals.

17. *Past life regressions*

Before I learned about the things of God, I believed in reincarnation. I tried past life regressions through hypnosis while I was in college. Many people are as duped as I was, and I didn't learn the truth about this demonic activity until after I was filled with the Holy Spirit years later.

18. *Worship of angels*

The New Age movement has opened the door to familiar spirits by creating a frenzy of interest in angels, which often includes praying to them or worshipping them. This is strictly forbidden in the Bible.

19. *Certain types of visualization and inner healing*

Some visualization and inner healing is from God and occurs through the blood of Jesus. However, any other type is demonic in nature. In addition, if you are attempting to visualize things through your natural mind, you're in danger of inviting familiar spirits.

20. *Ouija boards*

This has been discussed. It is a very subtle trick of the devil.

21. *Other demonic games*

Dungeons and Dragons, Magic-the-Gathering or Everquest Role Playing Game are other examples of demonic games. If you have children at home, do your research and keep them away from these open doors. If you've played, you will need to close the doors and cast out the associated demons. Other examples of games inviting in the demonic are included in the Adolescent and Child Keys in Appendix A, Sections 2 and 3.

22. *Conversing with demons during deliverance*

People can become fascinated with demons and with talking to them. There is only one instance in the Bible where Jesus conversed with a demon and all He did was ask it its name. In fact it is addressed in Luke 4:41: "And devils also came out of many, crying out, and saying, Thou art Christ the Son of God. And he rebuking them suffered them not to speak: for they knew that he was Christ" (KJV). Because of the inherent risks of conversing with demons, we don't do it, even in deliverance.

We speak to them and command them to leave. We don't allow them to speak to us and we certainly don't converse with them. If they do speak, whatever they say is likely to be a lie.

23. *Praying to dead saints or ancestors*
Many people in Eastern religions and those in the Catholic Church have unwittingly committed this sin and opened the door for familiar spirits.

24. *A drawing spirit*
This type of familiar spirit draws to it another person with the same spirit. For instance, I once knew a nurse who was raped. The rape opened the door for familiar spirits of lust. She could walk into the room of a very elderly, ill patient while wearing loose, ill-fitting scrubs, not looking sexy in the least. She would leave the room blushing from the obscene things the patient said to her. This happened repeatedly. The spirit of lust in the elderly patient recognized and drew the familiar spirit of lust in her. Once the spirit was cast out, the pattern stopped. Spirits of abuse often draw the abuser and the abused to each other.

Jealousy is a strongman and has a much broader meaning than you might imagine. One example of the spirit of jealousy is found in Numbers 5:14 and involves a jealous spouse. Another example is First Samuel 18:10–12 where we see the evil spirit of jealousy come upon Saul and cause him to want to kill David. The *World Book Dictionary* defines jealousy as "full of envy, grudging, resentful and suspicious." It also means to dislike or to fear a rival. The root word for jealousy and zeal are the same, so jealousy is a type of perverted zeal.

The root of this spirit goes much further than simple jealousy; it is even linked with murder or the temptation to murder. One of the questions we ask is, "Have you ever been tempted to commit murder?" People are usually very candid and say, "Yes, I really meant to kill the person if I got the opportunity." To date, we've only prayed for one person who actually carried out the intent and killed someone. When you think of a spirit of jealousy, always look for a spirit of murder as well.

The spirit of jealousy is grudging and resentful. The most commonly held perception of jealousy is feeling suspicious, distrustful and possessive about another person. This is, in fact, related to the spirit of jealousy and these feelings can easily progress to more intense and even violent emotions.

Some characteristics of a person with a spirit of jealousy are a desire for revenge, competition, anger, rage, hatred, cruelty, strife, contention, envy and division. To know which facet of the spirit of jealousy you have encountered, it is important to understand the differences between them. Competitiveness, especially excessive competitiveness, can be an outcropping of the spirit of jealousy. Anger is just a feeling of displeasure, which reveals itself in a desire to fight back. Rage is a violent outburst of anger, which usually has a sudden onset. Most people can control anger as you would smother a fire in a frying pan, but rage is like an oil field fire and is much more difficult to control.

Envy is discontent or ill will at another person's good fortune. When envy is present, the jealous emotion has progressed from "I'm mad" to the beginnings of a more deep-seated problem in which they wish another person ill will. It may have nothing to do with the individual, but may develop because of envy for the person's position or possessions.

Hatred is loathing, detestation, malice, spite and animosity. The word malice implies going beyond anger and really wanting something bad to happen to the person who is the object of the hatred.

Rancor is the next step in the process. By now the person is extremely, viciously angry. It has progressed to bitter hatred. Rage can come and go in a flash, but rancor is something that hangs on and eats at the person. Rancor involves malice and wishing harm to the person who is the target. Hatred and rancor can involve cruelty and evil acts.

The final step is murder, which is the desire to kill someone. This is more than the desire for that person just to drop off the face of the earth. When you're dealing with a person with a spirit of murder, he wants the person dead and in most cases he wants to do the job himself. Even if the person has never committed murder, if he has thought about it or wished he could kill someone, you must cast out a spirit of murder.

The spirit of jealousy can enter a person's life when extraordinary feelings of anger, envy and the like are experienced. Frustration can turn to anger and even rage. Temper tantrums in children may indicate a spirit of jealousy or may open doors for it. You will find the spirit of jealousy when a person says he wants to control his temper, but finds it impossible. He may wish he could get over his intense dislike for another person, but isn't able to do it. A wife may know intellectually that it isn't logical for her to be so possessive and jealous that even though he has given her no reason to be suspicious, she distrusts and even spies on her husband. She knows it doesn't make sense and may be damaging her marriage, but she repeatedly finds herself checking up on him or accusing him.

When the person wants to control the behavior, but can't, you are dealing with a spirit of jealousy. Some people may be able to force themselves to control the behavior, but they have to fight against it every day. These people are having some success at disciplining the spirit of jealousy, but they need deliverance from it.

THE SPIRIT OF HEAVINESS OR DEPRESSION

What we commonly call depression, in the Bible is called a spirit of heaviness. We see this in Isaiah 61:3, "To appoint unto them that mourn in Zion, to give unto them beauty for ashes, the oil of joy for mourning, the garment of praise for the spirit of heaviness" (KJV). The New International Version translates the word mourning as "despair." *Strong's* defines heaviness as, "despondent, to grow dull, to darken, to be dim, to fail, faint, feeble or obscure."

Psalms 69:20 says, "Reproach hath broken my heart; and I am full of heaviness" (KJV).

CHARACTERISTICS OF A SPIRIT OF HEAVINESS OR DEPRESSION

The characteristics of this strongman are despair, dejection, hopelessness and, mentioned above, depression. One of the first signs is often the loss of interest in God or the loss of joy in the Lord. It can be a feeling of heaviness, a broken heart that won't mend, self-pity or a victim spirit. A victim spirit is one that causes the person to feel everyone is against him or that his problems are worse, larger and more numerous that anyone else's. The victim spirit comes under the strongman of heaviness, but you need to address self-pity and a victim spirit individually.

Suicidal thoughts or the wish to die are almost always related to a spirit of heaviness. It may also include inner hurts, a torn spirit or insomnia. If you are dealing with someone who is on medication for any of these things, *never* tell him to stop taking his medication. That is out of the realm of deliverance and is not our job. Tell him to go back to his doctor and work it out with him. There are several reasons for doing this. First and foremost, there can be serious side effects from withdrawing from a medication too quickly. Secondly, the manifestation of the result of a deliverance can be gradual and you would hinder his recovery by removing the medication too soon. Also, giving instructions or advice regarding any medication or medical treatment can expose your ministry to legal risk. Always refer the person to his doctor in matters of medication.

In addition, I believe that it's a good witness to the doctor if someone goes back after deliverance and the doctor can see such an improvement that the doctor discontinues the medication or reduces the dose. Stopping the medication without the doctor's approval may be presumption instead of an act of faith. If he goes back to the doctor in worse shape and says, "I had some people pray for me, and I stopped my medication," it damages the credibility of the ministry.

After deliverance, the best defense the person can have against the spirit of heaviness is praise. He should spend as much time in praise of the Lord as possible and learn to use praise to drive away the spirit if it tries to reenter. First Samuel 18 and 19 describes how Saul was often taken with a spirit of depression and David played psalms of praise on the harp to lift the attacks of heaviness. During deliverance, if the spirit of depression resists leaving, it can be helpful to speak or even sing praises to God during the casting out process.

SPIRITS OF SORROW AND GRIEF

A spirit of grief can enter a person's life following excessive mourning after losing a loved one. The spirit of grief is not a strongman, but can often be linked to the strongman of heaviness. We prayed for a woman who had opened the door for a spirit of grief when her brother died. When we prayed for her, she wept so bitterly that you would have thought that he died yesterday. In fact, he died when she was a child. She shouldn't have been suffering that way after twenty years. Protracted or prolonged mourning is a clue to the spirit of grief. There is no set limit, but generally after a year there should be a lifting of the grief over the death of a loved one.

A spirit of grief and sorrow can enter following a divorce, due to prolonged mourning over the loss of the marriage. Even the end of a bad marriage can trigger this response as it represents an upheaval in lifestyle and the death of the dream of living happily ever after. This can happen to either of the people getting a divorce and we also see it in children whose parents divorced. The child may mourn for the parent who leaves the home almost as if the parent had died, especially if following the divorce the child sees the absent parent very infrequently.

The spirit of grief can gain a foothold when someone becomes physically or mentally disabled. This can be true when it is the person himself who becomes disabled or when it is a loved one. In either case, the life he knew before has, in effect, died. The spirit of grief can take root anytime you lose something or someone that you care about deeply.

As with the spirit of heaviness, once the spirit of grief and sorrow has been cast out, explain that praising the Lord will keep the door shut.

According to the Bible, the spirit of fear is a strongman that brings a host of problems and opens the door to oppression and torment. The world accepts fear as a fact of life, but the Bible says that the only righteous fear is the fear of God. In addition, according to scripture, faith is the *only* way to please God, and fear is the opposite of faith. So except for the fear of God, there is no way that God is pleased with fear. Lastly, fear is the devil's domain.

The Bible says, "For God hath not given us the spirit of fear; but of power, and of love, and of a sound mind" (Second Timothy 1:7, KJV). Clearly, the spirit of fear is not from God, therefore, it should be dealt with and cast out.

We should recognize that there is a difference between caution and fear. Being cautious at times is wise and can represent God's method of protecting us from danger. But, any fear, except the fear of God, gives Satan a legal entrance into your life, especially if it is extreme, prolonged or exaggerated beyond common sense.

THE FACES OF FEAR

Fear has many faces, and once it is seemingly overcome, often disguises itself and returns in another form. There is the fear of failure, the fear of success, the fear of people, fear of the dark, fear of poverty, fear of abandonment, and the list goes on. The spirit of fear will take advantage of a crisis in our lives to spring on us. Fear can also progress to a phobia.

For instance, I don't like snakes, but I'm not afraid of them. However, for years I suffered a phobia involving, of all things—grasshoppers.

Don't ask me why, because I don't know. I remember playing with grasshoppers as a child and I wasn't afraid of them then. But somewhere along the line, I developed not only a fear, but a phobia of them. There wasn't any decision making on my part, nor even a part of me that could be rational about grasshoppers—if confronted with one, I screamed and became paralyzed by fear. That, of course, is one of the characteristics of a spirit of fear: It's irrational. Fear also opens the door for anxiety and panic attacks.

I was never afraid of the dark. I was never afraid of scary movies or spiders. But if I even thought a grasshopper was around, I screamed and broke out in a cold sweat. I'm not a stupid person, but I was unable to rationalize away my phobia of grasshoppers. For some inexplicable reason, my greatest fear was that a grasshopper would touch my neck, and I had even had nightmares about that. People who knew of my phobia thought it was funny to sneak up behind me and softly touch the back of my neck. It wasn't funny, and whenever that happened, I lost control.

I remember one time I was in my car about to leave for my office. I looked down, and there was a grasshopper at my feet. I was paralyzed by fear. I sat there crying and mumbling, "Grasshopper . . . grasshopper . . . grasshopper." I finally managed to get out of my car and stumbled to the neighbor's house. I literally couldn't go to work until someone got the grasshopper out of my car.

DREAD

Fear may begin as dread or distrust, but the end stage of fear is always torment. I experienced torment with my fear of grasshoppers and suffered nightmares about them.

Most people don't understand how demonic dread can be. There was a period of time when every morning I awoke with a pain in my neck that progressed to a debilitating headache. I changed pillows. I bought orthopedic pillows. I did everything that I knew to do, but the cycle of pain and headaches continued. There was something about the way I slept that hurt my neck, and eventually I started dreading morning so much that I had a hard time going to sleep at night. In time, I didn't get more than two or three hours of sleep a night, because I was in such dread of the pain I would suffer when I awoke in the morning. I didn't realize that I'd opened the door to a spirit of dread. I became afraid to go to sleep because of the pain I would experience when I awoke.

Finally, I got into a healing line at church and fell under the power of the Holy Spirit. The Lord finally had my attention and said, "You're expecting it and you're accepting it." I realized that dread had opened the door for fear.

Dread can also enter when there is a threat of something distasteful happening or when you know something bad is going to happen and you have time to wait and worry. For example, if you are concerned that you may be about to lose your job, a feeling of dread can descend on you that eventually turns to fear. In people who are unable to pay their mortgage and begin receiving threats of foreclosure, dread and fear are common.

DISGUISED FEAR

The list of fears people suffer is almost endless; common fears include fear of snakes, spiders, the dark, ghosts, water, crowds, enclosed places, fear of public speaking, heights and flying. We also frequently encounter the fear of death, the fear of being injured, the fear of emotional pain, the fear of physical pain, the fear of rejection and the fear of losing a loved one. Fear is fear; all of these fears are caused by the same spirit—the strongman of fear.

When my mother became ill with a debilitating and progressive illness, I stood by her, took care of her and did everything I knew to do to help her until she died. While I was doing my best to stand in faith for her recovery, her doctors agreed that recovery was not possible. That prediction wore on me and I started dreading her death. This is an example of the spirit of fear taking advantage of a crisis in my life to take hold.

Unknowingly, that opened the door for me to fear losing other people I loved. I found myself thinking of my family and friends and wondering which one of them was next. I had to quit watching the television show *ER,* because I would see something happen on the show and think, *That could happen to someone I love!* I even mentally calculated how long I could expect loved ones to live based on their current age. I didn't speak any of this aloud, but as the spirit of fear became more and more entrenched, I found myself less and less able to control the fearful thoughts.

Long before we started this ministry, I knew that demonic spirits were behind my fears and we cast them out. However, we didn't know how to close the doors. So when I finally cast out the fear of grasshoppers, that spirit changed clothes and returned in the form of fear of losing a loved one. When I finally figured out what was going on, we cast that fear out, but it changed disguises again and returned as a phobia of wet roads.

I hate to even admit the wet road phobia, because it was so peculiar. I have always been a good driver and have never been involved in wrecks. Driving on snow, ice or slick roads had never bothered me. But now suddenly, if it rained just a little bit, I found myself white-knuckling the steering wheel. I finally realized that I was dealing with a spirit of fear when I found that I was afraid to walk across an asphalt parking lot because it had rained.

We cast out the spirit of fear once again. Later, when we started our deliverance ministry and learned about the doors I had standing wide open, I did it right and closed the entry points. That put a stop to the spirit continuing to reassert itself in my life wearing different disguises. However, it tried occasionally for awhile to sneak back up on me.

An example was one night as I was coming into my house after participating in a lengthy deliverance session. It was dark, my hands were full and I was tired. As I unlocked my front door, I saw a grasshopper sitting on the porch. Having been delivered from that fear, I was able to make a conscious decision not to allow it to frighten me. But, the spirit of fear had another trick up its sleeve. I opened the door partway and, because my hands were full, backed into the dark house. As I got part of the way inside, something suddenly hit me on the behind. I was caught off guard and having just seen the grasshopper, my mind screamed *"grasshopper attack!"* I shrieked, dropped my books and papers and prepared to take off running.

It took only a few seconds for me to realize that my dog had greeted me at the door by jumping up and putting his front feet on my rear. Because the spirit of fear did not have a hold on me, I was again able to calm myself. I immediately closed the entry point that had just opened up and cast the spirit of fear out. In the days when the grasshopper fear was operating, that episode would have given fear a big foothold in my life.

Remember all the horrors that Job suffered? When his nightmare began, Job said, "For the thing which I greatly feared is come upon me, and that which I was afraid of is come unto me" (Job 3:25, KJV).

Job's fear opened the door for Satan to bring those very things upon him. Any fear, except the fear of God, gives Satan a legal entrance into your life.

ENTRY POINTS

Some entry points for the spirit of fear might be the following:

1. Fear can enter from the womb, especially with a difficult or emergency birth.

2. A memorable experience that caused fear. Look for the first time the person remembers experiencing a particular fear and any particularly powerful experiences.

3. Thinking about doing something can bring intense fear. The possibility of losing your job or waiting for the results of a medical test are examples.

4. Dread

5. Public speaking – According to recent statistics, the thing Americans fear most is public speaking. Fear of death takes second place. I heard someone say that means that most people attending a funeral would rather be in the casket than giving the eulogy.

It's good to develop a "no tolerance" policy where fear is concerned, because the end stage of fear is always torment.

18 - LYING, SEDUCING, ERROR AND ANTICHRIST

LYING SPIRIT

In Second Chronicles 18:22 we see, "Now therefore, behold, the Lord hath put a lying spirit in the mouth of these thy prophets, and the Lord hath spoken evil against thee" (KJV). As you can see from this scripture, a lying spirit is not limited to someone who tells lies; a lying spirit is a strongman that lies about the things of God.

There is also a spirit of deception linked to it. The person with a lying spirit may have opened the door to it through a spirit of deception. Clues to the presence of a lying spirit are superstitions, divinations and familiar spirits.

Accusations against God, religious leaders or the body of Christ are all doors and clues to the presence of a lying spirit. Slander is also linked to a lying spirit, and goes deeper than accusations.

Some very good Bible teachers have gotten into false doctrine, because they were deceived by a lying spirit. Not everyone who tells a lie has a lying spirit, but certainly each lie is a step in that direction.

Gossiping can be the work of a lying spirit or the spirit of deception. Some people seem to thrive on gossip and you frequently find the same people in the middle of it repeatedly. Character assassination and false accusations can be an extreme example of gossip driven by a lying spirit.

One of the places we learn about seducing spirits is in First Timothy 4:1, "Now the Spirit speaketh expressly, that in the latter times some shall depart from the faith, giving heed to seducing spirits, and doctrines of devils; Speaking lies in hypocrisy; having their conscience seared with a hot iron" (KJV). The New International Version translates that verse, " . . . deceiving spirits and things taught by demons." Simply put, succumbing to the strongman of seducing spirits is listening to demons and taking your religious doctrine from them.

The prime target of the strongman of seducing spirits is the believer. People who aren't in covenant with God don't believe the right thing anyway, so seducing spirits don't bother targeting them. Instead, their goal is to seduce Christians into believing lies. If Satan can't entice Christians into sin to ensnare them, he will attempt to entangle them in false religion. Seducing spirits are linked closely with the strongmen spirits of error and antichrist.

I mentioned earlier that I once believed in reincarnation. A seducing spirit recognized my immaturity and vulnerability, and set out to seduce me into believing a lie. That tactic not only opened the door for other spirits to dominate me, but it also rendered me no threat to the devil.

Seducing spirits cause people to be fascinated with evil ways, objects or people, and can lead them from the truth. We are told in Deuteronomy 13:6–8,

> If thy brother, the son of thy mother, or thy son, or thy daughter, or the wife of thy bosom, or thy friend, which is as thine own soul, entice thee secretly, saying, Let us go and serve other gods, which thou hast not known, thou, nor thy fathers; Namely, of the gods of the people which are round about you, nigh unto thee, or far off from thee, from the one end of the earth even unto the other end of the earth; Thou shalt not consent unto him, nor hearken unto him; neither shall thine eye pity him, neither shalt thou spare, neither shalt thou conceal him. (KJV)

Proverbs 1:10 says, "My son, if sinners entice thee, consent thou not" (KJV). And James tells us that seducing spirits draw people away from the faith and into death, which is to eternal damnation (James 1:14–15).

Another open door to seducing spirits is fascination with false prophets and demonic signs and wonders. Seducing spirits were behind cults such as the one led by Jim Jones and also the Branch Davidians. Entertainers like Shirley McClain have gotten off into false religion and brought a lot of people with them.

Certain television shows like *Buffy, the Vampire Slayer* and *Angel* cooperate with seducing spirits because they twist wrong and portray it as right. Anything that twists the truth into a lie is connected with a seducing spirit. This could be teachings, books, games, movies or television. The current secular interest in angels is an example of seducing spirits taking something good, that God has created, and twisting it into something untrue. Some recent movies portrayed angels with human emotions and weaknesses; an obvious attempt by seducing spirits to dilute the status and twist the truth regarding God's heavenly host.

People looking for "power" in their lives and not understanding enough about God to recognize a counterfeit, may be seduced into believing in "signs and miracles" performed by false prophets. We are warned of this in Mark 13:22.

An individual with a seducing spirit would be a disaster in deliverance ministry. There would be a temptation to become fascinated with demons and even to want to converse with demons. This might be done in the name of gaining knowledge, but it is an objectionable practice and someone susceptible to lying spirits should avoid exposure to such a risk.

SPIRITS OF ERROR

James 1:4–6 tells us that there is a spirit of Truth and a spirit of error. The New International Version calls error a spirit of falsehood. People with a spirit of error are not teachable, not submissive and believe false doctrine. For this reason, it often opens the door for religious spirits and legalism.

We get a broader look at the spirit of error in Second Timothy 4:3–4, "For the time will come when they will not endure the sound doctrine;

but, having itching ears, will heap to themselves teachers after their own lusts; and will turn away their ears from the truth, and turn aside unto fables" (ASV). This scripture shows that the spirit of error will increase as the day of the Lord approaches.

People with the spirit of error tend to be defensive, argumentative and contentious. Sometimes they are still so in error that it's hard to get them to renounce it, because they are absolutely convinced that they are right. New Age is a prime example of the spirit of error at work. Believers in New Age are convinced they know so much that they actually point out where the Bible is in error. The spirit of error must be broken, renounced and cast out.

THE SPIRIT OF ANTICHRIST

The strongman of antichrist nips right on the heels of the spirit of error and the seducing spirits. The assignment of the spirit of antichrist is to keep people away from understanding, praying to and accepting Jesus. The spirit of antichrist denies the deity of Christ. It opposes Jesus and all of His teachings.

The spirit of antichrist is mentioned in First John 2:22, "Who is the liar but he that denieth that Jesus is the Christ? This is the antichrist, even he that denieth the Father and the Son" (KJV). First John 4:3 tells us that "every spirit that does not acknowledge Jesus is not from God. This is the spirit of the antichrist that you have heard is coming and even now is already in the world" (NIV).

There is often a spirit of lawlessness rooted in the spirit of antichrist. The Bible says, "Let no one deceive you in any way; for that day will not come, unless the rebellion comes first, and the man of lawlessness is revealed, the son of perdition" (Second Thessalonians 2:3, RSV).

Another trait you'll find when the spirit of antichrist is present is a pattern of prayerlessness. They may *try* to pray, but can't seem to do it. They may go to church, but leave without really understanding the message. They may sit down and try to read the Bible, but they either are blocked from reading it, or are blocked from understanding it. You will often hear them say, "I can't read the Bible, I get blocked." They may say, "Every time I try to pray I fall asleep or get distracted." The spirit of antichrist can cause people not to understand the things of God; they may hear the words, but they don't really grasp their meaning. It goes right over their heads, because they have a spirit of antichrist blinding their eyes. They aren't able to fully enter into praise and worship. Often these people used to be able to do these things, but now find it difficult or impossible.

In extreme cases, people with the spirit of antichrist won't even walk inside a church, not even to attend a funeral. They won't pick up a Bible for any reason. They just avoid anything to do with God.

19 - DEAF AND DUMB, INFIRMITY AND DEATH

The Bible records that Jesus cast a deaf and dumb spirit out of a boy after His disciples could not. This is found in Mark 9:17–29:

> And one of the crowd answered him, "Teacher, I brought my son to you, for he has a dumb spirit; and wherever it seizes him, it dashes him down; and he foams and grinds his teeth and becomes rigid; and I asked your disciples to cast it out, and they were not able."
>
> And he answered them, "O faithless generation, how long am I to be with you? How long am I to bear with you? Bring him to me." And they brought the boy to him; and when the spirit saw him, immediately it convulsed the boy, and he fell on the ground and rolled about, foaming at the mouth.
>
> And Jesus asked his father, "How long has he had this?" And he said, "From childhood. And it has often cast him into the fire and into the water, to destroy him; but if you can do anything, have pity on us and help us." And Jesus said to him, "If you can! All things are possible to him who believes." Immediately the father of the child cried out and said, "I believe; help my unbelief!" And when Jesus saw that a crowd came running together, he rebuked the unclean spirit, saying to it, "You dumb and deaf spirit, I command you, come out of him, and never enter him again."

And after crying out and convulsing him terribly, it came out, and the boy was like a corpse; so that most of them said, "He is dead." But Jesus took him by the hand and lifted him up, and he arose. And when he had entered the house, his disciples asked him privately, "Why could we not cast it out?" And he said to them, "This kind cannot be driven out by anything but prayer." (RSV)

There is a great deal to be learned from this passage of scripture, but one thing you probably noticed is that the boy had all the symptoms of epilepsy. He fell, he convulsed, he gnashed his teeth and foamed at the mouth, which are all classic symptoms.

However, it's important that you understand: Some people with epilepsy have a deaf and dumb spirit; others do not. If the person has been diagnosed with epilepsy, do not encourage him to stop his medication. Your job is to determine if he has a deaf and dumb spirit and deal with it. His doctor will adjust his medication based on the presence or absence of seizure activity.

SUICIDAL TENDENCIES

Deaf and dumb spirits are strongmen that are often linked with heaviness and depression, and may also be linked with suicidal tendencies. A lot, but not all, of mental illness is connected to deaf and dumb spirits. If you take a close look at the above passage of scripture, you'll notice something interesting. One translation of the Bible says he *often falls* into the fire and often into the water (Matt 17:15, RSV).

The deaf and dumb spirit caused the boy to throw himself into life-threatening situations. We've talked to people with deaf and dumb spirits who say they were driving their car when a thought popped into their mind, "Why don't you drive off that cliff?"

These suicidal tendencies are not associated with depression or despondency. The deaf and dumb spirit overtly attempts to cause its victim to commit suicide. Failing that, it will attempt to get its victim to hurt himself.

In extreme cases, the person with a deaf and dumb spirit is so confused that he cannot follow directions enough to pray with you. When that happens, you must bind the spirit so the person can hear and understand what you're saying.

In one version of the Bible, Jesus said that this kind (deaf and dumb spirits) come out only by prayer and fasting. In other translations, like the one you just read, it says, "this kind comes out only by prayer." We have cast out this spirit without fasting, but you should be led by the Lord. Jesus was giving the disciples this admonishment and reminding them they must prepare by praying and building their faith prior to undertaking the casting out.

INFIRMITY

The strongman spirit of infirmity is characterized by chronic medical disorders and lingering illness. It may include chronic conditions like allergies, asthma or hay fever. It may involve arthritis and is often linked with Freemasonry. However, not all instances of these chronic illnesses stem from a spirit of infirmity. The individual may just have a physical problem. In deliverance, your job is to challenge the spirits and find out if there is a spirit of infirmity, so you can cast it out.

Symptoms of a spirit of infirmity may include frailty (generalized ill-health and weakness), lameness, impotence, bent or twisted body or spine, arthritis or cancer. It is quite common for a spirit of infirmity to be generational. In these cases you might find the same medical problems passed down from grandparent, to parent, to child. The medical community recognizes that the inclination toward certain medical conditions is inherited. Familiar examples are heart disease and diabetes. It is easy to understand that if the spirit of infirmity is behind those conditions, the demon would also be passed down through heredity.

One thing that can block deliverance from a spirit of infirmity is if the person's identity is tied up in the disease or in the attention he gets from the illness. Jesus asked a blind man, "What do you want from me?" The man had to say, "I want to be healed."

The problem you may encounter are people who really *don't* want to be healed. They may think they do, but their identity may be so connected with the infirmity that they don't want to let it go. Being ill may get them sympathy, attention, special treatment, set them apart from everyone else. In a twisted, unconscious logic, these people may rather keep the pain and disability of the illness than lose the identity it gives them. Sometimes you have to ask, like Jesus did, "Do you want to be healed? Do you want to get rid of this thing?"

SPIRIT OF DEATH

Although the strongman spirit of death isn't mentioned in scripture by name, it's clear that this is more than just a condition. Exodus 12:23, Revelation 20:13 and Revelation 9:11 are all scriptures that describe a spirit of death.

In the questionnaire and interview process, you are looking for any pattern of premature death in the person's family. One related question on the questionnaire is, "Has anyone in your family died before the age of 60?" A spirit of death may take people prematurely.

One open door to a spirit of death is a near-death experience. Another open door might be if you were with a person as he died. That spirit of death will be looking for a new habitation. A couple from our church perceived that my husband (a doctor) and I (a nurse) needed deliverance from a spirit of death because we were around so much death. For eight years as night supervisor in a large hospital, I attended every death on the shift, so I was happy to have that door closed.

A spirit of death will enter any time someone has attempted suicide or had a death wish. As soon as you come against the spirit of death, immediately pray the spirit of life back into him. Watch the person closely as you cast it out. If he shows any signs of fainting or weakness, be prepared to remind the spirit of death that it has been commanded in the name of Jesus not to harm the person or anyone else and ask the Holy Spirit to give the person renewed life and strength.

The word perversion means to make crooked, to do amiss, to bow down, to commit iniquity, to pervert, to trouble and to do wrong. The strong-man of perversion is characterized primarily by a broken spirit. The ultimate form of perversion is an atheist, who has perverted everything God intended for his life: Instead of serving and worshipping the Lord, he does just the opposite.

The spirit of perversion is linked to the spirit of error. The Bible says, "The Lord hath mingled a perverse spirit in the midst thereof: and they have caused Egypt to err in every work thereof, as a drunken man staggereth in his vomit" (Isaiah 19:14, KJV). Very often, this brings about doctrinal error.

Another form of perversion is perverting or twisting the Word of God. For instance, God instructs His people to take the cares of this world to Him in prayer, and release them. We are instructed to live in peace by faith in God. Therefore, a chronic worrier, for example, has perverted God's intended will.

Unless the act was entirely involuntary, all acts of perversion require genuine repentance and a turning away from that sin, whether it is unbelief in God, doctrinal error, twisting God's word or sexual acts. In addition, sexual acts require the breaking of soul ties.

You may have heard someone jokingly say, "You old reprobate!" and not known what the word really meant. The Bible talks about people who God has turned over to a reprobate mind. "And even as they did not like to retain God in their knowledge, God gave them over to a reprobate mind, to do those things which are not convenient" (Romans 1:28, KJV). In other translations, the word convenient is translated as, "to do what ought not to be done."

A person with a reprobate mind's thinking is so perverted that he believes that his lifestyle is right. An example might be a pedophile who believes that he is just showing the children "love." That is a reprobate mind. Churches that cater to practicing homosexuals and attempt to twist the scriptures and justify their lifestyle is another example.

SEXUAL SIN

By far, sexual sins are the matters with which we deal most often in deliverance from a spirit of perversion. Door openers to the spirit of sexual perversion might be incest, pornography, homosexuality, bestiality, adultery and fornication. God's will for the human race is that sex belongs in the marriage bed. Fornication—sex outside of marriage—is a perversion of God's intended purpose.

A characteristic of a spirit of perversion is a filthy mind. A person whose every thought is centered on sexual fantasies, lust, fornication and adultery, is operating from a spirit of perversion.

A SPIRIT OF LUST

A spirit of lust is one of the primary ways that a door gets opened to a spirit of perversion. Any sexual act outside of marriage is a door opener for the spirit of lust and perversion. As was addressed in the discussion of Soul Ties in Chapter 11, as the deliverance minister, you will need to prepare yourself for conversations that are indelicate and often uncomfortable. You should keep your manner as objective and neutral as possible and avoid any sign of shock or disapproval. You will have to ask pointed questions as it is your responsibility to identify the issues that must be handled. Still, you don't need a lot of detail and I recommend obtaining just the information you require to clarify the spiritual matters so you don't subject the individual to any more embarrassment than absolutely necessary.

Lustful thoughts and fantasies are an open door for a spirit of perversion. If someone has engaged in these types of fantasies, they need go back and repent for them, and close that door.

Adultery is sex between two people when either of them is married to another person. According to *Vine's Expository Dictionary of New Testament Words* the word adulterer is *moichos*. The meaning of *moichos* denotes one who has unlawful intercourse with the spouse of another. The secular definition of adultery is narrower, and considers that only a person who is married to another person actually commits adultery. The Bible definition is broader; God considers both parties to have committed adultery if only one party is married. By either definition, adultery is sexual perversion.

A spirit of lust can open the door for incest in a family—whether voluntary or involuntary. Either way, incest is a sexual perversion, and it needs to be cast out.

Homosexual acts bring in spirits of homosexuality as well as perversion. As with all sin, if an individual comes for deliverance, he must be willing to repent and give up the act before deliverance can take place. If necessary, show the person a few scriptures such as Leviticus 18:23, "You shall not lie with a male as with a woman. It is an abomination" (NKJV), and First Corinthians 6:9–10, "Do you not know that the unrighteous will not inherit the kingdom of God? Do not be deceived. Neither fornicators, nor idolaters, nor adulterers, nor homosexuals, nor sodomites, nor thieves, nor covetous, nor drunkards, nor revilers, nor extortioners will inherit the kingdom of God" (NKJV). If he is willing to give up the lifestyle, proceed with the deliverance using the verse of freedom and hope that follows those above (verse 11), "And such were some of you. But you were washed, but you were sanctified, but you were justified in the name of the Lord Jesus and by the Spirit of our God" (NKJV).

With homosexuality, as with any sexual sin, if he is unwilling or reluctant, postpone the deliverance and refer him for follow up teaching and prayer. People who are engaged in ongoing sexual sin are not candidates for deliverance until they are ready to turn from that sin. We have had people arrive for deliverance who were living out of wedlock with another person. We have explained that to do deliverance while they are living in that manner would be a disservice to them because the door would be standing wide open for the reentry of demons.

Bestiality is sex with any animal, "Nor shall you mate with any animal, to defile yourself with it. Nor shall any woman stand before an animal to mate with it. It is perversion" (Leviticus 18:23, NKJV). I don't really want to know the details about how they do this. I just want to know that they did it, so I can cast it out.

Pornography is derived from the Greek word for prostitute. This illustrates that there is very little difference between looking at pornography and actually having sex. I thought that was interesting, because if you have a married man looking at pornography, he is committing the sin of adultery. Jesus said, "But I say unto you, that whosoever looketh on a woman to lust after her hath committed adultery with her already in his heart" (Matthew 5:28, KJV).

Sometimes you have to do a little teaching on this, especially with men who have never been physically unfaithful to their wives. Pornography is still a form of adultery.

Pornography is one of those sneaky, dark sins that like to hide from the light. It's also very addictive and quickly becomes bondage. Sometimes an individual can see one pornographic image one time and can't get rid of it. It's as though the image is burned in his mind with a branding iron. Therefore, one of the things you need to pray is for God to cleanse his memories using Isaiah 65:17, Isaiah 54:4 and Philippians 31:13–14. We also anoint his eyes with oil. Although deliverance will set the individual free from the bondage, sometimes walking out his freedom means retraining what he allows himself to see or think.

Very often, the spirit of perversion is generational. For instance, sometimes you'll see a child who begins masturbating at a very young age. Clearly, that is a generational spirit of perversion.

Another open door to perversion is anal sex. I read a book entitled *Wicca: Satan's Little White Lies* by William Schnoebelen, a former high priest in Wicca, a witchcraft organization, exposing that cult. In the book, he said that at the higher levels of Wicca they have anal sex with one another for the specific purpose of inviting demons into their lives. According to the precepts of Wicca, anal sex opens pathways or channels for the demons to enter. As a general rule, I don't believe anything that comes from Satan's camp. While I absolutely will not get my doctrine from demons, it does seem reasonable that if a group has asked for demonic counsel and the demons told them they could open channels for demons to enter in this way, there's a good chance it's true. Therefore, if you are praying for someone who has engaged in anal sex, it might be wise to pray, "In the name of Jesus, I close any pathways or channels that have allowed demons into this person's life."

PEDOPHILIA

The statistics on pedophilia are staggering: Some statistics show that as many as one in three girls and one in five boys are sexually molested. Often these victims will molest other children and the cycle will be repeated. Many people in the prison system do not believe that pedophiles can be rehabilitated. That's because there are a cluster of demons associated with this behavior, and neither prison cells nor counseling will get rid of them. Examples of these spirits might be: a predator spirit, a victim spirit, a spirit of lust, a spirit of control, a spirit of perversion, a spirit of pornography and addiction.

As mentioned earlier, by law, you must report to legal authorities if you learn the identity of any victim of pedophilia. If someone confesses this sin generally, make sure he understands that if you are given specifics you will report him. In some jurisdictions, you may not be required to report general information about a pedophile to legal authorities, but you should report it immediately to your pastor, so that the person will not be allowed to work with children or teens in the church. It would be wise to research the specific laws governing this subject in your local area.

In addition to being victimized by pedophiles, many children see pornography and sexually stimulating movies and act out what they've seen. If this is the case, those doors should be closed during deliverance as well.

PART FIVE

OTHER DEMONIC SPIRITS AND ISSUES

SPIRITS OF GUILT AND SHAME

A great many people deal with guilt and shame on a daily basis. Because this is so prevalent, we see evidence of it all through the deliverance session. We find that the most effective and time efficient method of dealing with the spirit of guilt and shame is to have the individual renounce it as soon as we recognize it. We do this throughout the interview and deliverance process. Whenever we recognize a door opener for the spirit of guilt and shame, we have the individual say, "I renounce the spirit of guilt and shame that entered my life when I . . ." Then we go ahead with the rest of the deliverance. We don't cast out guilt and shame until the very end of the session, but by then all the entry points are closed.

A spirit of guilt and shame is usually born out of rejection, and may enter anytime a person feels guilty or ashamed of himself or his circumstances. When searching for clues to this spirit, you might hear some of the following remarks:

- I still feel bad about that.
- I was so ashamed . . .
- I tried to hide the fact that I was . . .
- I didn't want anyone to know that I was pregnant . . . illegitimate . . . poor.
- My father was an alcoholic.
- I cheated on the test.

- I don't like to talk about that.
- I don't like to think about that.
- I still can't believe that I did that.
- I can hardly look her in the eye.
- How could I live with myself after that?
- I felt it was all my fault.

THE LEPER

Before we got our first television, my favorite entertainment as a child was to listen to the radio. My favorite programs were *Father Knows Best* and *Ozzie and Harriet*. One Saturday afternoon when I was about nine years old, I remember listening to a program about a man who thought he'd contracted leprosy. I didn't understand the word "leper" and thought they were saying, "leopard." I couldn't understand how someone could touch another person and turn into a leopard. Finally, I asked my dad about it.

My father had been in the Coast Guard during World War II, and had been stationed in the Philippines where there were leper colonies. In an effort to help me understand what a leper was, he pulled out an old photo of a woman with leprosy. That picture is still burned in my mind. It was a black and white photo of a woman sitting with her hands in her lap. She had no skin on her face.

A few days later, my younger sister came in from playing in the mud and kept putting her dirty feet on me. In frustration, I turned around and said, "Keep your feet off of me. You're a leper!" This was pretty startling because in my family we seldom called each other names, least of all such a distasteful one. I felt awful after I said it.

Now fast forward forty-seven years. We flew to Maui for a vacation with our pastors, John and Judith Benefiel. There is a leper colony on an island near there and my husband, who is a doctor, wanted to visit it. I found myself strangely disquieted by the idea and said, "I don't know if I can go to a leper colony," and I told the story about my sister and how I was still ashamed of having called her a leper.

Pastor Judith wisely said, "Pat, you need to forgive yourself." I did just that and I did tour the leper colony, but it wasn't until we started our deliverance ministry that I realized that I'd been operating in a spirit of guilt and shame all those years. It was the spirit of guilt and shame that had caused that simple incident to haunt me all my life. This story also illustrates that doors are opened to demons differently in different people. In some people, calling their sister a leper wouldn't have fazed them. They may not have experienced the least bit of guilt or shame over the incident, but for me it was a prime opportunity for that spirit to take hold of me.

OPEN DOORS

Whether you are an adult or a child, an open door for this spirit occurs when someone says to you, "You ought to be ashamed of yourself." This is especially true when the person is someone in a position of authority over you or it is someone you admire or want to please. Being too late and not making it to the bedside of a loved one before he dies can also open a door for guilt and shame. The spirit of guilt and shame can enter when you do something you know is wrong, or a situation exists in your life or family that you feel you must hide from the world. It can enter if you are arrested, jailed or in some way publicly humiliated.

It can enter retroactively if you have committed an act, not knowing that it was wrong, and later find out it was sinful, immoral, hurtful to someone else or unethical. We often see this with people who became believers late in life and realize some of the things they used to do were sins. In these cases, some education on God's grace and forgiveness is sometimes necessary in order to shut the door on the spirit of shame.

It may help to remind them that God told us, "Do not fear, for you will not be ashamed; Neither be disgraced, for you will not be put to shame; For you will forget the shame of your youth, And will not remember the reproach of your widowhood anymore" (Isaiah 54:4, NKJV), and, "Instead of your shame you shall have double honor, And instead of confusion they shall rejoice in their portion. Therefore in their land they shall possess double; Everlasting joy shall be theirs" (Isaiah 61:7, NKJV).

The spirit of guilt and shame can enter even when you were totally without fault in the situation. Satan doesn't play fair, remember? Although it wasn't their fault, victims of rape, molestation or any type of abuse suffer from guilt and shame. Children, especially, tend to blame themselves for mistreatment. Any sexual sin opens the door to this spirit, especially the sin of bestiality or homosexuality. Anyone, especially a Christian, who deliberately disobeys God, opens a door to guilt and shame.

CASTING THEM OUT

During the deliverance session, have the individual renounce "the spirit of guilt and shame that entered when . . ."

Sometimes you'll have to do some teaching in order for him to take this step. For instance, we prayed for a man once who had committed an improper act earlier in his life. He had carried the spirit of guilt and shame and, in fact, almost welcomed it. He felt as though he would be shirking his responsibility for the act if he stopped feeling guilty about the sin. It had become his manner of atonement. Reminding him of God's grace had not helped get him past the issue. In the session, we had learned that he had a young daughter who he loved very much. Finally, I said, "Imagine that your daughter has done something wrong, but she came and said, 'I'm really sorry about this.' Would you want her to go away feeling guilty?"

"Of course not!" he answered immediately. I asked, "Even if it were something very wrong?" He was still adamant, "No."

"You are God's child and He doesn't want that for you either," I explained. We could see in his face that he suddenly understood and he was ready to let it go.

A CRITICAL SPIRIT

Another spirit we encounter a great deal is a critical spirit, which is often linked to a judgmental spirit. We even see this in good, church-going people. These are often the people who seem to find fault in everything the church leadership does or complain about other members of the congregation. No one seems to measure up to their standards.

Part of your detective work during deliverance will be to find out how this spirit operates in an individual's life and to what other demons it may be linked. For instance, self-criticism is usually born out of rejection. If the person is primarily critical of the people closest to him, this can result in unforgiveness. If he's critical of people or things in relation to God, this is tied to a religious spirit.

However the critical spirit got in, if left to its own devices, it often progresses to a judgmental spirit. I will show you the progression. A critical spirit begins by finding a flaw. You may go to someone's house and find it a mess. Your reaction may not be demonic at all or you may indulge a critical spirit. You might just think, "Mmmm, her house is dirty." You found a flaw.

If you form an opinion about the flaw, it progresses to a judgment about the person. You might think, "Her house is dirty. She must be lazy." The next step might be, "Her house is dirty. She must be lazy and a bad mother to let her children live in such a mess." You are beginning to judge her.

The next step might be, "Her house is dirty. She must be lazy and a bad mother. I'm a better mother than she is." Now you've exalted yourself, which is definitely judgment and judgment is linked to pride.

Taking it a step further, you might say, "I'm not going to let my kids play with her kids, and I'm not going back to her house." Now you've progressed from criticism to judgment and on to condemnation. The whole thing may have been rooted in pride to begin with, and pride can be rooted in rejection.

Critical and judgmental spirits are frequently passed down in families. They also seem to "rub off" onto an individual who spends a great deal of time with critical people. If the spirits of criticism and judgment are rooted in pride, rejection or a religious spirit, it will probably be necessary to command those spirits to unlink in order to cast them out.

SPIRIT OF LAWLESSNESS

If you see lawlessness in someone's life, you generally see a pattern of unwillingness to submit to authority. The individual might constantly be at odds with those in authority over him: bosses, pastors, parents or teachers. He may quit a job because, "That guy always wanted to tell me what to do."

The person may not recognize his behavior as a problem at first. Unwillingness to submit to authority can disguise itself as being independent, self-reliant, a free thinker, a leader rather than a follower. The difference is that the person with the spirit of lawlessness insists on being independent when he should be submitted to authority, such as to a boss or pastor. In order to maintain his deliverance and resist falling into the behavior again, he may need some follow up teaching on spiritual authority as found in Romans 13:2 in which we are told "Therefore whoever resists the authority resists the ordinance of God, and those who resist will bring judgment on themselves" (NKJV).

Lawlessness can be rooted in rebellion, pride or an antichrist spirit. Those are the spirits that may need to be unlinked when coming against a spirit of lawlessness. Lawlessness is also often passed down generationally in families.

22 – RELIGIOUS, NATIVE AMERICAN, WARRING SPIRITS, WORD CURSES AND NAMES

The assignment of a religious spirit is to weaken the body of Christ by fragmenting, alienating and creating divisions between congregations or denominations. The religious spirit is legalistic (unbending or ritualistic) and may be linked to pride. Intolerance, legalism and judgmentalism are all characteristics of a religious spirit.

Characteristics of a religious spirit include:

- Bondage to a specific form of worship, while rejecting all others. For instance, in some churches the people raise their hands in worship. If someone who is used to a more formal church setting walks in and judges the worship to be improper, this is a religious spirit speaking. The religious spirit prevents the person from researching it in the Bible and learning that the definition of the word praise includes "extending or raising the hands." The person simply rejects the practice with a closed mind.
- Another characteristic might be defensiveness about denominationalism which separates the church. Regardless of how differently we may express our worship, we are all a part of the body of Christ and need to be united. Anyone who is judgmental about another church is usually dealing with a religious spirit.
- A religious spirit is also behind doctrinal imbalances, where people focus on one or a few aspects of serving God to the exclusion

of all others. A group may believe that they are the only way to heaven, forgetting that Jesus is the only way to heaven.

- Another characteristic is reliance on church doctrines which offers false security. These people may not feel the need to grow in their Christian walk. Any clues that suggest the individual is stuck on one way of doing things or putting his faith in good works instead of the Lord Jesus, indicate the presence of a religious spirit. An individual with a religious spirit may be following the traditions and routines of his church, but his focus is more on the routine than on how those things further his relationship with Jesus. This person may be a very active member of his church. However, he may be focused on what he feels is right and proper, rather than on whether or not he is doing it at God's direction. You may hear the following type of comment:

  - I'm loyal to my church—that's all I need.
  - I take communion every week.
  - I go to mass and receive absolution.
  - I'm very active in my church.

When interviewing this person, you will hear him make statements about what he does, but the statements won't be followed with a declaration such as how he felt closer to the Lord or that he felt as if his burden were lightened afterward. If asked why he does any of those things, the answer is usually something that amounts to "that's just the way it's done."

Entry points may be attending churches with lots of tradition, lots of do's and don'ts not found in scripture, condemnation, pride, prejudice or controlling church leaders. Of course, any cult is rooted in a religious spirit.

NATIVE AMERICANS

There has been a misconception in the body of Christ that all Native American religions are wrong. That's simply not true. However, if the individual has been involved in a vision quest, sweat lodges, dream catchers, god's eyes, fetishes or other religious props, you should consider a spirit of false religion. Look for superstitions or Shamanism.

We prayed for a woman with a Native American background and cast out a spirit of false religion. The spirit told her, "If I leave, you won't be able to minister to your people." She had a heart to evangelize the Native American community and the spirit was trying to convince her she wouldn't be able to relate or connect with them if she no longer "understood their religion." She knew that was a lie, and she renounced it and we cast it out. An interesting thing happened the moment that spirit left. She was overwhelmed by grief and sorrow. She began weeping as if her heart were breaking. In her spirit, she saw a woman weeping and hugging a tree. Through the help of the Holy Spirit, we recognized it as a scene from the Trail of Tears; a tragic procession in which thousands of Native Americans were forced to walk from their home in Georgia to resettle in Oklahoma. Many died along the trail and those who survived had been torn from their homes and thrust into a strange place against their wills. The minute the blinders of false religion were removed from this woman, the spirit of grief and sorrow manifested. This was a generational spirit passed down to her because of the abuse to her Native American ancestors during the Trail of Tears.

We have seen the same thing in a number of different deliverances. In each instance, a spirit of false religion masked a spirit of grief and sorrow. You need to be aware of that possibility in anyone with a Native American background. This is especially prevalent here in Oklahoma because Oklahoma was the termination point of the Trail of Tears and because so many covenants (treaties) between the United States and the Native American tribes were broken here. Due to abuse and rejection in past generations, there is a high incidence of alcoholism and suicide among Native Americans and a notably low percentage are born again.

The Oklahoma Apostolic Prayer Network is making great strides in overcoming the demonic strongholds at the "strategic" level (see Chapter Six). However, individually, Native Americans need deliverance in order to live free from these torments.

Don't neglect forgiveness and rejection issues with Native Americans. Many have an inherent distrust of non-natives, especially Caucasians. You will sometimes find that well-meaning Christians, in an attempt to evangelize Native Americans, have left them feeling insulted and disrespected. They may need to forgive the government, Caucasian Americans in general, as well as the Church.

Warring spirits are a very interesting phenomenon. This occurs when, within one person, there are certain types of mixed blood or mixed heritages that were once in opposition. Some examples of this occur when a person has a mixture of Caucasian and Native American in his bloodline. Other examples might be Caucasian and African American, slave and slave owner or conquered and conqueror. If the blood lines warred with one another, the individual may have a warring spirit which results in confusion and anxiety and needs to be cast out.

WORD CURSES

Just in case you have any question in your mind about the power words have over our lives, look at what the Bible says about it. Proverbs 18:21 says, "Death and life are in the power of the tongue: and they that love it shall eat the fruit thereof" (KJV).

You can't wield more power over anyone than the power of life and death.

Proverbs 6:2 says, "Thou art snared with the words of thy mouth, thou art taken with the words of thy mouth" (KJV).

And in Psalms 34:13 we find, "Keep thy tongue from evil, and thy lips from speaking guile" (KJV).

In Matthew 12:36–37, Jesus said, "But I say unto you, That every idle word that men shall speak, they shall give account thereof in the day of judgment. For by thy words thou shalt be justified, and by thy words thou shalt be condemned" (KJV).

These are only a few examples of what the Bible has to say about our words. My theory about words is this: Everything you say about someone is either a blessing or a cursing. If you say, "You are always late," or if you say, "You always do your best," you have either blessed or cursed the person. The tongue has the power of life and death. In the same way, the words of others affects you, what you say about yourself has a positive or negative effect on your life as well.

The above are just a few examples. As you ask the Holy Spirit to help you, you will be able to identify many more. One of the reasons Satan gets away with cursing us through our words is that few Christians understand how important our words are. Often we think words don't have an effect because they are true *(I always have too much month left at the end of my paycheck),* we were just kidding *(I want to die young and leave a good-looking corpse)* or we didn't say it in front of anyone else *(I wish I were dead)* and other subtle lies of the devil. Make no mistake—Satan and his cohorts will take any and every opportunity to get a foothold in your life. If a potential word curse surfaces during a deliverance session, it is probably because the Holy Spirit has brought it to your attention so that it can be broken.

SEARCHING FOR CLUES

During the interview, you are looking for clues to word curses. Some word curses may have been spoken by the individual over himself. Some may have been spoken by other people in his life. Some may even have been pronounced by witches.

The following is a sampling of word curses:

- I'm so accident prone.
- You could trip over a chalk line.
- If you leave this church, you'll never grow with God.
- You'll never fulfill God's plan for your life.
- If you marry that man, you'll always be poor.
- You'll always be miserable.
- Their marriage will never work.
- I always attract men who abuse me.
- I always attract men who leave me.
- I always attract men who are unfaithful to me.
- You'll never get off drugs.
- You're just like your father. You'll never amount to anything.

- I can never remember anything.
- My memory is getting worse by the hour.
- My Alzheimer's is showing.
- You ought to be ashamed of yourself.

Medical reports and doctors' words can not only bring a curse but also allow spirits of fear, hopelessness, anger, depression and others to enter. For example, imagine the effect of hearing words such as incurable, terminal, permanent disability.

In order to break a word curse, have the individual renounce the words and break their power though the name of Jesus. It might go something like this, "Father, I repent for joking around about having Alzheimer's. I renounce those words, and break the power of them in the name of Jesus." For prayers for breaking word curses and hexes, vexes and incantations see Appendix B, Section 1.

NAMES

A type of a word curse can occur if the root meaning of a person's name is a negative confession or has an association with the demonic. This is another example of how sneaky the devil is. Our name is something that is spoken every day by ourselves and others and can be the source of an ongoing word curse without anyone realizing it. For instance, the name Dennis or Denise means "revelry or wine." They are derivatives of "Dionysis," the god of revelry. This may be a clue if you're praying for someone named Dennis or Denise who has a problem with alcohol.

If someone walks up to you and says, "Hello, I'm Sheila," she is actually saying, "Hello, I'm blind." Gladys, Claude and Claudia all mean "lame," Calvin means "bald," Lola means "sorrows." Some names are the names of false deities. For example, Cynthia, Selina, Gwendolyn and Delia are all names for the goddess of the moon.

It's interesting to study the etymology (study of the origin) of names. I've noticed in many modern "baby names" books, the meanings have been "sanitized" making it even more difficult to rid ourselves of the word curse. You will often see the meaning of Cynthia listed as "moon" or "the moon personified," when in fact it is the name of the Greek goddess of the moon. Not all sources list all meanings. In order to learn the full meaning, it is necessary to do some research into the actual etymology of the name.

I keep a partial list of names and their meanings in my notebook, and if I see a connection between the root meaning of a person's name and a pattern of behavior that might be tied to it or if the name honors a false god or has occult connections, I have him renounce the spiritual significance of his name and redeem it. Names are obviously important to God as there are examples in the Bible of God changing people's names to be representative of the person and God's calling on his life (Genesis 17:5, 17:15, 35:10). You don't have to get out of balance on this subject. It isn't necessary for him to change his name, but it is a good idea to renounce any negative spiritual significance, close any doors that might be open because of the name and cancel any word curse the name has brought.

Since I am a nurse and my husband is a physician, at one time or another we've treated burn victims, shooting victims, those with a broken leg or severed spine from a fall on the ski slopes. We have seen or treated patients with acute heart attack, pulmonary embolus, amputees, flesh-eating bacteria and viruses, AIDS patients, birth defects and head injuries from motorcycle and car wrecks. If you spend most of your adult life working in or around a hospital, you will see the effects of trauma.

For each of the conditions listed, we could reel off a plan of medical care. The burn victim would be lowered into a whirlpool while nurses scrubbed away charred flesh. An AIDS victim would be given drugs to boost his immune system. A patient with a head injury would lie on a cooling blanket to decrease the temperature and swelling in the brain. Broken bones would be put in a cast. Antibiotics would be given for flesh-eating bacteria. For every medical condition there is a treatment plan, even if only to make the patient comfortable.

It wasn't until I enrolled at Wagner Leadership Institute in Colorado Springs that I became acquainted with the work of Peter Horrobin. Peter is the founder of Ellel Ministries and is an internationally known speaker and author. Taking a novel approach, he developed a strategy for treating the soul and spirit of anyone who suffered shock or trauma. I realized that while every broken leg would be treated medically, nothing was done for the spiritual and emotional fracture that occurred at the same time. The core of what we've learned in dealing with accident and trauma has stemmed from Peter Horrobin's teaching.

According to the Bible, we are tri-part people. We are made up of a spirit, a soul and a body. The first question we must ask is the obvious: Can a spirit or soul be broken? Proverbs 18:14 says, "The spirit of a man will sustain him in sickness, but who can bear a broken spirit?" (NKJV). Clearly, a spirit can be broken.

The Bible also says that the Lord wants us whole; spirit, soul and body. "Now may the God of peace Himself sanctify you completely; and may your whole spirit, soul, and body be preserved blameless at the coming of our Lord Jesus Christ (First Thessalonians 5:23, NKJV).

In the following verse, King David, a man after God's own heart, talks about how the enemy damaged his soul, how his spirit was overwhelmed and his heart distressed. "For the enemy has persecuted my soul; He has crushed my life to the ground; He has made me dwell in darkness, like those who have long been dead. Therefore my spirit is overwhelmed within me; my heart within me is distressed" (Psalm 143:3–4, NKJV).

Here, it sounds like Ezekiel was talking to those of us who have not treated the fractured inner man.

> The weak you have not strengthened, nor have you healed those who were sick, nor bound up the broken, nor brought back what was driven away, nor sought what was lost; but with force and cruelty you have ruled them. So they were scattered because there was no shepherd; and they became food for all the beasts of the field when they were scattered" (Ezekiel 34:4–5, NKJV)

Finally, Jesus said, "The Spirit of the Lord God is upon Me, because the Lord has anointed Me to preach good tidings to the poor; He has sent Me to heal the brokenhearted, to proclaim liberty to the captives, and the opening of the prison to those who are bound" (Isaiah 61:1, NKJV). The word "broken" means shattered into separate pieces. The word "hearted" refers to the entire personality which includes the spirit and soul. Jesus was sent to heal these shattered personalities.

SHOCK AND TRAUMA

Having established that internal wounds and fractures exist, we'll look at the definitions of trauma, shock and inner brokenness. Trauma is a severe wounding to the body that affects the spirit and soul as well. A shock is a severe and sudden impact on either the physical body or the emotions. Inner brokenness is a loss of Godly integrity of soul and spirit.

You can't have anything happen to the body that doesn't affect the spirit and soul. Although the body may have long recovered from the effects of shock or trauma, the spirit and soul may still be shattered. These inner wounds open the door to demonic spirits and can give place to fear. Fear on the inside can create fear on the outside, without anyone realizing why. In the situations mentioned, shame, rejection, anger, unforgiveness and other demonic influences would be expected. Often, when the trauma occurred in childhood, the emotions surrounding the incident are impeded in their development. The person may remain emotionally immature in those areas.

Also, strong emotional shocks or distress can wound the spirit and soul when no physical trauma takes place. An event or series of events that caused the person anguish, sorrow, intense humiliation, terror or emotional torment of any kind can be expected to damage the spirit and soul. As you pray, the Lord will show you what spirits are involved so you will be able pray over them as outlined below.

TREATMENT PLAN

The following is Peter Horrobin's treatment plan for ministering healing to the inner wounds caused by accidents and trauma. I recommend that when you begin this prayer, you tell the person for whom you are praying to take his time and to let you know anytime he needs more time to allow the Holy Spirit to bring healing. This is one time we ask the person to close his eyes as it may help him to focus.

1. Confirm the Lordship of Jesus Christ and ask for His protection.

2. Confess any responsibility for the accident or trauma (disobedience, wrong relationship, self-pronouncements). For example:

   A. A person on the way to commit adultery has a wreck.

   B. A person has spoken a death wish over himself.

   C. A person's drunkenness is the cause of an accident resulting in his injury.

3. Forgive everyone possibly involved. If a car hit you, forgive the driver. If a deer darted in front of your car, forgive the deer.

4. Sever soul ties with anyone involved in the accident, either alive or dead.

   A. A soul tie is created because of the trauma. It will be necessary to break soul ties with any people involved in the accident whether the individual for whom you are praying met them or not; an example would be the driver of the other car.

   B. In the example in number 3 above, it would be necessary to break soul ties with the deer if you hit one.

   C. It is necessary to break ties with the land or the area where the trauma occurred so that revisiting that place will not recreate the trauma in the person's emotions. We are not suggesting that there is an actual soul tie with the land, but a tie would be created because of the trauma.

5. Break any curses that may have been spoken by others. (For example: "He'll probably never walk again." "He'll never overcome his fear of the water after almost drowning.")

6. Ask Jesus to touch and heal the inner brokenness that occurred during the accident.

7. Ask Him to bring together that part which was broken during the accident and heal the part of the spirit and soul that were damaged. Then ask Him to grow that healed part up to the per-

son's present age and then ask God to bring the body into line with the healed spirit and soul.

8. Ask the Lord to separate the demons from the trauma.

9. Bind the demons in the name of Jesus.

10. Ask Jesus to remove all trauma, shock, fear, pain and wounding.

11. Ask that the Lord bring to the person's consciousness what happened during the trauma. Deal with all of the emotions first, then bind up the broken-heartedness and pray for physical healing.

12. Ask Jesus to heal the memories of the trauma and the aftermath, if any.

13. Break and expel any demonic authority and power attached. This might be fear, infirmity, panic, death or others. The enemy can sometimes lock part of the individual's emotions or personality into the trauma. Sometimes a recurring dream is a key to a past trauma.

14. Be alert to generational and territorial demons.

   A. Attack "black spots," break the power of the curse that is in that place where the accident occurred. (An example of a black spot is a particular geographical location to which a territorial demon has attached itself, such as an intersection where an unusual number of accidents have occurred).

   B. An example of a generational demon or curse at work would be the trauma of a diagnosis of cancer occurring when the person becomes 25, as happened with his father and grandfather.

15. Break the power of any curse attached to the trauma.

16. Ask the Lord to bring the soul and spirit into Godly order and unity.

17. Pray for physical healing and ask the Lord to bring the body into alignment with the soul and spirit.

18. Give God time to bring the healing.

Too often we pray for a person to be healed without ever asking, "Why is this person sick?" That's a lot like a doctor prescribing medicine without doing an exam. We must become spiritual diagnosticians. Often, unresolved pain is due to untreated inner wounds.

When praying for a victim of trauma, you must rely heavily on the Holy Spirit. Sometimes you will be dealing with the effects of old trauma, like not being wanted at birth, a failed abortion attempt, or the individual was fired from his job. In all these situations, the ruling spirit is shame. You may also find fear and rejection present.

In addition, be quick to recognize and pray for the trauma associated with the death of a loved one, witnessing a crime or accident, miscarriage, abortion, divorce, receiving a bad diagnosis or anything that created an emotional trauma.

BLOOD TRANSFUSIONS

The need for blood transfusions is generally associated with some type of medical trauma. If this has occurred, you will need to explore with the person the nature of the trauma and deal with the emotional and spiritual wounds involved. In addition, soul ties should be broken with the blood donor(s). This is also true with organ transplants. How to identify and break these soul ties was discussed in more detail in Chapter 11.

THE TRAUMA PRAYER AND THE DELIVERANCE SESSION

The prayer we use for healing of accidents and traumas is included in Appendix B, Section 2. We usually pray the trauma prayer after casting out rejection, but before casting out the rest of the strongmen, because the person is often able to release the demons more easily after he has been healed. However, this must be by the leading of the Holy Spirit. We have had sessions when we have started praying for the healing of trauma and had to stop and proceed with the deliverance and complete the trauma prayer at the end of the prayer time.

When praying for a current or ongoing trauma like a terrible marriage, current debilitating illness or a loved one who is ill, you pray in the same manner. You ask God to heal every wound that has occurred to date, then ask Him to give the person strength and wisdom to endure what is to come.

PART SIX

THE DELIVERANCE SESSION: STEP BY STEP

24 – UNDERSTANDING THE QUESTIONNAIRE

It's not necessary to use a questionnaire in deliverance, and nothing can replace the gifts of the Holy Spirit, particularly the gift of discerning of spirits. But you would have to be exceptionally gifted to discern everything that you can discover using a questionnaire. We've found that the most thorough deliverance is one where you cover the obvious open doors identified in a questionnaire as well as those things the Holy Spirit reveals.

The questionnaire we use was originally developed by Noel and Phyl Gibson. Doris Wagner reprinted it with permission in her books, and we obtained it through her. This questionnaire is a wonderful place to start, but is constantly evolving. We have revised it at least 13 times, and it has grown from 15 pages to around 28. We've found that the more detailed the questionnaire, the shorter the interview time and the more open doors you can identify.

Before we move on to the "how to" of a deliverance session, it's important to understand what the questions and the subsequent answers on the questionnaire mean. In this chapter I will list some of the questions and explain what open doors, or entry points, they might reveal. Copies of the complete questionnaires with explanation keys for adults, adolescents and children are included in Appendix A, Section 1–6. It may be helpful for you to refer to those pages as you read the information below.

Both the questions and the interview are detective work. There are no black and white answers about what you'll discover.

ITALICS AND BOLD PRINT

As you read through the questionnaire keys, what you see in italics are spirits you might find associated with that question. The bold black print contains notes that we thought might be helpful. They are to provide help for the deliverance minister something like the teacher's answer key to a test and are not on the copy of the questionnaire given to the person coming for deliverance. Of course, the information we've included in the keys is not absolute. In actual practice, you will find that not all of the spirits noted will be encountered; then again, you will encounter issues and spirits not listed. It is important to remain flexible and sensitive to the Lord's leading while you use the keys as guidelines, tips and clues.

QUESTIONS ABOUT CHURCH BACKGROUND:

The first several questions deal with the person's church background. The purpose of these questions is to look for a religious spirit or a spirit of legalism. We also ask about his conversion experience—was he baptized as a child or since he's been born again? If he hasn't been baptized since he was born again, that's something we need to know. In that situation, we always recommend that he follow the Lord's command to be baptized in water.

DO YOU HAVE A PROBLEM WITH DOUBT AND UNBELIEF?

One person might have a problem with doubt and unbelief because he is a new believer who has never been taught how to live by faith. On the other hand, you may discover that doubt and unbelief stems from a spirit of antichrist. Doubt and unbelief can be inherited, or the result of Freemasonry, witchcraft or intellectualism. There are a lot of things that might result in doubt and unbelief. You'll need to ask the questions to find the answer.

QUESTIONS DEALING WITH REJECTION:

All of category A deals primarily with rejection. Some questions in this category are as follows: Were you a planned child? Were you the right sex for your parents? Did your parents favor one of your siblings over you? Were you conceived out of wedlock? All of these questions are on the trail of a spirit of rejection. Also, if the individual was conceived out of wedlock, there will probably be a generational issue with lust and perversion.

WERE YOU ADOPTED? WERE YOU THE RESULT OF A VIOLENT CONCEPTION?

There are huge issues of rejection in adopted children, because they were rejected by their birth parents. Rejection, fear and emotional trauma can all enter from the womb, so we probe with questions about complicated or difficult birth.

WERE YOU A BREAST-FED BABY?

Breast-fed babies generally have fewer rejection issues and bonded early with their mothers.

ARE YOUR PARENTS LIVING?

This line of questioning is geared to finding a spirit of premature death in the family line. We ask the age that parents or grandparents died. If you see a pattern of early death in the answers to these questions, jot down "spirit of death, premature death" on your battle plan and in the deliverance, deal with the spirit of premature death. This question may also bring up issues of grief and rejection.

ARE YOU A PEOPLE PLEASER?

This is one of the questions on which we had to expand, because most people answer "Yes," they try to please others because everyone wants to be liked. However, that's not what we're looking for here. A more accurate question is, "Do you please other people to your own detriment?"

A positive answer may indicate the presence of a people pleasing spirit. There may also be issues of performance and perfectionism. Performance involves jumping through hoops for another person, working so hard to please that person that you loose sight of your own needs. Perfectionism involves performing to a standard that is not reasonable. Perfectionism is pressure from within the person himself.

ARE YOU A CRITICAL PERSON?

You're looking for a critical, judgmental or condemning spirit here. You need to know what form his criticism takes. Ask of whom he is critical. Find out if he feels superior to the people he criticizes. You will want to distinguish between self-criticism which would be tied to self-rejection, criticism of people close to him which may indicate unforgiveness and criticism of people in issues related to the church which may indicate a religious spirit or legalism. Simply finding flaws and expressing disapproval may evolve into being judgmental which would involve forming an opinion of people based on the flaws. You may also be dealing with condemnation if he has exalted himself and felt superior to others because of these perceived flaws. Judgmental and condemning spirits can be linked with the spirit of pride. In dealing with this area, you may be dealing with anything from a shortcoming in his personality to the strongman of pride.

QUESTIONS ABOUT SELF IMAGE.

You'll find a list of things the individual can circle if he feels it applies to him. How he answers may indicate a low self image, self condemnation or feelings of worthlessness. We've seen people circle every single one and add some more to the list. Those people have felt rejected every single day of their lives. We've had other people who didn't circle a single one of them, because either they didn't experience rejection or they didn't receive the potential rejection in a situation. Watch for people who circle that they hate themselves. These people may actually have a spirit of self-hatred and self-rejection that causes them all kinds of problems.

WAS YOURS A HAPPY HOME DURING CHILDHOOD?

Here you're trying to find out any information that will alert you to open doors. If they're vague, be more specific in the interview and ask questions like, "What was bedtime like?" He may think about it and say, "There was a lot of scuffling and fighting," or "I cried myself to sleep a lot." You may find out the home was peaceful or you may discover that as a child he was on his own a lot, responsible for siblings at a young age, or that there was violence in the home.

You will get people—especially men, God love them—who will answer with such vague answers that they tell you nothing. You may ask, "How was your relationship with your mother?" They respond, "Fine."

"How was your relationship with your father?"

"Okay."

When you get one word answers, you know that you'll be stuck there for a while, because you have to dig until he tells you what those relationships were really like. Sometimes it's helpful to ask him to describe some element of the relationship. For instance, you might ask him to describe a typical conversation when he asked his father to help him with his homework or asked his mother if he could have an extra dessert. Watch carefully for hints of violence.

HOW WOULD YOU DESCRIBE YOUR FAMILY'S FINANCIAL SITUATION AS A CHILD?

This question is important for a variety of reasons. If the family was poor or struggling financially, that's almost automatically a rejection issue. If they were affluent, you may be dealing with pride. You may also be dealing with a spoiled child.

It's possible for an overly spoiled child to also be very rejected, depending on how he was raised.

WERE YOU LONELY AS A TEENAGER?

Loneliness is a rejection issue. If you probe, you may find that there are forgiveness issues here as well.

DO YOU EXPERIENCE A MIXTURE OF ANGER, RESENTMENT, BITTERNESS, RAGE OR FEELINGS OF VIOLENCE?

If they answer "Yes," get them to explain. Everyone's definition of violence is different. For instance, I spent 50 years feeling guilty for once calling my sister a leper. That was extremely violent for me and I had to repent and deal with it.

We had one lady who was very contrite over her violence. By her remorse, I pictured her hitting her husband over the head with a rolling pin and giving him a skull fracture. This woman was so ashamed of her behavior that we had to press to get her to give us the details. She finally confessed, "I slid an ashtray across the floor at him!" Compared to other answers I'd heard, I didn't personally define that as violent, although I guess it could have hurt his toe or something, but this woman felt extremely guilty and ashamed of her behavior, so we dealt with it like we would deal with any violent act.

HOW MANY TIMES HAVE YOU BEEN MARRIED?

This question was not in the original questionnaire. We often found ourselves three hours into the deliverance when the person mentioned an ex-husband. We'd stop and say in surprise, "You've been married before?" She might answer, "Yes, three times. Why?" As you can well imagine, three marriages gives us a lot of things with which to deal that we almost missed simply because we hadn't asked the question.

Get her to tell you about her current spouse and how long they have been married. What's the marriage like? Ask about any previous spouses. What were those marriages like and why did they end? You're looking for covenant breaking, abuse, anger, rejection and lots of forgiveness issues. Sometimes they need to forgive themselves for failing at a marriage.

HAVE YOU BEEN INVOLVED IN A SERIOUS, ROMANTIC RELATIONSHIP WHERE YOU WERE NOT MARRIED?

Interestingly enough, people may tell you all about their marriages, but unless you specifically ask, most won't mention the person that they lived with out of wedlock. Here again, find out how long the relationships lasted and why it ended. You'll probably find a lot of rejection, anger and forgiveness issues. Fornication and soul ties are certain.

HAS LYING OR STEALING BEEN A PROBLEM FOR YOU? IS IT CURRENTLY A PROBLEM?

You're looking here for a spirit of deception and you might see a whole gambit of answers. If lying or stealing was a problem in the past but isn't now, find out if he went through deliverance or if he disciplined his flesh (and possibly a spirit). If he hasn't been through deliverance, go ahead and cast it out.

When you ask if this behavior has been a problem for him, you'll find some people who are pathological liars and others who just feel guilty over a whopper they told as a child.

Anytime you tell a lie, you've opened a door for the enemy, but that doesn't necessarily mean you're dealing with a spirit of deception. But I would err on the side of caution and cast it out just in case it's there.

DO YOU EXAGGERATE?

Exaggerating can be another clue to a lying spirit or a spirit of deception. If possible, find the motive behind the exaggeration. The kind of exaggeration with which you're trying to deal is when people exaggerate to make the situation appear different than it actually was.

Some people exaggerate because they're sort of dramatic and funny. They may say, "I didn't get a thing done yesterday, because the phone rang 13,000 times." Okay, everyone pretty much knows that the phone didn't ring 13,000 times. It might have rung 13 times, but 13,000 sounded more dramatic and funny. If the exaggeration is not expected or meant to deceive anyone, it would not be related to lying. Whatever the motive, though, exaggeration can open a door to the enemy if we're not careful.

DO YOU HAVE TROUBLE GIVING OR RECEIVING LOVE?

These questions help you see if the person has built up an inner wall to protect himself. That barrier can keep him from giving or receiving love. There are a lot of situations that can create this; one of them is Freemasonry.

DO YOU HAVE AN ADVANCED EDUCATION?

You're looking for a prideful spirit here. Some people can get a doctorate degree and be very humble. Others can attend a Vo-Tech after high school and get so puffed up about their achievement that they fall into intellectual pride.

You should also be looking for intellectualism, which may be the basis for doubt and unbelief.

DO YOU HAVE A HISTORY OF CONFLICT WITH THOSE IN AUTHORITY OVER YOU?

A positive answer to this question could indicate a spirit of lawlessness and/or a spirit of rebellion. You're looking for a pattern of behavior. Having one boss that he couldn't get along with doesn't make a pattern. So that doesn't necessarily mean he has that spirit, but you will need to explore further to determine if a pattern exists.

DO YOU HAVE, OR HAVE YOU HAD, PROBLEMS WITH IMPATIENCE, RACIAL PREJUDICE OR VIOLENCE?

These may be aggressive reactions to rejection, but they may also indicate a spirit of rebellion, a spirit of jealousy, anger, rage or murder. We've seen a lot of good Christian men and women who know these things are wrong, so they have disciplined their flesh not to react that way anymore. If you cast out the spirits behind the situation, they'll find it a much easier to discipline their flesh.

Remember, you don't have to kill someone to have a spirit of murder. We've seen wonderful, gentle people who half a dozen times in their lives wanted to kill someone. Even though they never acted on the feeling, it may well have stemmed from a spirit of murder.

HAVE YOU BEEN GIVEN TO SWEARING, BLASPHEMIES AND OBSCENITIES, AND DO YOU NOW?

Very often swearing and obscenities are linked with anger. That's usually where it comes from. But if it's not clear, ask the person, "What makes you swear?" We've seen people who began swearing because of anger, but then it became a habit. Regardless of the reason it started, it can become a spiritual stronghold.

Some people started swearing because their friends were swearing. Most of the time, when they make new friends they stop swearing. In that case, it may not have been demonic, but rather a bad choice. However, if swearing continues for years it is far more than a choice.

ARE YOU EASILY FRUSTRATED? IF SO, DO YOU SHOW IT OR STUFF IT?

Frustration is often linked to depression, anger or pride. You might begin by asking what frustrates him. It could also be linked to a critical spirit.

ARE YOU AN ANXIOUS PERSON? ARE YOU A WORRIER? DO YOU GET DEPRESSED?

You are looking for a pattern of ongoing behavior, not a transitory episode related to a specific situation or event that ended when the situation ended. If he answers positively on any of these, ask if anybody in his family experienced these things. These often relate to fear and depression. Later on in the questionnaire, there will be a question about thoughts of suicide.

HAVE YOU EVER HAD SHOCK TREATMENT, PSYCHOANALYSIS, BEEN UNDER ANESTHESIA, BEEN INTOXICATED, USED DRUGS INDUCING A PASSIVE MIND STATE OR HAD FEVER WITH DELIRIUM?

All these questions are looking for a passive mind state. Having a passive mind is like opening a garage door and letting in anything that wants to come inside. It creates a huge open door for the enemy.

Once during my nursing career, a woman came into the hospital with toxic shock syndrome. She was a very nice woman and very normal. Then her fever spiked out of control and she lost consciousness.

When she awoke, she came out biting, scratching, spitting, cursing and being obscene. This behavior was unlike anything she'd ever done prior to the fever and loss of consciousness. When her mother walked into the room, she'd bite her and say horrible things to her.

The nurse taking care of the woman came to me and said, "If I didn't know any better, I'd think this lady's head would start turning around on her neck."

I went to check on the woman and said, "Yes, this is definitely demonic."

Another nurse and I knew what to do about the situation, so we went back and prayed for the woman. I was the supervisor so I left soon after to make rounds, but I got paged back to the nurses' station. The woman's nurse was crying. "I saw something sitting on her face! It was bloody and it stunk!" I realized immediately that the demon was now no longer inside the woman, but outside because of our prayer.

"You saw a demon," I explained.

"I didn't want to see it!" she cried.

"You needed to see what you're dealing with," I said.

The point of this story is that any time your mind is unguarded, demons can take advantage of the situation and come in. In deliverance, we've seen mean, ugly things that spit and snarl on their way out, and others that leave with a little yawn. I don't always know what they are. I don't really want to know. As long as they leave, I don't care.

HAVE YOU EVER BEEN HYPNOTIZED?

Once again, this question is looking for an open door due to a passive mind state.

HAVE YOU OR ANY CLOSE FAMILY MEMBER BEEN A FREEMASON?

Freemasonry, Odd fellows, and all secret societies are wrought with the demonic and can bring with them a whole host of symptoms. We dealt with Freemasonry thoroughly earlier in the book, but just understand that any link to Freemasonry or other secret societies is a huge open door. One of the things often linked with it is a spirit of infirmity.

DO YOU FEEL MENTALLY CONFUSED?

This would point toward a spirit of confusion, Freemasonry or a spirit of antichrist, all of which result in confusion. If he has generalized confusion, it could be linked with depression or any number of other things. If, however, the confusion is often linked with the things of God, you are most likely dealing the spirit of antichrist.

DO YOU DAYDREAM, AND IF SO, WHAT IS THE NATURE OF YOUR DAYDREAMS?

The next question, "Do you have mental fantasies?" is linked with this question on daydreams. Daydreams, mental fantasies and bad dreams can all be linked with Freemasonry, but they can also be symptoms of other things as well. Some people daydream as they plan their day. But some people daydream to escape, and they make up scenes in their minds that often include sexual fantasies or other things that are ungodly. If he daydreams to escape, you're looking for escapism, which might be bondage.

Ask what he daydreams about, and how often he daydreams. How many hours a day does he spend daydreaming? Some people daydream in order to get to sleep at night; this is usually not a problem depending on the content of the day dream. You will occasionally run into people whose daydreams are more real to them than their life. Some live a whole fantasy life with themselves on center stage—in which case you're dealing with a lot of self-deception. Some daydreams can be harmless, but daydreams used as a means of escape, involving ungodly subjects, or that are a significant part of the person's life are signals of spiritual issues.

HAVE YOU EVER BEEN TEMPTED TO COMMIT SUICIDE? HAVE YOU EVER WISHED TO DIE AND SPOKEN IT OUT LOUD?

If he has attempted to commit suicide, you need to find out why. It was probably depression, but it could also be other things such as hopelessness and despair. In any case, you'll need to cast out a spirit of death. If he has spoken his desire to die out loud, you need to have him break that word curse that he spoke over himself.

HAVE YOU HAD A STRONG OR PROLONGED FEAR OF ANY OF THE FOLLOWING?

There is a long list of things people fear, and sometimes they will add to the list. When you're dealing with fear, you have to explore to find the entry point. For instance, if he listed that he is afraid of the dark, you might ask if he remembers the first time he was ever afraid of the dark. Ask if there is a particular moment he remembers that is linked to that fear. There isn't a question listed here that would reveal a generational or heredity element to the fear, so cast it out anyway.

HAVE YOU EVER MADE A PACT WITH THE DEVIL?

Category C deals with witchcraft and the occult. If you run across someone who has made a pact with the devil, don't be intimidated, just deal with it. It's just a demon and the blood of Jesus will drive it out. However, you need to know how to go about it. In order to get the doors closed, you'll need to have him repent of and renounce the curse that he placed upon himself. We usually apply anointing oil in these cases, but if he made a blood pact, I would definitely get out the anointing oil and symbolically apply the blood of Jesus to replace the pact. You are looking for spirits of divination, witchcraft and control that can come through such a pact.

TO YOUR KNOWLEDGE, HAS ANY CURSE BEEN PLACED ON YOU OR YOUR FAMILY?

This isn't something that people always know, but we have had people who knew that an infidel kind of curse was put on their family. Other curses that have been put on people are a little more subtle, but you deal with them just as you would any word curse.

TO YOUR KNOWLEDGE, HAVE YOUR PARENTS OR ANY RELATIVE AS FAR BACK AS YOU KNOW BEEN INVOLVED IN OCCULTISM OR WITCHCRAFT?

You are looking for inherited spirits and familiar spirits. Remember to always deal with inherited spirits when a familiar spirit is involved.

HAVE YOU EVER READ ANY BOOKS ON OCCULTISM OR WITCHCRAFT?

If he has, ask him why he read it. For instance, I read a book on WICCA (an association of witches' covens). It was written by a Christian for the purpose of exposing Wicca and I read it to learn how to stand against them. Because my purpose was research this did not open a door to the occult in my life. But when I was in the ninth grade, I read a book about astral projection. Although I never practiced what I learned, my motive for reading the book was curiosity and I was open to the idea. This was an open door that I had to close when I went through my own deliverance.

HAVE YOU EVER PLAYED GAMES SUCH AS DUNGEONS AND DRAGONS?

Dungeons and Dragons is a demonic game that is a door opener for anyone who plays it. There are a lot of other demonic games, many of which are on the adolescent questionnaire. If you've ever played those games, read dark novels or novels with an occult theme, you need to close those doors and deal with whatever spirit is associated with it.

Demonic films, movies and extremely violent scenes are linked to spirits of violence, familiar spirits of witchcraft and can open the door to a spirit of fear.

HAVE YOU EVER BEEN INVOLVED IN TRANSCENDENTAL MEDITATION?

Transcendental Meditation has its roots in Eastern religions and you may need to deal with false religion spirits that came in during a passive mind state as well as the other spirits involved. Also ask if he had a mantra—a phrase, word or sound which he repeated over and over while he meditated. Many mantras are actually the names of demons that the person is repeating over and over. If he had a mantra, be sure and have him repent of it, renounce it and cut off anything that came into his life that was associated with it.

HAVE YOU EVER VISITED HEATHEN TEMPLES?

If he has visited these temples, ask why. Chances are pretty good that if he once toured the Taj Mahal and took a couple of pictures, you may not be dealing with anything demonic. Ask if he gave any offerings, took part in a ceremony or experienced anything unusual associated with the visit. If so, at the very least, he needs to repent of honoring false gods and there may be spirits of idolatry, false religion and the occult to handle.

HAVE YOU EVER DONE ANY FORM OF YOGA?

Yoga has its roots in false religion and often involves both meditations and mantras associated with a passive mind. The exercises in Yoga are also demonic. Each position invokes the presence of a demon. You will need to evict the spirits associated with Eastern religions and the occult.

WERE YOUR PARENTS OR GRANDPARENTS SUPERSTITIOUS, AND WERE YOU?

Superstition is the opposite of faith in God and is connected with witchcraft. Find out to what degree their lives were governed by superstitions. Did they ever walk across the street to avoid going under a ladder? Did they ever change their plans because the morning sky was red?

There were all sorts of superstitions in my family when I was growing up. For instance, if you were walking side by side and you had to split to go around a sign post, you had to say, "Bread and butter," before you split. Otherwise, it meant you were going to have a fight with that person. We could never walk with one shoe on and the other shoe off. Anything that is avoided because it's considered bad luck or that is done to ward off bad luck should be repented of, renounced and the associated spirits of divination, witchcraft, the occult, fear and doubt and unbelief cast out.

HAVE YOU EVER WORN OR KEPT ANY OF THE FOLLOWING?

This gives a list of things you might have around the house that are associated with witchcraft, charms, enchantments and fetishes. This leads to a bit of spiritual housecleaning.

DO YOU HAVE IN YOUR POSSESSION ANY SYMBOLS OF IDOLS OR SPIRIT WORSHIP SUCH AS A BUDDHA, CARVING OR GARGOYLES?

A lot of Native American art is beautiful, but you need to beware of fetishes. Fetishes, like necklaces with little carved birds, turtles and bears, are used in false worship, and you need to get rid of them. Much Native American and Eastern art contains images related to false religion and false deities.

I know of one woman who destroyed of thousands of dollars worth of stunning art, because it had demonic associations. It must have been a very difficult thing to do, but how much money would you pay to keep that curse off of your life?

ARE YOU DRAWN TO ANY OF THE FOLLOWING MUSIC?

Perhaps because Lucifer was originally a musician, music can be a huge open door to the satanic. We ran across one girl who said she would be perfectly normal until she listened to certain kinds of hard core heavy metal music. Within two hours of listening to her favorite music, she said she was looking for someone to "hurt."

The power that music has on our minds and emotions is obvious if you notice how music is used in movies and television shows to control our responses to scenes and subject matter. Many types of music stir up all kinds of demonic activity. There are many Christian musicians who record good music as a substitute. But some of it is a gloom and doom type of Christianity with no grace in it. So you have to be watchful over all music, and be careful about what you recommend to the person with whom you are praying.

HAVE YOU LEARNED ANY OF THE MARTIAL ARTS?

A lot of Christians want to learn martial arts because they are peaceful, provide a method of self-defense and keep them from getting into fights. That's probably all true, but our purposes here are to close every possible open door to the enemy, and martial arts have their roots in Eastern religion and at their roots were based on anger and violence, although that may not be how they are used today. I go with the philosophy that if the roots are bad, the fruit is bad.

HAVE YOU EVER HAD ANY PREMONITIONS?

A positive response on this question might reveal a perversion of the prophetic gift, such as déjà vu or psychic sight. He needs to repent, renounce it and pray that God would raise that gift up in his life in a godly way.

HAVE YOU EVER BEEN INVOLVED IN FIRE WALKING OR VOODOO?

Basically voodoo is divination and witchcraft. But you may need to go after it a little differently. We've only run into a couple of cases, so we're not experts on the subject. It involves domination over other people's spirits and it may involve mind control. If you have voodoo operating in your area, you might want to look into it more closely before the deliverance.

DO YOU HAVE ANY TATTOOS?

We've had some interesting experiences with tattoos. Most of the time, the reason someone gets a tattoo is rebellion against authority or against society. Since God told the children of Israel not to get tattoos, it might even be rebellion against God. Today, it is also thought to be a fashion statement. Explore with the person the reason behind getting the tattoo and proceed accordingly. We always anoint the tattoo with oil when we cast out any associated spirits.

In addition to the motive, you need to come against the message the tattoo gives. For instance, a heart with a knife piercing it may be a symbol of violence or hatred. We've seen lots of people with a dragon tattoo which is both a symbol for and one of the names of Satan (Revelation 20:2).

On one occasion, a young woman came in for deliverance who had gotten her tattoo as a teen when she was rebellious. It was very pretty and we discerned that she had an underlying pride in it. As always in dealing with tattoos, we anointed it with oil and prayed. When she renounced the pride associated with it, an interesting thing happened. A spirit of rebellion, that she didn't even realize was still attached to her, finally left.

HAVE YOU EVER BEEN IN THE MILITARY?
HAVE YOU EVER BEEN TRAINED FOR COMBAT?

We are especially looking for any experience in combat. In order to be a good soldier, there are some things with which people trained for combat have to deal. You may encounter spirits of anger, violence, fear, murder and guilt, just to name a few. Many of them will also have "survivor's guilt" (a feeling of guilt because they lived and others died) which they don't understand, but can allow a strong spirit of guilt and shame to enter. When dealing with people who served in Vietnam, we have to remember how some groups in America treated them with contempt and understand the rejection and anger that may have resulted. It's important to show no condemnation for anything they reveal that they may have done.

They will need to forgive everybody from the Vietnamese government, our government, Jane Fonda, the protestors at home, and the guy next door who waited it out in Canada, to the Vietnamese man who is trying to make a living by running the corner store. And they will need to forgive themselves.

When you do deliverance on men and women who were in the Vietnam War, you will likely run up against a brick wall. God love them, they have often been so bruised and traumatized by the experience that they don't want to talk about it. They don't want to think about it. They don't want to remember it. They surely don't want to tell you about it. You have to be very gentle, but you absolutely cannot let them wiggle off the hook, because there's so much that has to be dealt with, not the least of which is forgiveness.

One of the things that will often break the stalemate is asking, "Have you ever been to the wall?" (National Vietnam Veterans Memorial). Often that's when the tears start to flow. If on the questionnaire they have answered that they have seen someone die or have killed someone, you may need to remind them of God's grace and forgiveness. They need to understand that it is not an accident that they survived; God had His hand on them. They may fear they have broken the commandment "Thou shalt not kill" (Exodus 20:13, KJV). Explaining that the word "kill" is more accurately translated as "murder" should help.

Sometimes these people have stuffed their feelings so deep and drug it around so long, that you have to beg them to deal with it. I mean practically on bended knee, beg them to deal with it. The statistics on suicides, divorce, imprisonment, alcoholism and drug abuse in the soldiers following the Vietnam War are just astronomical. Many of these people have really suffered.

One of the men for whom we prayed started out saying that there wasn't anything about his experience in Vietnam that was bothering him; later, after some gentle probing, he broke down and the tears and weeping seemed to go on forever. After it was all done, he said the most astounding thing. He said, "I never realized how horrendous that war was."

I was shocked at the depth to which he had shoved it, stuffed it, covered it and refused to face the reality of it for over thirty years. So whatever you do, care enough to refuse to let them stuff it any longer.

Break the word curses that were spoken by Buddhist monks over American troops in Vietnam declaring that they would be wanderers for the rest of their lives, they would be angry and would never find peace. These curses were spoken in an organized, concerted effort by groups of monks over American troops. Even if the person is unaware it was being done, the curses must be broken. In addition to forgiveness, you may need to deal with guilt and shame, both "survivor's guilt" and shame over their own actions. Also common are fear and distrust, anger, rage and murder, and the spirit of death.

HAVE YOU EVER HAD A NEAR DEATH EXPERIENCE?

Here again, you're tracking a spirit of death.

HAVE YOU EVER HAD A LOVED ONE DIE?

You're looking for a spirit of grief and mourning. They may need to forgive the person who died for leaving them.

HAVE YOU EVER BEEN EXTREMELY COMPETITIVE?
IS IT OUT OF CONTROL?

You're looking for a competitive spirit or a spirit of pride.

HAVE YOU EVER STUDIED VISUALIZATION
OR USED INNER HEALING?

There are some types of inner healing that are done under the blood of Jesus, but there are a lot of times when it is demonic.

DO YOU HAVE LUSTFUL THOUGHTS AND FANTASIES?

Find out what they are. The fantasies might involve homosexuality, adultery or violence.

DO YOU MASTURBATE AS A COMPULSIVE PROBLEM?

You're looking for bondage. If the problem is compulsive, there will be a spirit of whoredoms. If it involves unhealthy fantasies, there may be a spirit of lust and perversion.

HAVE YOU EVER COMMITTED FORNICATION? HAVE YOU HAD SEX WITH PROSTITUTES? HAVE YOU COMMITTED ADULTERY? HOW MANY SEXUAL PARTNERS HAVE YOU HAD? LIST THEM.

You are looking for spirits of perversion, guilt and shame. Break soul ties with each individual involved.

The question they will balk at is naming their sexual partners. All you need is the first name. They need to understand no one is going to contact the other parties or ever discuss it again once the deliverance is over. Remind them that the questionnaire will be destroyed as soon as deliverance is done. But you will need to lead them in prayer to break the soul ties with each partner. Sometimes they'll get to the point that they can't remember names. In those cases, they can just list "the guy at the gas station" or "the hitchhiker who smoked cigars." As long as they, God and the demons know who they mean, it is adequate.

Don't get shocked. We've had people whose lists of sexual partners was several extra pages. If you miss one sexual partner, you'll cover it at the end by breaking soul ties with anyone with whom they've ever had sex at any time.

HAVE YOU EVER HAD AN ABORTION?

If she has had an abortion, she must repent and forgive herself. She must forgive anyone who pressured her into it or contributed in any way. You'll want to deal with a spirit of death, a spirit of murder, and probably guilt and shame. If you're praying with a father who did not want his child aborted, he needs to forgive the mother and everyone involved in the abortion.

HAVE YOU EVER HAD INNER SEXUAL STIMULATION AND A CLIMAX OUT OF YOUR CONTROL, ESPECIALLY AT NIGHT?

This is not just asking about sexual fantasies. Find out if he ever sensed a presence that had sex with him while he was asleep. If the spirit came in the form of a man, you are dealing with a spirit of incubus. If it came in the form of a woman you are dealing with a spirit of succubus. Have them repent, renounce it and then cast out incubus or succubus.

DO MEMBERS OF THE OPPOSITE SEX MAKE UNINVITED COMMENTS TO YOU?

It's one thing if the person is flirting with someone when the comments occur. It's quite another if the comments were totally unprovoked. He may have been minding his own business when someone started making off color remarks to him. You're looking for a familiar spirit. If it seems that everywhere he goes people make inappropriate remarks or tell him dirty jokes, it's probably a familiar spirit.

DESCRIBE YOUR SEXUAL RELATIONSHIP WITH YOUR SPOUSE.

You may or may not find anything that needs to be dealt with. In addition to information related to sexually-connected demons, you may learn about the relationship in general and find deliverance issues unrelated to sex. Listen and pray.

CATEGORY F IS GENERAL QUESTIONS ABOUT THEIR FAMILY.

The country or culture from which their family originates may point to spirits inherited in their bloodline. For example, if you find someone who is prideful and warlike, and especially if this is a pattern in their family, you may discover that their roots are German. According to some literature, there are spirits of pride and imperialism in Germany. Other countries have prevalent spirits of poverty, idolatry, the occult, etc.

HAVE YOU EVER BEEN IN A COUNTER CULTURE?

You may find people who were bikers, hippies, surfers, in the New Age movement or a member of a cult. If they answer this with an affirmative, ask what the culture was like. That will give you a clue as to how to pray.

DESCRIBE YOURSELF IN AS MANY ONE OR TWO WORD PHRASES AS YOU CAN.

You are again trying to get this person's self image. You may find a lot of rejection or they may paint a prideful picture. Sometimes you'll see a list of all bad phrases, and at other times people will list only good things about themselves—and everything in between.

When we started our deliverance ministry, the only people for whom we prayed were the members of our church and that is still our primary ministry. I don't recommend ministering deliverance to people who aren't submitted and accountable to a local church where you are confident they will receive the proper spiritual support and follow-up. Since our pastor urges everyone in our church to go through deliverance, and requires it for those in leadership positions, that can be a full time responsibility for the team. At the time of this writing, we have 24 members on our deliverance team and twelve intercessors. Thank God! But even with that team, we usually have a waiting list of about three months.

Our pastor, Dr. John Benefiel, leads the Oklahoma Apostolic Prayer Network, which is a network of hundreds of churches of various denominations that are linked by prayer for this state and nation. Eventually, Dr. Benefiel expanded the people for whom we pray to include the regional leaders of the Oklahoma Apostolic Prayer Network and their representatives. We also train them to start their own deliverance ministries. Whenever we minister to individuals who are not members of our church, we require approval of both our pastor and the person's pastor.

In addition, there have been a few instances when Doris Wagner referred out-of-state cases to us. We have ministered deliverance to teens with schizophrenia and other diagnoses, with the prior approval of both our pastor and the teens' pastors. The details of ministering to the schizophrenic will be covered in a subsequent book.

I recommend always ministering deliverance in teams of at least two people. Our team never ministers solo. If evil spirits decide to be stubborn or troublesome, it is important to have spiritual support. In addition, it is often easier for the minister who is not talking to hear the direction of the Holy Spirit. Whenever possible, female teams minister to women and male teams minister to men. If this isn't possible, we never minister without a member on the team of the same sex as the person for whom we are praying. However, there is generally less embarrassment and more freedom for the person to discuss the intimate details of his life with a team of the same sex.

There have been a lot of excellent deliverance ministers quietly setting the captives free for years. But there have also been theatrical dog-and-pony shows that have given deliverance a bad name. We have no part in that sort of thing. Deliverance is one of the ministries offered by our church and the people who come to us for prayer are not charged a fee of any kind.

INDIVIDUAL PREPARATION

For those preparing to go through deliverance in our church, the first step is to pick up the questionnaire. At that time, they are also given both recorded and written guidelines to help them prepare for the deliverance. Included in the questionnaire packet is a legal waiver which they sign prior to their deliverance session. Copies of all of these forms, including the written guidelines and the script for the tape, are included in Appendix C, Section 1 of this book.

By far the individual's most difficult task will be answering the questions on the questionnaire. This process will dredge up many unpleasant memories and potentially painful experiences from the past. The purpose of the questionnaire is to alert the team to open doors to demonic spirits that must be closed. Completing the questionnaire should be done prayerfully and with total honesty.

When all the paperwork is complete, the individual seals the envelope and turns it in to our church secretary who keeps it safely locked away. The deliverance ministry leader then assigns a team of two to minister the deliverance. The assigned minister schedules the deliverance session. At this point we recommend that the individual coming for deliverance prepare himself further by prayer and fasting.

TEAM MEMBER PREPARATION

As the ministry team leader, I am the only person on our team who accepts completed questionnaires directly from individuals, as mentioned. They may also be given to our church secretary who keeps them in a secure place until she gives them to me. When I am given a questionnaire, I never let it out of my sight until I get home where I can put it in a safe place. I never lay it down on a chair and walk away. I log each questionnaire into my database, then assign a ministry team to schedule the deliverance.

When we call the person to schedule the deliverance session, we are extremely careful about what we say if we have to leave a message with a person or an answering machine. We may leave a message giving our name and say, "I'm calling to schedule your prayer time." Since we have no idea who might be listening to the message, we never use the word deliverance.

Prayer and fasting are an important part of the team members' preparation process. On one occasion Jesus' disciples couldn't cast out a demon, but He was able to do so. Jesus said, "This kind of demon won't leave unless you have prayed and gone without food" (Matthew 17:21, TLB).

Everyone should follow the leading of the Holy Spirit about fasting. When we first started our deliverance ministry, we fasted the day of the deliverance. However, when one of our team members almost fainted during a session due to low blood sugar, we switched to fasting *before* the actual day of the deliverance. That has worked better for us.

One hour before the deliverance session, the assigned team gets together to pray for God's direction and prepare the Battle Plan. One thing we specifically ask is which member the Lord wants to lead the session. We usually each take a section, at the Lord's leading. We only have one person in authority at a time. This prevents confusion and keeps authority from being diluted.

FORMING THE BATTLE PLAN

Our first order of business is to form a battle plan before the individual arrives for his deliverance session. Depending on the individual minister, this can be done well ahead of time or the ministers can meet to form the battle plan just before the session. There is a great deal of information on the questionnaire, and you'll need to sort it out in an orderly fashion so that you'll know how to pray.

If the ministers are going to prepare the battle plan together, we meet one hour before the session is scheduled to begin. One of us reads through the questionnaire aloud and the other takes notes. As we go through the questionnaire, we use a highlighter to mark places where we see an open door. As one of us reads and highlights, the other lists in categories what we find. We also make notes of any questions we need to ask the person to clarify or expand on his answers. If we decide to do the battle plan prior to the day of the session, one or both of the ministers can prepare a draft of the plan. They would meet one hour prior to the scheduled time of the session to go over their plans and combine their thoughts.

I want to assure you that there is no need to do this exactly the way we do. You can do whatever works for you. However, this might help get you started. *A sample battle is included in Appendix A, Section 5.*

I handle things in a particular order during deliverance, so I generally list the things I find in the questionnaire in the same order. For instance, I deal with Freemasonry first, then soul ties, followed by word curses, and then forgiveness. As I read through the questionnaire, I may see that the individual's mother did not protect her from abuse by her father. The mother may also have made her quit cheerleading. Under the category of forgiveness, I would jot "Mom" and a couple of words to remind me of the issue. That way when we get into the deliverance session, I won't forget to lead the woman in a prayer of forgiveness for her mother.

I do the same thing for rejection, fear, lust and perversion and on down the list. We deal with every spirit as though it were generational, just in case.

If I find that the woman's father left when she was a child, I would list "Father" under forgiveness, but that issue would also prompt me to list "fear of abandonment" under the category for fear as well as listing it under the category of abandonment and rejection.

Listing the open doors in an orderly manner provides you with a battle plan, and it also prevents you from having pages of notes and not knowing where to start. When you have finished dealing with something on your list, immediately mark through it so you'll know you've dealt with each item.

One word of caution: The battle plan, while extensive, is not meant to be a fixed, set-in-stone list. The Holy Spirit knows a lot more than what is written on the questionnaire or your battle plan. Listen carefully to His instructions. For example, the Lord may stop you from going through forgiveness because He knows the woman may need to break a soul tie with her mother before she can truly forgive her. Always follow His guidance on the order and method of deliverance. We never want to allow our "plan" or procedures to interfere with His plan.

Once the battle plan is established, you are almost ready for the deliverance session.

THE SETTING

Most of our deliverance sessions are done in our homes, usually at the kitchen table. This is a comfortable environment and tends to put people at ease. In addition, we like to sit at a table because we write notes to one another. We usually sit across or adjacent to the person, and try make sure he isn't looking into bright light. We have a glass of water, tissues and a lined trash can at hand for the person for whom we are praying and paper, pens, sticky notes and water or soft drinks for the team members.

We turn off the ringers on the phones in the house and ask that all cell phones be turned off as well. We attempt to remove any interruptions or distractions. We put a Do Not Disturb sign on the front door so that the doorbell will not be rung by neighbors or delivery men. We ask our family members to avoid coming into the area and not to cause disruption. Pets are kept out of the room.

Of course, a private room at the church is another option. The room should be quiet, private and out of sight of church traffic. The same steps as above should be taken to prevent interruptions and distractions.

We plan and prepare for a session to last several hours. It would be unfair and disturbing to the person for whom we are praying if the session had to be ended due to time limitations before the deliverance was completed. Some sessions take only three or four hours, but many take much longer. The longest personal deliverance session in which I can remember participating was fourteen hours. If a team member needs to leave early, he can quietly slip out without disrupting the proceedings as long as at least two members remain.

There is some opinion that extremely long deliverance sessions are a hardship on the person for whom you are praying. However, our experience has been just the opposite. We find that once the person has gone through all the preparation for the deliverance and anticipation of being set free, he wants to stay until it is done no matter how long it takes. This should, of course, be tailored to the individual involved.

26 - THE PERSONAL DELIVERANCE SESSION

In this chapter I will present the basic outline for the actual personal deliverance session as we administer it. Every session will be unique to the individual and his needs, but there are basic elements that we recommend be included in each session. As always, be sensitive to the leading of the Holy Spirit. He may want to make spontaneous changes in your plan.

When individuals show up for their personal deliverance sessions, you need to be aware that they will likely feel anxious and unsure about what will happen. One of your first priorities is to put them at ease. Make sure the atmosphere is light and friendly.

PRAY IN MINISTRY TEAMS OF TWO OR MORE PEOPLE.

As discussed in the previous chapter, it is unwise to attempt deliverance alone.

ONE MEMBER OF THE TEAM IS IN AUTHORITY TO LEAD AT A TIME.

This ensures orderliness and prevents confusion which can dilute the authority. Satan and his demons thrive on confusion and chaos; this method eliminates the disorder that can give the demons strength to resist deliverance.

The designated member leads the person in speaking forgiveness, breaking word curses, renouncing sins and closing doors, and casts out the demons. If it is felt that it is appropriate for another member to lead, the authority is passed to that person. If the authority should go back to the original leader or to another person, it is passed by agreement.

Unlike some deliverance styles, our team members don't interrupt each other while we are praying or conversing with the person for whom we are praying. Only one member speaks at a time. We don't have several people casting out various demons at the same time or calling out information or instructions. While the lead member is directing the session with the person, the other members pray quietly in tongues and listen to the Holy Spirit. They also watch the person for whom we are praying very carefully, especially his eyes, for signs of demonic activity. When a member sees something the leader should know or hears from the Holy Spirit some direction or information for the deliverance, that member writes it down on a piece of paper and passes it to the leader. The leader then handles it as the Holy Spirit leads. It may prompt the leader to ask the person a question, cast out a specific demon, or it may be appropriate for the leader to pass the authority to the note-writer to handle that particular aspect of the deliverance.

The session is conducted in an orderly fashion at all times. No theatrics or commotion is appropriate.

OPEN THE SESSION WITH PRAYER

Ask the Holy Spirit for direction, wisdom and protection. Specifically ask for protection for the people present and their families. Ask Him to bring events and information to the mind of the person for whom you are praying that need to be dealt with in the session and to give the team members wisdom. Ask that a complete work be accomplished in the deliverance.

Bind, muzzle and gag in the name of Jesus all demonic entities and forbid them from manifesting, talking or trying to injure anyone. This is a critically important step that both ensures the orderliness of the session and makes it easier to cast the demons out. Binding the demons prevents them from displaying the regrettable conduct that I've mentioned before. People being thrown into walls by demons and the news stories of people being beaten or tied up during deliverance sessions to subdue demons are the result of deliverance ministers failing to bind the demons and maintain control of the session. If, during the session, a demon starts to act up, the leader immediately reminds it that it has been bound in the name of Jesus and commands it to stop.

This would probably be a good time to tell you that we don't "rebuke" demons. The King James Bible says that Jesus rebuked demons. I don't know how that word translated into the English language, but in our experience, rebuking demons simply makes them act up and manifest. Other than that, it has no effect on them. It doesn't assist in making them leave. So we bind, muzzle, gag, renounce, repudiate and cast them out but we don't rebuke them.

WHAT WILL HAPPEN?

After we've invited the Holy Spirit to take over the deliverance and have bound the enemy, the next thing on our agenda is to tell the individuals what to expect. The following is a list of things we cover:

Educate them, if necessary, on the scriptural basis for deliverance and other elements of the process. Depending on their level of understanding and knowledge of the Bible, it may be necessary to conduct a rudimentary teaching on what the Bible says about deliverance. They don't need to know all the details of the process, but it is important that they understand that it belongs to them and that God wants it for them. They also need to know that they and the ministers have spiritual authority over demons.

It may be necessary for them to be given some education on some of the words and terms that will be used. We were praying with a young woman once who seemed to chuckle a little when we lead her to say that she renounced and repudiated the demon. After a couple of times we stopped and asked her why. "Repudiate," she said, "It's such a funny word. What does it mean?" It doesn't do much good to have someone repudiate a demon if she has no idea what she is doing.

Reassure them that the demons will not hurt them.
Most people's only experience with deliverance was seeing *The Exorcist,* or having experienced people flopping around on the floor during a deliverance session back in the 1970s. Reassure them that we do not allow manifestations like that.

Ask them not to pray during the session unless we ask them to do so.
We assume that they have prayed before they arrived, but now is not the time. Some people want to pray in tongues or repeat the name of Jesus during the deliverance session, but that will often block demons from leaving. As we've discussed in a previous chapter, demons frequently leave though the mouth and they don't want to pass over a tongue that is praying in the mighty name of Jesus.

Ask them to interrupt us and tell us of anything significant that comes to their mind during the session, or any physical sensations they experience.
While we do not interrupt another team member during a deliverance session, we instruct the individual to do so. The things that they tell us may lead us to pray in a different direction. For instance, if we're praying against a spirit of fear, and suddenly the individual starts feeling angry, that tells us that the spirits of fear and anger may be linked together, and we need to deal with both of them at the same time.

Ask that they not stifle anything during the session.
As we covered in the chapter on Dealing with Demons, they often leave in an expulsion of air. We explain at the beginning of the session that they may experience some physical symptom such as yawning, coughing, sneezing, belching, the need to clear their throat or similar displays. We also explain that they may not experience any physical response at all when the demons leave and if they don't, that doesn't mean the demons didn't go. We know by faith that demons have to leave when their legal right to stay has been taken away and they are commanded in the name of Jesus. We want them to understand that the physical response is not necessary; we certainly don't want them to force or fake anything. We do want them to realize what could happen so they don't suppress a yawn

or belch if they feel one coming on. Suppressing the physical manifestation could delay the demon's departure. We assure them that we will not be offended and that they need not apologize. If they understand this at the beginning, they are less likely to worry that we'll interpret a yawn as boredom or a belch as bad manners.

Explain why we will be passing notes.

As mentioned earlier, we do not interrupt one another while we are praying. However, each team member will be discerning things and hearing from God about how to pray. Therefore, we will jot notes and pass them back and forth. It's very important that we explain ahead of time that this will happen, and it's important that they understand why we do it. A person, for instance, who is very rejected will see us passing notes and think, "*Why are they writing notes about me? Is it something real bad?*"

Warn the individuals that we may seem stern when dealing with demons and not to take it personally.

Some people with the sweetest personalities and voices can sound very stern when dealing with demons. They might speak in a very commanding voice and even point a finger. It's important for the individuals to understand the difference between the minister speaking to them personally and speaking to the demon.

Warn the individual that he may feel like he's under a microscope.

When we do a deliverance session, we're watching for changes. We may watch the person's eyes or watch for a change in his complexion. When he arrives, we try to notice his coloring, eyes and demeanor, so that we'll recognize a change. For that reason, the individual may feel as though he's under a microscope. It may be uncomfortable for him if he feels like we're staring and he doesn't know why.

Educate him as you proceed so that he can help you identify issues to address.

Explaining what you are doing, what you are looking for and why, can help the person bring up subjects, memories and events that will tell the deliverance minister what needs to be done.

Remind the person that it is the Holy Spirit who is doing the work. Ensure that the person with whom you are praying doesn't look to you as his deliverer. It is easy for the person to transfer his feelings of gratitude and awe to the deliverance minister and this, of course, must be avoided. It is critical that ego is not allowed to play a part and that the person is reminded that you are just the minister of God's power and goodness.

Forgiveness—You will need to educate the person so he can recognize people he needs to forgive, not excuse the people who need to be forgiven, understand that needing to forgive them doesn't mean you don't love them, etc. You will also need to help them learn to forgive from the heart.

Open doors—Take some time to explain what open doors mean and how they can be opened. Help him identify door-opening events he may have dismissed as unimportant.

Closing doors—It is crucial that the person fully understand what happened to open the door, be completely willing to repent and turn away from the sin and fully comprehend what it means to renounce the demon.

The person should also understand that while he must make every effort to keep his deliverance by avoiding the sins and mistakes of the past, if he makes a mistake and reopens a door, he can repeat the renouncing and casting out process and start over. The corridor explanation is Chapter Six is a helpful tool.

THE INTERVIEW

You may recall that before the deliverance session began, we went through the questionnaire and formed a battle plan. During the interview process, we again update the battle plan. The purpose of the interview is to go through all the things highlighted on the questionnaire and ask for more specific information. One team member conducts the interview, while the other one updates the battle plan by adding to the list those entry points with which you need to deal.

It's important to listen very carefully as his story unfolds during the interview. For instance, you may stop and ask for more specific information and discover that Uncle Joe sexually abused him as a child. The person doing the writing will update the list to include forgiveness for Uncle Joe, and casting out the spirits associated with the assault as well as putting Uncle Joe on the soul tie list.

Sometimes the person gets carried away with the story and goes off on rabbit trails about Uncle Joe or Aunt Mary. In those cases, gently lead him back to the task at hand. You can't afford to spend too much time on a specific issue that was really his mother's story and may not have a great deal to do with this deliverance session.

THE DELIVERANCE

While there is no formula for a deliverance session, there are some basics that we always include. Below is the list in the order we usually follow. It is important to remember that the Holy Spirit may rearrange your plan.

1. Pray against Freemasonry.

2. Break soul ties.

3. Break word curses.

4. Forgive everyone involved, including self-forgiveness.

5. Deal with rejection and cast it out.

6. Pray for trauma

7. Identify the entry points and open doors for each specific demon.

8. Repent for the sin or iniquity that opened the door to the demon.

9. Renounce and repudiate the demons associated with the sin, iniquity or open doors.

10. Close the entry points and open doors.

11. Cast out the demons. Repeat for each demon, unlinking spirits as needed.

12. Ask the Holy Spirit to fill the vacancy left by the demons.

13. Pray protection over everyone involved.

14. Destroy the questionnaire.

15. Pray over the house and command any lingering demons to leave.

If the door was opened through the individual's sin, the first step is to have the individual repent of the act that was the entry point. As mentioned earlier, it's crucial that he recognizes the act as sin; otherwise it's not really repentance. If the entry point wasn't a sin on the part of the individual, ensure he has forgiven and broken any soul ties with any person involved.

The second step to closing doors is for the person to renounce the spirit that came in through that door. As mentioned earlier, we don't rebuke the demons; we renounce and repudiate them. You'll probably need to explain the definitions of these words rather than have people repeat them by rote.

"Renounce" means to give up entirely, to forsake, to relinquish, to cast off, to disown and to refuse to recognize it as your own. "Repudiate" means to refuse to accept, to reject, to disclaim, refuse to acknowledge, to cast off and to disown.

If there are multiple events for the same problem, close each door one by one. As he closes these doors, remind him of the corridor illustration and ask him to visualize himself slamming the doors closed one after another.

CROUCHING DRAGONS

As you go through this process, very often the individual will say, "I only did it one time!" Or he may say, "I was a child and I didn't know playing with Ouija boards and horoscopes was dangerous."

Don't just gloss over these objections, but rather, address them. In Genesis 4:7, God told Cain, " ... sin lies crouching at your door. It desires to have you" (NIV). The Hebrew word for "crouching" refers to a demon waiting to pounce.

First Peter 5:8 says, " ... Your enemy the devil prowls around like a roaring lion, looking for someone to devour" (NIV).

If the enemy goes to all the trouble to crouch, and wait for any opportunity to pounce on you and devour you, do you think he'll miss the opportunity you gave him when you were six years old and played with a Ouija board?

"But that's not fair, I didn't know it was dangerous!"

No one ever accused the devil of being fair. He takes advantage of unborn babies! He's not a nice guy. Derek Prince once said, "Just because poison isn't labeled, doesn't mean it's not poison. It will have the same effect on you whether it's labeled or not." Likewise, just because you only opened one door, and you didn't know it was dangerous, doesn't mean it didn't have an effect on you.

CASTING OUT DEMONS

Once the sin has been repented, the demons renounced and repudiated and forgiveness granted, casting out the demon is very simple. You command it to leave in the name of Jesus, carefully watching for any manifestations. Ask the Holy Spirit to show you when the spirit has left. You can also often tell by looking at the person. Many times you will see a change in his expression when he is set free.

Once you've gone through everything that turned up on the questionnaire or in the interview, and any spirits the Lord revealed to you along the way, use the name of Jesus to challenge any demon attempting to stay behind.

Occasionally, you will encounter an individual who is not ready to give up the behavior associated with the demon you identify to cast out, most commonly when dealing with addictions and from time to time with sexual sin. It is a trait of the spirit of bondage that the decision to give up the behavior is often a difficult, complex one and the person for whom you are praying may not be ready. This is particularly common when dealing with alcoholism and drug addiction. There is no point in pushing him to make a commitment he is not going to be able to fulfill.

If the individual tells you he is not sure he can stop the behavior or if you feel an uncertainty in your spirit, the best course is not to cast those spirits out at that time. Sometimes, you can conduct the rest of the deliverance, but refrain from casting out the spirit behind the addiction. If you cast it out, one of two things will probably happen. The demon may refuse to leave because the person is not willing to truly renounce it and close the door. Or the demon may leave because the person has renounced it, however, if the person later resumes the behavior, the door will be reopened and the spirit will come back in, probably stronger than before.

In these situations, explain to the individual why you intend to wait until another time to cast out the demon. Then bind the spirit in the name of Jesus and command it not to operate in the person's life. Command it to be silent, forbidding it to talk to him, put feelings in his heart or thoughts in his mind. Explain to the individual that he should now have more success in resisting the behavior and to give it his best effort in self-discipline and prayer. Ask him to return when he has confidence that he will be able to keep the door closed to the demon and at that time you will cast it out. You may find, though, that the demon is linked with other demons in the individual's life. In that case, you probably won't be able to conduct the rest of the deliverance effectively.

It is not necessary for him to completely stop the behavior on his own before you can cast out the demon. It is only necessary that he has a conviction that he will be able to discipline his flesh after deliverance to prevent return of the demon. Often we find that these individuals return in a short time and we are successful in completing the deliverance.

STUBBORN DEMONS

You will undoubtedly encounter demons that resist leaving. This is especially true of demons that have been unchallenged in the person's life for many years, have been consciously invited in, have been rampantly active in the person's life or are linked with other spirits that have not yet been cast out. There are several steps you should take when a demon is being stubborn.

- Review the battle plan and ask the Holy Spirit to reveal any spirits that are "linked" with the resisting spirit. If a spirit of fear came in at the same time as a spirit of death, they may be linked and gaining strength from each other. If a spirit of rejection later opened the door for a spirit of anger, they may resist leaving unless you cast them out together. If all the doors have been closed, you may need to instruct "In the name of Jesus, I command the spirits of anger and rejection to unlink from each other and any other kindred spirits and leave now."

- If lead by the Holy Spirit, lay hands on the person when you cast it out. (Luke 4:40–41). Always explain to the person what you are going to do and ask his permission before you touch him. If any physical manifestations are taking place such as discomfort in the back or headache, you may need to lay hands on the place of the manifestation. It may be appropriate for more than one member of the ministry team to lay hands on the person at the same time at the direction of the leader. *Never, never* touch the person on private places of his body even with his permission or at his request. There is no need or excuse for roughness with the person, such as holding him down, hitting him or wrestling with him.

- Anointing the person with oil is often appropriate to enforce the commandment for a demon to leave.

- Review the interview and questionnaire to identify any doors left open or any areas in which the person was ambiguous about renouncing the sin. It may be necessary to have the person repeat his renunciation of the spirit and to be more aggressive and forceful. Sometimes the demons don't believe the person if he has simply repeated what you led him to say if it wasn't earnest and heartfelt.

- Look for unrepentant sin that may have been overlooked. Be alert for any current sin, especially willful sin, that may not have been evident.

- Ask the person to deliberately cough or take and release a few deep breaths. This sometimes helps push the demon on out.

- Have a member of the ministry team read scriptures aloud that apply to the specific spirit and the authority of Jesus' name while another member commands the demon to leave. *Useful scriptures are included in Appendix B, Section 2.*

- If the demon is talking to you through the person and you feel it necessary to respond, say the opposite of what it is saying. For example, if the demon is telling the person that he isn't a good enough Christian to receive deliverance, tell it Jesus already earned deliverance for this child of God and he is completely entitled to it. Don't, however, allow yourself to be drawn into a conversation or debate with a demon. Once you know the tactic it is using, command it to be silent and remind it that it was bound, muzzled and gagged in the name of Jesus at the beginning of the session.

- Perform whatever "prophetic" or symbolic acts the Holy Spirit might direct. If the hands were involved in the sin, the Holy Spirit may have the person wash his hands and declare himself cleansed in the name of Jesus. If the person has a history of being a victim, he may need to stand up and stomp his feet, declaring that he will no longer submit to the spirit of victimization.

There is no need to yell, shout or scream at demons. The authority of Jesus' name is as effective in a whisper as in a shout. You must be firm and resolute and you may speak sternly to demons. But demons are not hard of hearing and if you find yourself yelling or even raising your voice, you should be aware you are allowing the demon to take control of the session. Stop yourself immediately, take a break, if needed, and regain control of the session. You may find that it is appropriate to pass the authority to lead the session to your ministry partner, at least temporarily. The same is true of physically touching the person. With the exception of gently laying anointed hands on him, touching him is not necessary. Never touch him roughly and, even if he asks, never touch him anywhere except the head, hands, shoulders, neck and back (above the waist) and the feet. Absolutely never touch a person on the front of his body from the shoulders down.

Ask the Holy Spirit to shine His light on any darkness still linked to the individual. Then ask the Holy Spirit to fill the person and every place vacated by demons.

Next, pray protection over the individual, each of you involved in the deliverance session, all your families and property—declaring that there will be no backlash. Especially pray over the property where the deliverance was held, forbidding the spirits to stay.

Sometimes people will ask that we provide prayer support for them after the deliverance session. We agree to pray if the Lord brings them to mind, but because we may do three or four deliverances in a week and we can't honestly spend hours in prayer for all those people, no matter how willing we might be. That's part of the reason that we urge everyone in the church to be part of a home fellowship group, because that home fellowship pastor and the believers in the group will provide most of the prayer support.

DON'T ASK HOW THEY FEEL

We recommend that you *don't* ask, "How do you feel?" That's a mistake on many levels. First, depending on *feelings* will get you in trouble. This is a step of faith, and many times the changes in a person's life are not instantaneous. In addition, if you ask how he feels, and he doesn't feel any different, it could derail his faith in the deliverance.

Having said that, don't be surprised if people volunteer that they feel different. The most common thing we hear is, "I feel so much lighter!" In addition, after what may have been several hours of deliverance, they'll often have a happy smile on their faces and appear extremely relaxed, sometimes so relaxed they can hardly stand up. We call this the "rag doll" effect.

DESTROY THE QUESTIONNAIRE

When everything else is finished, hand the individual his questionnaire and have him destroy it. This accomplishes two things. First, for obvious reasons, no one should ever see that document. Second, having the individual shred the questionnaire is a prophetic act that puts a "period" on the past and frees him to step into his future. The Battle Plan and all notes of all ministers present are also destroyed.

Occasionally, the individual asks to keep the questionnaire himself. We discourage this. While I understand the desire to have some kind of record of what he has been set free from, I prefer that he leave with no reminders of the old baggage.

AFTER CARE

You will give the individual the Post Prayer Instructions and discuss with him the importance of staying connected to his spiritual support network. After Care is discussed in more detail in the After Care chapter and the Post Prayer Instructions are included in that chapter.

Unlike adults, you generally only get one shot at getting teens delivered; you can't play games and you must earn their respect. Therefore, special consideration must be given when assembling a teen deliverance team. Some traits of people who would work well with teens are as follows:

- Must have an easy-going personality
- Must have some rapport with teens
- Must be flexible in their communication style
- Must be able to understand the teen's lingo and be up to date on their terms
- Must be very accepting and non-judgmental
- Must be able to minister on the teen's level
- Must be one who is not afraid to directly confront behavior

We suggest that the team work with the teen apart from the parents. Parents are welcome to fill out a teen packet and give us their observations. They may even write notes or a letter stating concerns, insights and family history. This helps flesh out the information. It can often show where the two are not in agreement. However, it's vital that the parent allow the teen to fill out a packet of his own and have the privacy to turn it in without losing his confidentiality.

Before taking a teen through deliverance, we require that at least one parent go through his own deliverance and have walked it out for six months. There have been exceptions when a teenager has taken the initiative to give his life to the Lord, but although he may go to church regularly, he doesn't have parents who are Christians. In these cases we make sure he is connected to a spiritual mother or father in the church who works closely with him to provide a spiritual covering and accountability. This has worked very well in keeping our teenagers free and moving forward because they know they are being watched over and have a mentor to speak into their lives. However, if the teen is under the age of 18, it is necessary that a parent or guardian sign the waiver before the deliverance session.

After taking a teen through deliverance, if there are issues between him and his parents, we visit with them about the problem. At that time, we attempt to help direct each of them to see the other's point of view and come to a Godly resolution. Our main focus is to help strengthen the family relationship. If the parents are focusing on an issue that is difficult for the teen, we try to help them come up with a plan that won't spiral him into rebellion.

We often see communication problems between the parent and teen. In these situations, we help them come up with strategies for a healthy, open relationship. We talk about styles of parenting, ideas of how they can grow together and gain one another's respect. It is important to note that we always ask the teen's permission to speak to the parent on any issue. That way we do not violate his trust or privacy. However, if the teen states he does not want us to speak to the parent, we have to help him realize that nothing will change in the family relationship unless both parties agree to change. When you talk with the parent about changes that need to be made, it's important that the teen always be present. This ensures that he doesn't feel that you are ganging up against him.

This has made a huge impact on our teens. It is not unusual for them to seek out our team members and confess when they've made mistakes. It is a giant step of maturity when they ask for help because they want to be accountable.

INCEST AND SEXUAL ABUSE

A three-year-old victim of incest doesn't know what to do with the shock and trauma associated with the abuse. He can't process it, so the body and spirit endure it while his mind goes to a safer place. The emotions go underground, but are still being carried around when the child becomes a teen.

Incest and other sexual abuse open the doors for a spirit of grief and shame, perversions, control and others. Soul ties must be broken.

When after ministering deliverance, lead the teen through the trauma prayer and ask God to heal the following:

- Body memories
- Emotional memories
- Flashbacks–ask God to erase and stop
- A torn spirit
- Inner hurts
- Fractured emotions

TRAPS FOR TEENAGERS

We know that drinking and drugs are issues for teens. This will, of course, open doors to whoredoms and bondage, if there is an addiction, and create a passive mind state. Cigarettes are marketed with youth in mind and are highly addictive. The fear of rejection by their peers causes many teens to stumble into addictions.

With the advent of computer games the stakes are raised. Kids as well as adults step into a fantasy world and take on a mystical role of another person or being that has magical power. This is very enticing for someone who feels he has little success or control over his life. It becomes a place where he can feel powerful and mighty. It is very addictive because the fantasy becomes reality to him. Many teens don't think they are affected by this. However, the real story is that these games are door openers to rebellion, suicide, death, divination, murder and, in extreme cases, can cause loss of personal identity and loss of touch with reality. Many specific games are covered in the questionnaire key in the Appendix. However, the game market changes rapidly and it is important that the deliverance ministers stay up to date on new games.

DIVINATION

Teens also regularly get invited to visit cemeteries, attend séances and generally creep each other out. They are unaware that a familiar spirit of divination or a spirit of death might follow them home. Teens are turning to various forms of divination looking for power and control that they are not finding in their local church or their lives in general. Sometimes they can be teens from a Christian family who rebel and find they gain power and a sense of belonging in this new group. There are many good informative books on divination, witchcraft and Wicca written by Christians. If you will be ministering to a large number of teens who are heavily into witchcraft in some form, I suggest you research the specific problem so you can help them. The following are questions you may want to ask the teens:

- Have you set up an altar with candles in your room?
- Have you cast spells?
- Do you have crystals, stones, metals, and powders in your possession?
- Do you have pouches where you put items related to spells?
- Do you have a book of Shadows (their personal collection of spells, potions, curses, hexes, vexes, and incantations)?

If they have answered "yes" to any of these questions, they need to repent, agree to burn or otherwise destroy the items and pray cleansing over their room. The parent's assistance may be required to burn the items.

PASSING-OUT GAMES

Teens often play passing-out games. One form of this game is to hold their breath. In another slant to the game, they put a rubber band around their necks and hang upside down. They choke one another, they create a hangman's noose or use plastic bags over their heads.

The purpose of the game is to become so lightheaded from a lack of oxygen that they feel a "rush". This can also be connected with sexual bondage, where the sexual stimulus is heightened by anoxia (lack of oxygen).

Satan's tactic in enticing them to play these games is that when they pass out, they are in a passive mind state which opens the door for demons. If sexual perversion and divination are practiced together, demonic power is increased.

Demonic strongholds may include rejection, thrill seeking, people pleasing, self-hatred, control and divination.

ANOREXIA AND BULIMIA

Anorexia and bulimia are disorders predominantly found in teenagers and young adults. The spiritual roots of anorexia and bulimia are self-rejection, self-hatred, control, whoredoms, abandonment, death and fear of rejection. Because the person with anorexia or bulimia is very fractured and will need continued support to build self-esteem and gain coping skills, after the deliverance we refer them to counseling for follow-up. If they won't agree to counseling, bind the demons and strip them of their power, but do not cast them out until the person is ready to change.

SELF-MUTILATION

Self-mutilation may include cutting, head banging, biting and clawing oneself. This is a mechanism that allows the victim to disassociate from his inner pain, by transferring it into physical pain which he can endure. You might hear statements like:

- I don't know how to handle the emotional pain, but I do know how to handle the physical pain.
- All the pain leaves my body when I see the blood drip out. Then there is relief.
- I don't know how to say what I feel.
- I want the pain to stop but I don't know how to make it end.
- Look what you (they) made me do.

These people usually isolate emotionally and will not share their real feelings for fear of what people would think. Self-injury may be their only coping mechanism and may be associated with some form of abuse. You will often find that those who self-mutilate have a great deal of difficulty communicating their feelings and emotions as many of them do not have a safe environment in which they are able to express what they are going through without suffering rejection or persecution. They may feel they have no power to change what is hurting them emotionally. Self-mutilation gives them what they see as something they can control. The spiritual roots are self-rejection, self-hatred, deep sorrow or grief, familiar spirits, a spirit of death or control.

CLOSING

In closing, we have seen some wonderful results in teens walking out their deliverance. Many teens have made a commitment to live a holy life and remain sexually pure as well as improve their relationship with their Heavenly Father. One of the most important things to remember in teen deliverance is to help foster and mend family relationships. One of the key roles of the deliverance minister is to help the teen and parents learn to make the necessary changes needed to walk out their deliverance. This will help the teen with all of his relationships including his relationship with God.

28 – CHILDREN'S DELIVERANCE

Children are such a blessing and a gift from God. Getting them set free from demonic baggage at an early age will help them fulfill God's plan for their lives. Let's face it, children are born into iniquity. If that generational sin is not dealt with, it will affect them for the rest of their lives. Therefore, taking care of this at a young age helps the child reach God's full potential without having to go through unnecessary heartache. As you will see, children's deliverance is more complex than you might think.

Our children's deliverance ministry is for those children from birth to twelve years old. Because of their age, we have two requirements for children to go through deliverance.

First Requirement: At least one parent *must* go through deliverance and walk out their freedom for six months before we will minister to their child.

It's necessary for a parent to go through deliverance first because they are responsible for the child's spiritual welfare. If they haven't shut their own spiritual doors and learned to walk out their own freedom, it will be hard for them to help the child.

Second Requirement: One parent or guardian must be present during the deliverance.

It is important that the parent be there to repent of any generational sins and learn what the child has received so he/she can help the child walk out his deliverance. If there is more than one child in the family, each child will go through deliverance separately unless the children are no more than two years apart and have similar issues. We have found that with very young children having a sibling there leading the way will help them. The youngest child we have taken through deliverance is three. The child must be able to understand the process and work with you. In dealing with children younger than three, we pray over them and teach their parents how to pray prayers of deliverance for them.

TOOLS

There are two primary tools that we use in working with children. The first is a questionnaire that we created specifically for children, which is filled out by the parent. A copy of the children's questionnaire with the key is in Appendix A, Section 3 of this book. Children between the ages of nine and twelve who are mature enough to express themselves and their feelings, may also fill out some portions of the questionnaire. It is imperative that the parent does not read what they write. The child needs to feel safe to write down his perception of things without feeling the parent would become angry or upset.

The second tool we use is the book, *The Little Skunk,* written by Sue Banks. This book tells the story of three children who are left at home while Mom goes to the store. The boys go outside and forget to close the door. A little skunk gets into the house and starts to leave his stinkies. The girl, who has a spirit of anger, yells at the boys and they all chase the skunk trying to get it to leave. The brother, who has a spirit of fear and the neighbor boy who has a spirit of gluttony are involved in the chase. They open all the windows and doors and pray for God to help them. The skunk runs out the door but the house smells terrible.

That evening the kids' dad used the skunk incident to teach the children about deliverance. Comparing the little skunk to demons, and the house being our bodies, he explains that there are doors that allow demons to come into our lives.

Children relate well to this story and can identify the "little skunks" in their own lives. Children as young as three have no trouble understanding this concept.

In our church everyone who works in any children's ministry area must have been a member of the church for at least six months and have passed a criminal background check. We continue this standard with our children's deliverance team. An additional rule is that no adult is left alone with a child; there are always at least two adults present. This keeps the child safe and shelters the team from the risk of any accusations of behavior that could be misinterpreted.

One of the most important attributes of a children's deliverance minister is the ability to be led by the Holy Spirit and to make the process *fun!* This is not the place for any religious spirits! We have rolled on the floor, had burping contests and fallen out of our seats to help the child get free.

Characteristics of a good children's deliverance minister include:

1. Very discerning
2. Young at heart and able to relate well to children
3. Free from self-consciousness
4. Able to confront issues

    Occasionally we have to challenge parents concerning discipline, parenting styles, communication, programs they allow the children to watch, games they are allowed to play and putting certain rules into place that may be more constructive.

5. Great wisdom
6. Able to communicate well
7. Spontaneous and fun
8. Free from religious spirits
9. The ability and authority to cast out demons with a smile
10. Led by the Holy Spirit

Under no circumstances should a children's deliverance minister ever raise his voice or yell at a child. This experience must never be a frightening one as fear could further demonize the child and keep him from being set free. The whole experience should be fun.

THE TEAM

The children's deliverance team consists of a prayer leader for the parent (known as the adult's leader), a prayer leader for the child (known as the children's leader), and an intercessor. It is vital that these two prayer leaders—one for the adult and one for the child—work well together, without any pride or control.

RESPONSIBILITIES OF THE ADULT'S PRAYER LEADER

1. Cast out demons that were inherited through generational curses.

2. Lead the parent through repentance and break all demonic assignments that came through open doors in the parent's life.

3. Lovingly confront the parent about issues that could reopen spiritual doors. An example would be if shame is used as a form of discipline.

4. Teach new parenting skills.

RESPONSIBILITIES OF THE CHILD'S PRAYER LEADER

1. Explain the process to the child.

2. Ask questions to form lists for forgiveness, soul ties and word curses.

3. Read *The Little Skunk* and explain ways to make the skunks leave.

4. Lead the child through forgiveness.

5. Break ungodly soul ties, word curses and death wishes.

6. Lead the child to repent for doors he may have opened through lying, having an imaginary playmate or watching certain television shows or playing certain games.

7. Help the child understand he has to change certain behaviors or "skunks" will return.

8. Teach ways to change behavior such as how to control anger, give up nail biting or watching certain television programs.

9. Be willing to be "goofy," if it helps.

10. The prayer leader will never be alone with the child. They will remain in the same room as the parent and adult leader, and always within eye contact, but out of ear shot if possible. When necessary, the child leader may go into another room and pray with the child but *only* if a third person such as an intercessor is with them.

Children often burp during a deliverance session. We find it helpful to give them a soda because it makes the process seem more natural. Warn the child that sometimes our faces might look serious if we're looking for a skunk that's hiding. I refuse to have anyone on my team who can't cast out demons with a smile. Again, it is vital that you not make this process frightening, but one that makes the child want to come back for prayer.

You can't say the same things in a children's deliverance that you could discuss openly in one for an adult. For instance, don't say anything that might make the child feel confused or rejected. If you need to discuss that the child was conceived through a rape, that the child was not the desired sex, or that a spell was put on him at birth, ask these questions privately. These things are discussed and repented of when the child is away from the parent with the children's prayer leader.

The role of the intercessor is to pray and intercede with the leader. This is a great place to start, and it's a great way to be trained to work in children's deliverance ministry.

THE PROCESS

Once the parents and child arrive, the team prays with them together. At that time we spend a few minutes with the child making sure he is comfortable with the children's leader. We explain to the child that the parent will be staying with the adult leader and he will go with the children's leader and intercessor to read a story and pray. Each goes to his own separate area as mentioned previously, the child is never left alone with one adult; there are always two adults with the child at all times. At this time each leader assumes the responsibility listed above.

CAST THOSE SUCKERS OUT!

Come together as a team and begin casting those demons out. I cast out everything that the parent and child have repented over being mindful to avoid saying anything or using words that would be frightening or upsetting to the child. Ask God to fill him up with His Spirit.

Don't think that just because you're dealing with a child that the devil has given him any breaks. Children have often suffered a lot of trauma and will need the trauma prayer. On one occasion we prayed for a girl who was into witchcraft. She had been so traumatized, and felt so controlled by demons, that she invited them in. She mistakenly believed that if she invited the demons in that she could control them. She was eight years old.

SEAL THE DELIVERANCE

Pray and thank God for overcoming the obstacles in the child's life such as fear, rebellion, fear of sleeping alone and anger, etc. Ask God to do a complete work in the child's life. Pray that all of God's plans and purposes for the child's life come to pass. Pray that God will give the parents and child wisdom in the days to come. Ask the Lord to heal and bless family relationships. Pray blessings over the child.

Review the After Care packet with the parents. Explain the process of spiritual housecleaning and getting rid of certain toys. Discuss changes both the parent and child will need to make. Write down a plan for them to stay free.

We want the deliverance process to be a positive experience for the child. I like to give the child a hug and a treat, if his parent approves.

29 - AFTER CARE

Just as important as the actual deliverance in the lives of the people for whom you pray is their following the necessary steps to "keep" their deliverance. When they leave your deliverance room they will be as free as they've ever been and the doors and entry points will be closed tight. It is crucial that you help them understand that they must now make the changes in their lives that will keep the doors closed. As we have said in a previous chapter, our deliverance team only prays for deliverance with individuals who are planted in a church where they will receive the spiritual support, teaching and prayer covering they need. As the individuals walk out of your deliverance room they must make a personal decision to stay close to God and their spiritual support network. Leading a holy life is critical to remaining free from demonic control.

As his deliverance session concludes, we give each individual a copy of the After Care Instructions that follow and discuss with him the importance of the advice contained in them. Our church also offers After Care classes in which people who have been through deliverance are taught techniques for walking out their deliverance and are given an opportunity to ask specific questions regarding challenges they are facing.

It is our goal in every deliverance session to ensure that a complete work is done and that the individuals are totally free from all demonic control when they leave. However, it is not uncommon for someone who has been through "full-personality deliverance" to need some additional prayer at a later time.

Our human personality and spiritual make up is quite intricate so, *get counseling if you need it*. The deliverance you receive freely was bought and paid for by the precious blood of Jesus and the enemy of your soul doesn't like it one bit. You must understand that he will try to ensnare you again. He will try to trick you and deceive you. Those attacks *will* come. But you'll find that there is a big difference now. Before deliverance, the battle raged within you. The attack itself came from within. Now you'll find that the battle and the attacks are no longer within. Now you'll be able to see them coming so that you will immediately be able to confront the situation with the Word of God.

It's crucial that you follow up your deliverance with discipline. Don't open a door for the devil to enter. Stay submitted in the local church and remain submitted to authority. If home groups or prayer groups are available in your church, join one immediately and ask for prayer support. Know who you will call on to pray for you when you need help. Ask the Lord to help you recognize the devil's attempts to reclaim your life, and be quick to repent and shut every spiritual door. Put the following steps into effect in your life immediately.

Don't allow one negative thought germinating space. Confess the general areas in which you have received freedom positively and gratefully in prayer.

> Romans 10:9–10: "that if you confess with your mouth the Lord Jesus and believe in your heart that God has raised Him from the dead, you will be saved. For with the heart one believes unto righteousness, and with the mouth confession is made unto salvation." (NKJV)

Renew your mind daily and learn to take every thought into captivity to Christ. The enemy can use your thought life to re-establish a foothold in your life. Ask God to help you recognize wrong thoughts, then take control of them immediately. You don't even have to finish a thought that you have recognized as wrong. The prayer "Renewing the Mind" will help you to take control of your thought life and re-train your thinking.

> Second Corinthians 10:5 "Casting down arguments, and every high thing that exalts itself against the knowledge of God, bringing every thought into captivity to the obedience of Christ." (NKJV)

Make right choices. Meet each new day trusting in God's power to help you to make the right choices. Don't let your feelings deceive you.

> Galatians 3:3 "Having begun in the Spirit, are you now being made perfect by the flesh?" (NKJV)

Don't even glance over your shoulder at what is now in the past. Move forward and expect continuous and increasing freedom where Satan has previously bound you or used you for his purposes.

> Philippians 3:13–14 "Brethren, I do not count myself to have apprehended; but one thing I do, forgetting those things which are behind and reaching forward to those things which are ahead, I press toward the goal for the prize of the upward call of God in Christ Jesus." (NKJV)

Use your faith-shield against the devil. Remember, anything the devil whispers in your ear is a lie. That's his profession and he's very good at it. If he tries to convince you that your freedom didn't really happen but was just in your mind or was emotional, use your faith-shield against him and tell him what God does to liars. He will soon give up.

> James 4:7–8 "Therefore submit to God. Resist the devil and he will flee from you. Draw near to God and He will draw near to you. Cleanse your hands, you sinners; and purify your hearts, you double-minded." (NKJV)

All condemnation comes from Satan. Never believe him; you have been blood-cleansed and are blood-protected. Don't hesitate to use the name of Jesus, the blood of the Lamb, and your confession of faith against all Satan's temptations and condemnation.

> Revelation 12:11 "And they overcame him by the blood of the Lamb and by the word of their testimony, and they did not love their lives to the death." (NKJV)

> Romans 8:1 "There is therefore now no condemnation to those who are in Christ Jesus, who do not walk according to the flesh, but according to the Spirit." (NKJV)

Avoid deliberate sin like the plague. If you realize you have been pulled back into sin, no matter how small, repent immediately. This will stop Satan from weighing you down with guilt, one of his favorite habits.

> First John 5:18 "We know that whoever is born of God does not sin; but he who has been born of God keeps himself, and the wicked one does not touch him." (NKJV)

> First John 1:9 "If we confess our sins, He is faithful and just to forgive us our sins and to cleanse us from all unrighteousness." (NKJV)

Rely upon the Holy Spirit to control your life, your emotions, your desires, and your imaginations together with your will, by deliberately giving Christ Lordship over them each day.

> Romans 12:1–2 "I beseech you therefore, brethren, by the mercies of God, that you present your bodies a living sacrifice, holy, acceptable to God, which is your reasonable service. And do not be conformed to this world, but be transformed by the renewing of your mind, that you may prove what is that good and acceptable and perfect will of God." (NKJV)

> Ephesians 5:18 "And do not be drunk with wine, in which is dissipation; but be filled with the Spirit." (NKJV)

Galatians 3:5 "Therefore He who supplies the Spirit to you and works miracles among you, does He do it by the works of the law, or by the hearing of faith?" (NKJV)

Meditate on God's Word every day. Take time or make time to read and learn. If time is limited, carry scripture verse cards with you for your free times.

Joshua 1:8 "This Book of the Law shall not depart from your mouth, but you shall meditate in it day and night, that you may observe to do according to all that is written in it. For then you will make your way prosperous, and then you will have good success." (NKJV)

Colossians 3:16 "Let the word of Christ dwell in you richly in all wisdom, teaching and admonishing one another in psalms and hymns and spiritual songs, singing with grace in your hearts to the Lord." (NKJV)

Wear the armor of spiritual warfare every day. Put on each piece thoughtfully and prayerfully and be protected at all times. Don't forget the seventh piece of the armor is "prayer."

Ephesians 6:10–18 "Finally, my brethren, be strong in the Lord and in the power of His might. Put on the whole armor of God, that you may be able to stand against the wiles of the devil. For we do not wrestle against flesh and blood, but against principalities, against powers, against the rulers of the darkness of this age, against spiritual hosts of wickedness in the heavenly places. Therefore take up the whole armor of God, that you may be able to withstand in the evil day, and having done all, to stand. Stand therefore, having girded your waist with truth, having put on the breastplate of righteousness, and having shod your feet with the preparation of the gospel of peace; above all, taking the shield of faith with which you will be able to quench all the fiery darts of the wicked one.

And take the helmet of salvation, and the sword of the Spirit, which is the word of God; praying always with all prayer and supplication in the Spirit, being watchful to this end with all perseverance and supplication for all the saints." (NKJV)

Keep your eyes and ears open for all the sneaky traps the devil will leave around for you. Then "holler for help" to your Heavenly Father, and He will answer and give you the victory.

James 4:7–8 "Therefore submit to God. Resist the devil and he will flee from you. Draw near to God and He will draw near to you. Cleanse your hands, you sinners; and purify your hearts, you double-minded." (NKJV)

Beware of thinking you can make it alone. You never will because God never intended you should. Be smart; admit you can't, and then do it with His help.

John 15:5 "I am the vine, you are the branches. He who abides in Me, and I in him, bears much fruit; for without Me you can do nothing." (NKJV)

Hebrews 13:5 "Let your conduct be without covetousness; be content with such things as you have. For He Himself has said, 'I will never leave you not forsake you." (NKJV)

Break wrong friendships and choose positive, clean-living friends who put Jesus first. The enemy will use the people with whom you associate to influence your thinking, habits and behavior. You need to spend your time with people who will influence you in the right direction. Attend church regularly and faithfully.

James 4:4 "Do you not know that friendship with the world is enmity with God? Whoever therefore wants to be a friend of the world makes himself an enemy of God." (NKJV)

Break former habits that led to sin. Avoid magazines, movies and television programs and things on the Internet that you should not see. Turn away from the strong, fleshly desires that created sinful habits.

> Philippians 4:8 "Finally, brethren, whatever things are true, whatever things are noble, whatever things are just, whatever things are pure, whatever things are lovely, whatever things are of good report, if there is any virtue and if there is anything praiseworthy—meditate on these things." (NKJV)

Never let up on warring against the list of no-no's. Criticism, negativity, grieving over the past, over-sensitivity, doubt, selfishness, putting feelings before faith and prayerlessness are all on the list.

> Galatians 5:19–21,26 "Now the works of the flesh are evident, which are: adultery, fornication, uncleanness, lewdness, idolatry, sorcery, hatred, contentions, jealousies, outbursts of wrath, selfish ambitions, dissentions, heresies, envy, murders, drunkenness, revelries, and the like; of which I tell you beforehand, just as I also told you in time past, that those who practice such things will not inherit the kingdom of God. Let us not become conceited, provoking one another, envying one another." (NKJV)

Do a spiritual check to see if you are holding any unforgiveness or bitterness toward anyone. Hurts and injustices can occur at any time. You will need to search your heart frequently to be sure you have forgiven anyone and everyone for hurting you. Unforgiveness is an open door for the enemy to come back in.

> Mark 11:25 "And when you stand praying, if you hold anything against anyone, forgive him, so that your Father in heaven may forgive you your sins."
>
> Ephesians 4:32 "And be ye kind one to another, tenderhearted, forgiving one another, even as God for Christ's sake hath forgiven you." (NKJV)

Get rid of all items in your home or life that would connect with the demonic.
During your deliverance, physical items may have been identified that
defile your home with demonic influence. You must remove and destroy
at once those items and any others that you find.

(Taken in part from *Evicting Demonic Intruders* by Noel and Phyl Gibson, published by New Wine Press. Distributed in the USA by Gospel
Light.)

PRAYER FOR RENEWING THE MIND

Father, I thank you that you will help me walk out my deliverance as I
renew my mind daily. "For the word of God is quick, and powerful, and
sharper than any two edged sword, piercing even to the dividing asun-
der of soul and spirit, and of the joints and marrow, and is a discerner of
the thoughts and intents of the heart" (Hebrews 4:12, KJV). "And be not
conformed to this world: but be ye transformed by the renewing of your
mind, that ye may prove what is that good, and acceptable, and perfect,
will of God" (Romans 12:2, KJV).

I thank you, Lord, that Your Word says, "Trust in the Lord with all
thine heart; and lean not unto thine own understanding. In all thy ways
acknowledge him, and he shall direct thy paths. Be not wise in thine own
eyes: fear the LORD, and depart from evil" (Proverbs 3:5–7, KJV). As I
trust you, I will walk in truth and not fall back into sinful patterns. "For
the weapons of our warfare are not carnal, but mighty through God to
the pulling down of strong holds; Casting down imaginations, and every
high thing that exalteth itself against the knowledge of God, and bringing into captivity every thought to the obedience of Christ;" (Second
Corinthians 10:4–5, KJV).

I thank you, Lord, that Your Word says, "Be careful for nothing; but
in every thing by prayer and supplication with thanksgiving let your
requests be made known unto God. And the peace of God, which pass-
eth all understanding, shall keep your hearts and minds through Christ
Jesus. Finally, brethren, whatsoever things are true, whatsoever things are
honest, whatsoever things are just, whatsoever things are pure, whatsoever things are lovely, whatsoever things are of good report; if there be

any virtue, and if there be any praise, think on these things (Philippians 4:6–8, KJV).

I thank you that "we have the mind of Christ" (First Corinthians 2:16, KJV). I thank you that as I meditate on Your Word "This book of the law shall not depart out of thy mouth; but thou shalt meditate therein day and night, that thou mayest observe to do according to all that is written therein: for then thou shalt make thy way prosperous, and then thou shalt have good success" (Joshua 1:8, KJV). I thank you that Your Word says, "Commit thy works unto the LORD, and thy thoughts shall be established" (Proverbs 16:3, KJV).

Lord, I thank you for my deliverance, and I thank you for the life style of deliverance and freedom You will help me walk.

AFTER CARE FOR CHILDREN

After your child's deliverance, it is important that you help your child keep his or her freedom. Here are some guidelines.

1. *Pray for cleansing of your child's room:* Ask the Lord Jesus to cleanse the child's room from the influence of every oppressive spirit from which he has been freed.

2. *Deal with continued problem habits:* Established habits may take time to disappear. Encouragement is important as well as discipline to help your child break habits. It is helpful to pray over your child quietly, but audibly, after he goes to sleep.

3. *Keep the lines of communication open:* Children and teenagers need to talk. They are in the business of working out their beliefs and attitudes. As a wise parent, you will be the safe place for your child to share his thoughts and feelings. Without the freedom to communicate with you, your child will seek out peers or outsiders to help form his belief system.

    After the enemy has been defeated, young people usually want to talk. Making yourself available and willing to listen will help your child clarify his thinking, release emotional pressures, and be open to receive advice. It is important that you be ready to listen or discuss as needed. This will help your child avoid further potential crises.

4. *Set aside a time for worship if it is not part of the family routine:* This is one of the best ways to unite the family. The whole family should be involved, if possible. The timing is very important; it should be regular, interesting and not too long. It should be done in such a way that the children look forward to it. Family worship should include:

   A. *Worship and praise.* Children should be taught how to worship God for who He is and praise Him for what He has done in the world. They should also praise Him for their family and their own lives. To learn to be thankful in childhood will be a great spiritual asset in later life.

   B. *Bible Study.* The home is the Christian parents' first line of defense against secular humanism. Teaching the Bible early in life is one of our greatest weapons to fight Satan's onslaught against Christian standards.

   C. *Participation.* The children should be encouraged to participate. The reading material should be geared to your child's age and understanding. There are many good children's Bibles as well as stories for all ages that are helpful. The asking of questions and prayer time should also be suitable to the individual ages of your children.

ENGAGE IN SPIRITUAL WARFARE OVER YOUR CHILDREN

Parents need to be sensitive to the need for "instant" spiritual warfare. It is so important to pray when God gives the unction. There are testimonies of accidents that have been prevented and trouble avoided because parents have prayed when God gave them the leading.

Parents should learn to recognize when their children are coming under demonic oppression so they can engage in spiritual warfare for them. Below are some examples.

BONDAGE

The enemy prevents them from doing what they know to be right; for example, from saying they are sorry when they know that what they did was wrong, from forgiving others, or from being honest, obedient, respectful, and diligent.

DOMINATIONS

The enemy makes them do what they know to be wrong, although they may not want to. Examples include displays of anger, temper, stubbornness, disobedience, deceit, and lustful actions.

OPPRESSIONS

Satan often troubles children with a variety of fears. He also makes them anxious for no apparent reason, causes them to oppose spiritual matters, or stirs up an insatiable interest in occultic and psychic matters.

AFFLICTIONS

Children may have an unexplained series of mishaps or accidents, and suffer from repeated sicknesses or allergies of all kinds. Children are often the first to fall victim to family curses causing blindness, deafness, and mental problems particularly when they occur as an established family pattern.

EMERGENCY PRAYER

This prayer is taken verbatim from: *Deliver Our Children from the Evil One* by Noel and Phyl Gibson, published by Sovereign World Ltd. Tonbridge, Kent, England. Distributed in the USA by Gospel Light).

"I take authority over you, Satan, in the Name of Jesus Christ, and render you powerless in the life of . . . (child's name).

I bind your power, break your influence, and loose . . . (child's name) from your grip. All harmful hereditary, and other spirits . . . (name them) I break in the name of Jesus, and by faith I now take the blood of Jesus and cleanse the conscious mind, the subconscious mind, the emotions, the imaginations, the heart and will of . . . (name child).

I thank You for the power and authority of Your name and blood, Lord Jesus, and ask You to keep the heart of . . . (name child) open and tender to the leading of the Holy Spirit. Please fill . . . (name child) with Your everlasting love, Your peace, and Your joy, for Your glory. I ask this in the name of Jesus. Amen."

SUMMARY

1. Christian parents should be a child's first line of defense against any demonic activities in their lives. To be effective, parents need to be free themselves and see that their family home and possessions do not cause children to become oppressed.

2. Parents should keep a watchful eye on their children's friendships and where they spend time outside of school hours. Any change in behavioral pattern should be investigated thoroughly.

3. Parents can be very effective in seeing their children and teenagers released from bondages and dominations, and bringing them into new attitudes and habits.

4. Parents have a God-given responsibility to institute and maintain a time of family worship, and to protect their children by engaging in spiritual warfare on their behalf.

5. Discipline is essential to breaking habits associated with the problems from which the child has been set free.

(Much of this material was taken from *Deliver Our Children from the Evil One* by Noel and Phyl Gibson, Sovereign World Ltd, P.O. Box 777 Tonbridge, Kent TN11 0ZS, England)

PART SEVEN

APPENDICES

For copies of the contents of the Appendices plus usable copies of the questionnaires please log onto our website at:

www.DeliveranceRescuingGodsPeople.com

and follow the directions for free downloads for owners of this book.

APPENDIX A

SECTION 1

ADULT QUESTIONNAIRE KEY

Name:			Age:		Sex:	

Marital Status:	Single	Married	Divorced	Remarried	Widowed
How Many Times Have You Been Married?					
Current Profession:					
What is the best time to schedule your deliverance?	Weekday		Evening		Weekend

Please answer the following briefly:

1. What is your church background?

   Religious spirits, legalism, idolatry, worship of saints, pride, critical spirits, judgmental spirits, doubt and unbelief, skepticism.

2. Explain briefly your conversion experience. If you came to Christ as a teenager or older, was you life really changed?

3. Were you baptized or dedicated as a child?   Yes   No

   Were you baptized since you've been born again?   Yes   No

4. In one word who is Jesus Christ to you?

   Savior and Lord are ideal answers. God or Son of God are also satisfactory. Indirect answers such as example, friend, leader and redeemer usually indicate a general belief in the biblical Christ but not close relationship.

5. What does the blood of Jesus mean to you?

   Pray leaders should not accept theological definitions, but only spontaneous declarations of faith in the substitutionary and explainable death, burial and resurrection of Jesus Christ for them personally. If the person is not born again, lead him to the Lord before proceeding with the deliverance.

6. Is repentance part of your Christian life?   Yes   No

   Should the person being prayed for refuse to repent, the deliverance procedure will be a waste of time.

7. What is your prayer life like?

8. Do you have assurance of salvation?   Yes   No

Frequently victims of rejection are 'wobbly' about assurance. After deliverance from rejection, they usually confess assurance. Should doubts still remain, check for:

Hereditary spirits of anti-Christ, spirits of intellectualism, rationalism, humanism, doubt and unbelief.

After release; cleanse and minister faith to believe God's word. If positive responses are still not given, check the genuineness of their claim to salvation.

9. Do you have a problem with doubt and unbelief in everyday   Yes   No
   Christian living?

   Spirits of doubt and unbelief. If there is a blockage of the things of God, look for spirits of anti-Christ, stupor, error, and lying spirits. Anti-Christ spirits may also come from Freemasonry and witchcraft.

   Believers under oppression find faith difficult.

10. Are you satisfied with your Christian Walk?   Yes   No
    If not. How would you like to see it improve?

    Whatever is listed here, pray for this improvement at the end of the deliverance.

CATEGORY A   REJECTION

1. Was your relationship with your parents: (circle one)   Good   Bad   Indifferent
   Explain:

a. Was your father (circle)   Passive   Strong   Manipulative   Neither

   Were you friends?   Yes   No   Sort of

   Describe briefly your relationship with your father:

b. Any special problems with your father?

   Look for issues needing forgiveness. Spirit of rejection. Depending on relationship, look for fear, dread, guilt and shame, control, etc. Patriarchal bondages must be broken, and inherited spirits cast out; apathy, passivity, lack of motivation, anger, laziness, etc.

APPENDIX A

SECTION 1

c. Was your mother: (circle)   Passive   Strong   Manipulative   Neither

   Were you friends?   Yes   No   Sort of

   Describe briefly your relationship with your mother:

d. Any special problems with your mother?

   Look for issues needing forgiveness. Spirits of rejection. Depending on relationship, look for fear, dread, guilt and shame, control, etc. Matriarchal bondages must be broken, and inherited spirits cast out; apathy, passivity, lack of motivation, anger, laziness, etc.

2. a. Were you a planned child?   Yes   No   Don't Know

    Spirit of rejection.

  b. The "right sex" for your mother?   Yes   No   Don't Know

    The "right sex" for your father?   Yes   No   Don't Know

    Spirit of rejection. In extreme cases, self-hatred and homosexuality.

  c. Did your parents favor one of your siblings over you?   Yes   No   Don't Know
    Who and in what way?

    Spirit of rejection. Forgiveness issues of parents and the favored sibling.

  d. Were you conceived out of wedlock?   Yes   No   Don't Know

    Spirits of rejection, lust, fear, guilt and shame.

  e. Were you adopted?   Yes   No   Don't Know

    Spirits of rejection, abandonment; forgiveness of biological parents.

  f. The result of a violent conception (i.e. rape)?   Yes   No   Don't Know

    Spirits of fear, anger, rage, violence, lust, rejection.

g. If adopted, do you know anything about your biological parents?

Pray against any hereditary spirits associated with known characteristics or behaviors of biological parents, (i.e. spirits of addiction, lust, fear, etc.)

h. Do you know if your mother suffered any trauma during her pregnancy with you?
Physical trauma?
Explain:

Spirits of fear, rejection.

Emotional trauma?
Explain:

Spirits of fear, rejection.

i. Was your birth difficult or complicated?   Yes   No
If yes, in what way?

Spirits of fear, death, infirmity.

j. Were you held by your mother shortly after your birth?   Yes   No

If baby was kept in an incubator; spirits of rejection, fear.

A breast-fed baby?   Yes   No

If not breast-fed, look for spirit of rejection.

k. Do you have brothers and sisters?   Yes   No

Name:	Age:

Where do you fall in the sibling line?

Depending on the family, any position in the sibling line can allow in a spirit of rejection.

APPENDIX A

SECTION 1

How was your relationship with them growing up?

Look for forgiveness issues and spirits of rejection, jealousy, guilt and shame.

What is it like now?

Look for forgiveness issues and spirits of rejection, jealousy, guilt and shame.

Any special problems?

Look for forgiveness issues and spirits of rejection, jealousy, guilt and shame.

3. Are your parents living?

	Mother	Yes	No
	Father	Yes	No

Are they Christians?

	Mother	Yes	No
	Father	Yes	No

If not Christians, determine if they have rejected the faith of the person being prayed for. If so, spirit of rejection. If parents (or other loved ones) died unsaved, look for spirits of grief and mourning, fear, guilt.

Living together?	Yes	No
Divorced?	Yes	No

Forgiveness issues. Spirits of rejection, fear of abandonment, betrayal, covenant breaking.

Remarried?	Yes	No

Forgiveness issues. Spirits of rejection, betrayal, jealousy.

If parent(s) are deceased, at what age did they die?
Mother
Father

If grandparents are deceased, at what age did they die?
Maternal grandmother
Maternal grandfather
Paternal grandmother
Paternal grandfather

SECTION 1

Have any other members of your family died before the age of 60?   Yes   No
If so, who?

Look for premature death; (any death before the age of 60).

How is your relationship with stepparents?
Are they Christians?   Yes   No

Forgiveness issues. Spirits of rejection, control, jealousy.

How is your relationship with: Stepbrothers?   Stepsisters?

Are they Christians?   Yes   No   Yes   No

Forgiveness issues. Spirit of rejection.

How was your relationship growing up?

How is your relationship now?

Forgiveness issues. Spirit of rejection.

4. Are you a people pleaser (do you jeopardize yourself to please   Yes   No   Maybe
    others)?
    In what way?

    Strongman of pride. Spirits of performance, competitiveness, codependency; commonly born out of rejection.

5. Are you a critical person?   Yes   No   Maybe
    Of what activities or characteristics are you most critical?

    Do you feel superior to people of whom you are critical?   Yes   No   Maybe

    Spirits of criticism and judgment, envy, pride and jealously. May be born out of rejection, pride, fear, control, anger.

6. Do you feel emotionally immature?   Yes   No   Maybe
    What is your emotional age?

    May be symptom of rejection.

APPENDIX A

SECTION 1

7. Tell us about yourself-image (circle all that apply):

Low self-image	Feel insecure
Condemn myself	Hate myself
Feel worthless	Believe I am a failure
Feel inferior	Question my identity

Punish myself (if so, how?)
    Mentally
    Emotionally
    Physically
    Sexually

Low self-image is commonly a symptom of rejection. However, look for spirits of hopelessness, depression, despair, self-accusation, self-condemnation or punishment.

8. Was yours a happy home during childhood?   Yes   No
   Describe briefly:

Spirits of rejection. Forgiveness issues.

9. How would you describe your family's financial situation when you were a child?
   Poor
   Slight financial struggles
   Moderate income
   Affluent

Spirits of rejection, poverty, fear (of poverty, etc.), pride, shame, greed.

10. Did your parents tithe?   Yes   No
    Do you tithe?   Yes   No

Spirits of poverty, fear; God robbing spirits.

You don't have the legal ground to pray for prosperity for a person who isn't keeping his part of God's covenant concerning sowing and reaping.

11. Were you lonely as a teenager?   Sometimes   Yes   No
    Explain:

Forgiveness issues; spirits of rejection, rebellion, independence, abandonment.

APPENDIX A

SECTION 1

12. Do you experience a mixture of anger, resentment, bitterness, revenge, rage, feelings or actions of violence? (circle all that apply)
Explain:

Strongman of jealousy, spirits of anger, resentment, bitterness, revenge, rage, rancor, Violence; these feelings and actions may allow in a spirit of guilt and shame. Identify entry points and close them.

13. How many times have you been married?
Current spouse's name?

How long have you been married to your current spouse?
How would you describe your relationship?

Forgiveness issues. Spirit of rejection and any others depending on the relationship.

14. Previous spouse's name

How long were you married?
How would you describe your relationship?

Why and how did it end?

Forgiveness issues. Spirit of rejection, covenant breaking spirit; depending on relationship, guilt and shame, anger and others.

*Please use the back of this page to list other spouses and to describe your relationship(s).

15. Have you had any serious romantic relationships not involving marriage, i.e.   Yes   No
lived with someone, but never got married?
Name of person

How long were you together?
How would you describe your relationship?
Why and how did it end?

Forgiveness issues; spirits of rejection, lust and perversion (if sexual relationship). Depending on relationship, guilt and shame, anger, and others.

*Please use the back of this page to list other partners and to describe your relationship(s).

APPENDIX A

SECTION 1

16. How many children do you have?

Name:	Age		Relationship:
Name:	Age		Relationship:
Name:	Age		Relationship:

How is your relationship with them?
Any special problems, past or present?

Forgiveness issues. Also any elements revealing other spirits such as spirits of guilt, anger, etc.

17. Has lying been a problem for you?   Yes   No
     Is it now?   Yes   No

     Has stealing been a problem for you?   Yes   No
     Is it now?   Yes   No

     Do you exaggerate?   Yes   No

Strongman of lying, spirits of deception, guilt and shame; possibly spirits of rebellion, lawlessness.

18. Do you have trouble giving or receiving love?   At times   Yes   No

May be symptoms of rejection and fear of rejection. May have allowed in a spirit of fear (fear of being emotionally hurt, fear of abandonment, etc). Look for 'inner wall'.

19. Do you find it easy to communicate with persons close to you?

     I have real difficulty   I have problems at times   I am unwilling   It's easy

Difficulty may be symptom of rejection. Spirit of stubbornness. Look for 'inner wall'.

20. Are you a perfectionist?   Yes   No

     Were (are) your parents perfectionists?   Yes   No

Perfectionist spirit. May be born out of rejection, pride, fear, control, anger, obsessions (whoredoms).

APPENDIX A

SECTION 1

21. Do you come from a proud family?   Yes   No

Inherited strongman of pride.

22. Do you personally have a problem with pride?   Yes   No

Strongman of pride; identify entry points and close them.

23. Have you had advanced education?   Yes   No
If so, what?

Strongman of pride, intellectual pride, intellectualism, rationalism, humanism, atheism, skepticism, unbelief, argumentativeness, mockery.

24. Do you have a history of conflict with those in authority over you,   Yes   No
i.e. teachers, bosses, pastors, etc.
If so, please describe:

Strongman of pride, rebellion. If there is a pattern of conflict, spirit of lawlessness.

25. Do you have or have you had problems with (circle all that apply):

Below are the aggressive reactions to rejection (left side of the tree)

Impatience	Used to	Now	Irritability	Used to	Now
Racial prejudice	Used to	Now	Moodiness	Used to	Now
Violence	Used to	Now	Anger	Used to	Now
Defensiveness	Used to	Now	Rebellion	Used to	Now
Temper	Used to	Now	Stubbornness	Used to	Now
Temptation to murder	Used to	Now			

Strongman of jealousy, spirits of anger, temper, violence, murder

26. Have you been given to: Swearing   Blasphemies   Obscenities
Do you now?   Swear   Blaspheme   Use Obscenities

Blaspheming spirits, spirits of obscenity, anger, rebellion, lawlessness.

27. Think over your life and list any times you've been hurt or suffered an injustice. Ask God to remind you of specific incidents, large or small. These incidents can involve parents, family members, siblings, spouses, children, friends, pastors, bosses, teachers, neighbors, or even total strangers. Don't be concerned with *why* they did what they did; if it hurt you, please include it. For example, has anyone ever treated you unfairly? Has anyone ever done anything that hurt your feelings? Can you remember anytime when you cried or felt like crying because of something someone did to you? Did anyone ever embarrass you, leave you out, abandon you, or frighten you? *(Note: Please take your time with this. If it comes to your mind during this time, it is probably the Holy Spirit reminding you, so include it in the list).*

Pre-school years:
Grade school years:
Middle school and high school years:
College or young adult years:
Incidents in marriage:
Incidents at work:
Incidents at church:
Incidents involving friends:
Incidents involving people you dated or wanted to date:
Recent incidents:
Others:

All of the above must be dealt with in the area of forgiveness. Also look for entry points for the spirits below:

Spirits of rejection, anger, rage, jealously, control, fear.

CATEGORY B MENTAL AND EMOTIONAL PROBLEMS

1. Are you easily frustrated?   Yes   No

   Do you show it or bury it?   Show   Bury

2. Are you: An anxious person   A worrier   Get depressed

   Strongman of heaviness; spirits of anxiety, doubt and unbelief, depression.

3. Did either of your parents or grandparents suffer from depression?   Yes   No
   Father   Mother   Grandmother   Grandfather

   Inherited spirits of depression, anxiety, nervousness.

SECTION 1

4. Have you or has any parent, brother, sister, or grandparent suffered from   Yes   No
   acute nervousness or a mental problem, such as schizophrenia, bipolar
   disorder or obsessive compulsive disorder?

   Who?   Problem?

   Unless the person being prayed for obviously needs professional help, cast out the following:

   Hereditary or personal strongman of heaviness; spirits of anxiety, fear.

5. Have you personally ever had psychiatric counseling?	Yes	No
Hospitalization for psychiatric treatment?	Yes	No
Other hospitalization?	Yes	No
Shock treatment?	Yes	No
Psychoanalysis?	Yes	No
Been under anesthesia?	Yes	No
Been intoxicated (alcohol)?	Yes	No
Used drugs inducing a passive-mind state? (prescription or non-prescription)	Yes	No
Had a fever with delirium?	Yes	No
Been unconscious?	Yes	No
Other?	Yes	No

In people who are medicated, the demons often become sluggish and are slow to respond to deliverance prayer. If possible, it is better to pray after the effects have lessened or when no medication has been taken.

Deaf and dumb spirits, heaviness, depression; cast out any spirits that took advantage of a 'passive mind state' to enter the person's life. Close doors opened to any spirits that entered while in a hypnotic, drugged or unguarded mental state.

6. Have you ever been hypnotized?   Yes   No
   If so, when and why?

   Spirits that entered during a 'passive mind state'. Familiar spirits, spirits of deception, mind-control, confusion, spirits of antichrist are common, but any spirit can take advantage of a 'passive mind state'.

7. Are you currently taking any medication for depression, anxiety or pain, or   Yes   No
   an anti-psychotic drug? If so, what are you taking and how often are you
   taking it?

APPENDIX A

SECTION 1

8. Since you have been taking it, do you have difficulty concentrating and focusing or is it easier?

   Have Difficulty   It's Easier

   During the interview process, you need to find out if the person is taking anything that is mind altering in a way that would cause him to be unable to receive deliverance. Often a person needs to be on a medication in order to focus and receive deliverance. You can often tell by talking with him and determine if he can follow your conversation or if he is spacing out. Never tell anyone to stop his medication. If you feel that he is on so much medication that he can't receive deliverance; ask him to consult his physician to get his medications regulated so he will be able to concentrate and work with you. Then reset the appointment when that is accomplished.

9. Have you, your parents, or grandparents been in any cults (circle all that apply)

Christian Science	Myself	Others	Rosicrucian	Myself	Others
Armstrong Worldwide COG	Myself	Others	Gurus	Myself	Others
Christadelphians	Myself	Others	Unity	Myself	Others
Jehovah's Witnesses	Myself	Others	Mormons	Myself	Others
Children of Love	Myself	Others	Scientology	Myself	Others
Religious Communes	Myself	Others	Bahai	Myself	Others
Unification Church (Moonies)	Myself	Others	Theosophy	Myself	Others
Eastern Religions (specify)	Myself	Others	Anthroposophy	Myself	Others
Native Religions	Myself	Others	Spiritists Church	Myself	Others
Other:					

Spirits of false religion, doubt and unbelief, deception, and spirits with the name of the cult.

10. Have you or has any close family member been a member of:

Freemason	Odd Fellow	Rainbow Girl	Mormon
Eastern Star	Shriner	Daughter of the Nile	Amaranth
Job's Daughter	Elk	DeMolay	Fraternity
Sorority	Secret organization and societies		

If so, who?

Do you suffer from (circle all that apply)

Apathy	Hardness of Emotion	Confusion	Financial Disaster
Skepticism	Comprehension Difficulties	Unbelief	Doubt
Infirmities	Frequent Sickness	Allergies	

Spirits of Freemasonry. If no Freemasonry is identified, look for other causes.

APPENDIX A

SECTION 1

Is there any Masonic regalia or memorabilia in your possession? Yes No
If yes, what?

Ensure the person destroys any regalia or memorabilia.

11. Do you feel mentally confused? Yes No
    Do you have mental blocks? Yes No

    May be symptoms of Freemasonry; also may be spirits of occultism, witchcraft, Satanism, confusion. If mental blocks center around the things of God, spirits of antichrist, stupor.

12. Do you day-dream? Yes No
    If yes, what is the nature of your day-dreams?

    If day-dreaming is excessive, interferes with daily activities, or is used to escape reality, look for spirits of escapism, fantasy, false comfort, addiction. Other spirits as revealed by the content of the day-dreams. Also may be symptoms of Freemasonry.

13. Do you have mental fantasies Yes No
    If yes, what is the nature of the fantasies?

    If fantasizing is excessive, interferes with daily activities, is used to escape reality, or indicates a loss of grasp on reality; spirits of escapism, fantasy, false comfort, addiction, self-hatred, grandeur. Other spirits as revealed by the content of the fantasies. Also may be symptoms of Freemasonry.

14. Do you suffer from bad dreams? Yes No
    What is the content or nature of the dreams?

    Look for elements of the dreams revealing spirits such as fear, lust, etc. Also, may be symptoms of Freemasonry.

15. Do you suffer from sleeplessness? Yes No

    Symptoms of Freemasonry. Also, depending on the circumstances, spirits of fear, lust, depression, worry.

16. Have you ever been tempted to commit suicide? Yes No
    Have you tried? Yes No
    If yes, what did you do?

APPENDIX A

SECTION 1

Spirits of death, depression and any other spirits associated with the emotions which prompted the attempt such as self-pity, fear or shame. If the person felt out of control as if something were driving him to try to kill himself, deaf and dumb spirit. If the person was trying to get attention or get his way, spirit of control. Also symptom of Freemasonry.

Have the person repent.

17. Have you ever wished to die?   Yes   No

Have you spoken it aloud?   Yes   No

Break "Word Curse" of death. Spirits of death or depression. Look for any spirits associated with the emotions which prompted the death wish such as self-pity, fear, shame. If the person was trying to get attention or get his way, spirit of control. Also may be symptom of Freemasonry.

Have the person repent.

18. Have you had a strong and prolonged fear of any of the following? Please list the first time you remember experiencing fear in each area marked:

Failure	Used to	Now	Inadequacy	Used to	Now
Inability to cope	Used to	Now	Death	Used to	Now
Authority figures	Used to	Now	The dark	Used to	Now
Being alone	Used to	Now	Rape	Used to	Now
Satan and evil spirits	Used to	Now	The future	Used to	Now
Violence	Used to	Now	Women	Used to	Now
Crowds	Used to	Now	Heights	Used to	Now
Men	Used to	Now	Insanity	Used to	Now
Public speaking	Used to	Now	Accident	Used to	Now
The opinion of people	Used to	Now	Old age	Used to	Now
Enclosed places	Used to	Now	Insects	Used to	Now
Terminal illness	Used to	Now	Spiders	Used to	Now
Dogs	Used to	Now	Snakes	Used to	Now
Animals	Used to	Now	Pain	Used to	Now
Flying in an airplane	Used to	Now	Water	Used to	Now
Grocery stores	Used to	Now	Open spaces	Used to	Now
Death or injury of a loved one	Used to	Now	Rodents	Used to	Now
Divorce or marriage breakup	Used to	Now			
List any other fears not included above:					

APPENDIX A

SECTION 1

Name the demons by the particular fear they cause such as: 'a spirit of the fear of failure' 'fear of the opinions of people' 'fear of spiders', etc. Also symptoms of Freemasonry.

To find entry points, look for the first time the person experienced the fear or any times of intense or memorable fear. There may be multiple entry points for any given fear. Treat 'used to' fears the same as if they were current fears so that all entry points can be closed. Look for fears from childhood – specific and generalized. For example, a perfectionist mother may have instilled fear of failure and inadequacy in a child. Living with an alcoholic father may have instilled a generalized dread (or fear) in the child. Divorce of parents may open the door to a fear of the unknown or fear of abandonment. Some fears are simply taught, by parents or others in childhood by example or in an attempt to keep the child safe. For example, children who are constantly advised to watch out for snakes may develop a fear of snakes. If a parent is afraid of something, such as storms or water, children may develop a similar fear. Close these doors as they are recognized.

CATEGORY C   WITCHCRAFT AND THE OCCULT

1. Have you ever made a pact with the devil?   Yes No

    Brings on a curse, the person must repent.

    Was it a blood pact?   Yes No

    Very strong; apply oil representing the blood of Jesus to break the pact. The person must repent.

    What was it?
    When did you make it?
    Why did you make it?
    Are you willing to renounce it?   Yes No

    Have the person specifically renounce the pact, reversing specific words spoken. Familiar spirits, spirits of witchcraft, occult, anti-christ, manipulation, control, and other related spirits such as fear.

2. To your knowledge, has any curse been placed on you or your family?   Yes No
    By whom?
    Explain:

    Look for generational patterns such as: The eldest son of every married descendant is born blind. The first daughter of every family dies in childhood. Suicides take place in families at regular intervals.

    If family histories are unknown, but certain generational problems occur regularly, it would be wise to treat them as curses. Break their power, evict any oppressive demons and pray for healing of victims. All curses must be broken and every oppressive demon that has entered because of the oaths or curses, cast out, before praying for cleansing and healing.

3. To your knowledge, have your parents or any relative as far back as you   Yes No
    know been involved in occultism or witchcraft?
    Whom and doing what?
    To what extent?
    As a child, did any family member dedicate you to Satan or any demonic   Yes No
    worship?
    If yes, who, when and why?

Renounce the dedication. Inherited familiar spirits, spirits of divination, witchcraft, antichrist, spiritism, or any spirits associated with the particular activity.

4. Have you ever had involvement with any of the following? (circle all that apply)

Fortunetellers	Tarot cards	Ouija boards		
Astrology	Séances	Mediums		
Palmistry	Color therapy	Levitation		
Astral travel	Horoscopes	Good luck charms		
Black magic	Demon worship	Asked for a spirit guide		
Clairvoyance	Crystals	Done automatic handwriting		
New Age Movement	Reincarnation	Past lives regression		
Psychics	Iridology	Been to a curandero or native healer		
Been involved in any other witchcraft or demonic or Satanic things?			Yes	No
If so, what?				
To your knowledge have your parents, grandparents or other ancestors ever been involved in any of the above?			Yes	No
Which ones?				

Experiences, no matter how innocent they seem, must be taken seriously and the demon dominating each activity cast out.

Familiar spirits, spirits of divination, witchcraft, antichrist, spiritism, or any spirits associated with the particular activity.

5. Have you ever read books on occultism or witchcraft?   Yes No
    Why?

Those who read them out of fascination or a desire to learn to practice the craft need cleansing, and books should be destroyed. If the books were read solely for research, demonic entry would be unlikely.

Spirits of divination and familiar spirits; also, look for spirit of fear.

6.	Have you played demonic games such as Dungeon & Dragons, Fable Role Playing Game – X-Box, Starcraft Role Playing Computer Game, Everquest Role Playing Computer Game or other demonic-themed video games?	Yes	No
	Have you read "dark" novels, or novels with themes about the occult, the supernatural, ghosts or science fiction?	Yes	No
	Have you watched demonic films or films with themes about the Occult the supernatural, ghosts or science fiction?	Yes	No
	Have you watched films with extremely violent themes or scenes, or with scenes portraying graphic violence or injury to human beings or animals?	Yes	No
	If yes to any of the above, do you now?	Yes	No
	What when and how often?		

Strongman of fear; spirits of divination, familiar spirits, violence, murder.

7. Have you been involved in Transcendental Meditation?   Yes   No
   Do you have a mantra?   Yes   No
   What is it?
   Have you ever had acupuncture?   Yes   No

Spirits of false religion, Hinduism, Buddhism, idolatry, antichrist, deception, divination, familiar spirits; the person needs to renounce the mantra; mantras may be demonic names, calling up demon powers. Renounce any spirits that took advantage of the unguarded mental state to enter.

8. Have you been involved in Eastern religions?   Yes   No
   Which ones?
   Have you followed a guru?   Yes   No

Spirits of false religion, Hinduism, Buddhism, idolatry, antichrist, deception, divination, familiar spirits.

9. Have you ever visited heathen temples or a mosk?   Yes   No
   If so, when and why?
   Did you make offerings?   Yes   No
   What were they?
   Did you take part in any ceremony?   Yes   No
   Explain:

Look for the reason they visited the temples; if they were just tourists or were there to

pray against the false religion and did not participate in any offerings or ceremonies, there may have been no demonic entry. If they were required to remove their shoes or cover their heads in order to pay respect to the premises , this is considered a form of worship and must be renounced.

Spirits associated with the temple or mosk involved, Hinduism, Buddhism, Islam, etc.

10. Have you ever celebrated Halloween or Mardi Gras?   Yes No
    If so, when and in what way?

These are both celebrations honoring demonic powers.

Spirits of divination, occult, witchcraft, idolatry, familiar spirits, voodoo spirits.

11. Have you ever done any form of yoga?   Yes No
    Meditation?   Yes No
    Exercises?   Yes No

Spirits of false religion, Hinduism, idolatry, antichrist, deception, divination, familiar spirits. If meditation was involved, cast out spirits that took advantage of a 'passive mind state'. Each position of yoga exercises invokes a demon.

Repent and renounce any involvement with yoga and renounce any spirit that may have entered because of the positions taken.

12. Have you ever learned or used any form of mind communication, mind control   Yes No
    or ESP?
    Explain:

Familiar spirits, occult, divination.

13. Were your parents or grandparents superstitious?   Yes No
    If so, who?
    Were you?   Yes No
    If so, are you now?   Yes No
    Were their lives or your life governed by superstition?   Yes No
    Explain:

Spirits of divination, occult, doubt and unbelief, witchcraft, fear of the unknown.

APPENDIX A

SECTION 1

14. Have you ever worn or kept any of the following:

Signs of the Zodiac	Fetishes	Amulets
Peace Symbols	Ankh	Pyramids
Tai Chi Symbols	Swastika	Caduceus

Do you have any in your possession?   Yes   No

Ensure that the person destroys the item.

Spirits of divination, occult, doubt and unbelief, witchcraft, fear of the unknown; deal with spirits associated with the specific item.

15. Do you have in your possession any symbols of idols or spirit worship such as:

Buddha	Totem Poles	Masks
Carvings	Pagan Symbols	Fetish Objects or Feathers
Gargoyles	Obelisks	Statues or Pictures of Dragons or Snakes
Rosary	Zodiac Symbols	Statues or Pictures of Saints
Native American art or jewelry depicting spiritual subjects or symbols		

If so, what?

Where are they from, and how did you get them?

Ensure that the person destroys the item.

Spirits of divination, occult, doubt and unbelief, witchcraft, fear of the unknown; deal with spirits associated with the specific item.

16. Do you have any witches, such as "good luck witches" in your home?   Yes   No

Ensure that the person destroys the item.

Spirits of divination, occult, doubt and unbelief, witchcraft.

17. Are you drawn by any of the following music?   Yes   No
    Rock & Roll   Punk Rock   New Age
    Rap   Heavy Metal
    How much time do you spend listening to it?

Spirits of idolatry to each dominating musical art form. Spirits of lust, violence, occult, etc. associated with specific type of music, (ask what the lyrics are if you don't know), also, look for spirit of bondage if the person was drawn, compelled or addicted to the sound or beat.

APPENDIX A

SECTION 1

18. Are you drawn by demonic art, abstract art, or surrealistic art?   Yes No
    If so, which?

    Spirits of idolatry, occult, and spirits associated with the specific art form.

19. Have you ever learned any of the martial arts: Yes No
    If so, which?
    Do you practice it now?   Yes No

    Spirits of eastern religions, spirits of each martial art form, plus spirits of anger, violence, murder, idolatry, antichrist, control.

20. Have you ever had premonitions?   Yes No
    Deja vou?   Yes No
    Psychic sight?   Yes No
    If so, how frequently?

    Depending on frequency and content, familiar spirits, deception; look for false spiritual gifts, i.e. if the person is called to a prophetic gift, familiar spirits may have perverted it into psychic sight. Close the third eye.

21. Have you ever been involved in: (circle all that apply)
        Firewalking   Voodoo
    Any other form of religious pagan ceremony?   Yes No
    If so, what and when?

    Spirits of voodoo, occult, witchcraft; spirits associated with the specific ceremony such as spirits of the sun dance, rainbow serpent fire, Native American vision quests, sweat lodge, etc.

22. Do you have any tattoos?   Yes No
    If so, what?

    Spirits of rebellion and lawlessness; any spirits associated with the specific tattoo must be cast out and the power of the tattoo broken, i.e. tattoos of dragons symbolize Satan and/or rebellion and the occult, some tattoos have themes of violence, murder, lust. If the subject of the tattoo is demonic, it should be removed if possible.

23. Have you ever been in the military?   Yes   No
    If yes, where you trained for combat?   Yes   No
    Have you been in combat?   Yes   No
    Where and when?
    Have you ever seen anyone die?   Yes   No
    Have you killed anyone?   Yes   No

Spirits of fear, violence, murder, death, anger, rage, fear and guilt; if the person has been in actual combat, deal with forgiveness issues.

Look for the taking of any oaths making anything more important than God.

If oath was made; spirit of idolatry; break oath and repent.

24. Have you ever had a near-death experience?   Yes   No
    If so, when and what happened?

Spirits of death, fear, deaf and dumb spirit.

25. Have you had a loved one who died?   Yes   No
    If so, who and when?
    Did you mourn or grieve for them?   Yes   No
    Explain:
    Do you now?   Yes   No
    Women only: Have you ever had a miscarriage?   Yes   No
                   Have you ever had a stillbirth?   Yes   No
    Did you mourn or grieve for them?   Yes   No
    Do you now?   Yes   No
    Have you ever been with someone when they died?   Yes   No
    Describe your feelings about it:

Spirits of death, grief and mourning, fear, spirits that transfer as a person dies, especially death.

Usually normal grieving can last a year; any grieving past that time may open the door to a spirit of grief and mourning.

26. Do you have or have you ever had tendencies toward violent behavior?   Yes   No
    Have you ever acted violently?   Yes   No
    If so, when and towards whom?

Strongman of jealousy; spirits of violence, rage, anger, rancor, murder, guilt and shame. Look for forgiveness issues.

The person needs to repent.

27. Are you or have you been extremely competitive? I am now   I used to be
    Is it out of control?   Yes   No
    Explain:

    May be born out of rejection, pride, anger, fear. Identify the nature and reason for the
    competitiveness and deal with the spirit behind it.

28. As a child, did you have an imaginary playmate?   Yes   No
    Explain:

    Determine if the playmate talked to the person or gave him instructions, guidance, or
    advice. If so, familiar spirit and spirit guide.

29. Have you ever studied or used "visualization" or "inner healing"?   Yes   No
    Explain:

    Look for any technique that did not rely on the name of Jesus or a natural means of
    healing. If there was any supernatural aspect of the healing that was not based solely and
    specifically on the power of the Holy Spirit, deal with familiar spirits, new age, sorcery,
    witchcraft, mind control, and any other spirits associated with the specific technique.

CATEGORY D   **SEXUAL SINS, SEXUAL BONDAGES**

1. Do you have lustful thoughts?   Fantasy Lust?   Yes   No
      Heterosexual   Homosexual   Pedophilia   Bi-sexual
   Of what?
   Frequency?

   Strongman of perversion and lust, spirits of homosexuality, violence, and any other spirits
   associated with the content of the thoughts or fantasies.

2. To your knowledge, was there evidence of lust in your parents, grandparents or   Yes   No
   further back?
   If so, explain:

   Clues: Family history of pre-marital conceptions, marriages following pregnancies,
   incest, extra-marital affairs, pornography.

   Inherited strongman of perversion and lust; spirits of guilt and shame, depending on the
   nature of the behavior, homosexuality and violence.

APPENDIX A

SECTION 1

3. Do you masturbate?   Yes   No
   Frequency?
   Do you know why?
   Do you feel it is a compulsive problem?   Yes   No

   In children, usually the first evidence of hereditary lust. Strongman of perversion and lust; spirits of guilt and shame; if compulsive problem, spirits of bondage, whoredoms and addiction.

4. Were you ever sexually molested by someone outside your family as a child or   Yes   No
   teenager?
   More than once?   Yes   No
   Explain:

   Strongman of perversion and lust. Forgive the perpetrator and anyone who failed to protect the person from the molestation. Also, deal with all spirits allowed in due to the emotional response such as anger, hatred of the opposite sex, rejection, fear, guilt and shame. Break "soul tie." If pattern exists in the person's life, familiar spirit of lust and victim spirit.

   Were you actually raped?   Yes   No
   By whom?
   More than once?   Yes   No
   Explain:

   Spirits of violence, fear, victim, predator.

5. Have you ever participated in incest (sex with a family member)?   Yes   No
   With whom?
   Was it voluntary on your part?   Yes   No
   If not voluntary, were you actually raped?   Yes   No
   How often?
   Over what period of time?

   Strongman of perversion and lust; spirits of guilt and shame; forgive the perpetrator; if the act was voluntary, forgive himself. If a pattern of abuse exists, familiar spirit of lust and victim spirit; break "soul tie."

6. Men: Have you ever molested or raped anyone?   Yes   No
   First names:

   Strongman of perversion and lust; spirit of the predator; behavior may be born out of rejection, spirits of violence, anger, rage, pride, guilt and shame; break "soul tie."

APPENDIX A

SECTION 1

Women: Have you ever been raped?   Yes   No
          By whom?
          Explain:

Strongman of perversion and lust; spirit of violence, victim spirit; also deal with all spirits allowed in due to the emotional response such as anger, male hatred, rejection, fear, guilt and shame. Forgive the perpetrator. If pattern exists in the person's life, familiar spirit of lust and victim spirit; break "soul tie."

7. Have you ever committed fornication (sex while not married?)   Yes   No
    How many partners?
    First names and when:

Strongman of perversion and lust; spirits of guilt and shame; break "soul tie."

Have the person repent.

Have you ever been involved in oral sex outside of marriage?   Yes   No
With whom? (first names)

Strongman of perversion and lust; spirits of guilt and shame; break "soul tie."

Have the person repent.

8. Have you ever had sex with prostitutes?   Yes   No
    How many?
    When?

Strongman of perversion and lust; spirits of guilt and shame; break "soul tie."

Have the person repent.

9. Have you ever committed adultery (at least one partner married)?   Yes   No
    While you were married?   Yes   No
    While you single and your partner was married?   Yes   No
    First names and when?

Strongman of perversion and lust; spirits of guilt and shame; break "soul tie."

Have the person repent.

10. Are you currently involved in an illicit sexual relationship   Yes   No
    First name:

APPENDIX A

SECTION 1

Are you willing to break it off?   Yes   No

Strongman of perversion and lust; spirits of guilt and shame; break "soul tie."

Have the person repent.

11. Have you ever had homosexual or lesbian desires?   Yes   No
    Do you now?   Yes   No
    Have you ever had a homosexual or lesbian experience?   Yes   No
    With whom and when?
    Do you currently participate in homosexual or lesbian activity?   Yes   No
    If so, how frequently and with whom?
    Are you willing to stop?   Yes   No

Strongman of perversion and lust; spirits of homosexuality, guilt and shame, self-rejection; break "soul ties."

The person must be willing to repent and stop the activity.

12. Have you ever had tendencies toward transvestite behavior?   Yes   No
    Have you ever acted on transvestite tendencies?   Yes   No
    If so, when and how often?
    Do you now?   Yes   No
    Are you willing to stop?   Yes   No

Strongman of perversion; spirits of self-rejection, self-hatred, guilt and shame.

Have the person repent and the person must be willing to stop the activity.

13. Are you sexually frigid?   Yes   No
    Explain:

Determine the cause of an aversion to sex, i.e. fear (fear of sex, fear of men, fear of rejection, etc.), anger, hatred, unforgiveness, shame, self-rejection and self-hatred, "inner wall," etc. and deal with the associated spirits.

14. Have you ever sexually fantasized about an animal?   Yes   No
    Have you committed a sex act with an animal?   Yes   No
    Name all animals involved:
    How often and when?
    Very often hereditary. Strongman of perversion and lust; spirits of bestiality, fantasy, rejection, guilt and shame; name the spirit of the animal, (i.e. a dog would have a canine spirit, a cow would have a bovine spirit, etc.) and evict it. Break "soul tie."

APPENDIX A

SECTION 1

Have the person repent.

	Yes	No

15. Has pornography ever attracted you?
How did you become involved?
Name of persons involved:

If material was given to him, have him forgive the person who got him involved.

To what extent have you viewed pornography?
How frequently?
When?
Have you seen pornographic movies, videos or DVDs? Yes No
When and where?
Have you viewed pornographic magazines or photos? Yes No
Have you viewed live sex shows? Yes No
When and where?
Have you viewed pornographic material on the Internet? Yes No
Have you participated in sexually oriented "chat rooms" or Yes No
discussion groups on
the Internet?
Have you had a sexual fetish? Yes No
What is it?
Do you still view pornographic material? Yes No
What, when and how often?
Do you currently purchase or rent pornographic movies, videos or Yes No
DVDs or have such a channel on your home TV?
How frequently?
Are you willing to discontinue any use of pornography? Yes No

Strongman of perversion and lust; spirits of guilt and shame; depending on the content of the material, any spirits involved such as homosexual spirits, violence, pedophilia, etc. If sexual partner encouraged use of pornography during sex, spirit of rejection, forgiveness issues.

The person must be willing to repent and stop the activity. Pray for cleansing; pray for purging of the memories of what he saw and heard.

16. Have you ever been involved in anal sex? Yes No
With whom?

Strongman of perversion and lust; spirits of sodomy, control; if a homosexual experience, spirits of homosexuality. For women, common entry point for spirits of rejection, control, guilt and shame. Close all channels that were opened to demonic entry during anal sex.

APPENDIX A

SECTION 1

In all cases of sexual perversion, self-forgiveness, and forgiveness of the other party involved need to be emphasized, cleansing ministered and inner healing prayed for. They also need to receive love, and be encouraged to share it without shame or fear.

17. Women: Have you ever had an abortion?   Yes   No
    How many?
    Give dates and father's first name(s)

    Spirits of death, murder, grief, guilt and shame. Forgive father of the child and anyone who pressured her into having the abortion. Break "soul ties" with the baby.

    Repent and forgive herself. Causes a hostile environment in the womb for future pregnancies. Pray for cleansing and healing of the womb.

18. Men: Have you ever fathered a child that was forcefully aborted?   Yes   No
    How many?
    Give dates and mother's first name(s):

    Pray to forgive the mother.

    Were you in favor of the abortion?   Yes   No

    If no, forgive the mother. If yes, repent, pray for forgiveness and forgive himself.

    If the father knew of the abortion, and especially if he was in favor of it, spirits of death, murder, grief, guilt and shame.

19. Have you been plagued with desires of having sex with a child?   Yes   No
    Have you actually done so?   Yes   No
    If yes, how many times and when?

    Strongman of perversion and lust; spirits of pedophilia, control, guilt and shame.

    Repent and pray for forgiveness. May need to apologize to all concerned. May need to turn himself in to the authorities.

20. Have you ever had inner sexual stimulation and climax out of your control,   Yes   No
    especially at night? (By this I mean, do you have dreams of a personage
    approaching and asking to have sex with you, or just doing it, and you "feel" a
    presence in bed with you, then wake up with a sexual climax? This is some-
    thing other that a normal nocturnal emission).
    If yes, when and how frequently?

APPENDIX A

SECTION 1

Spirit of incubus (manifests as a male) or succubus (manifests as a female); these may be familiar spirits, or gain access through witchcraft ceremonies or satanic worship.

21. Have you ever gone to a massage parlor and been sexually stimulated?   Yes   No

Strongman of perversion and lust; spirits of guilt and shame; if there was genital contact, break "soul ties."

22. Have you had sexual fantasies?   Yes   No
    Do you now?   Yes   No
    How frequently?
    What are they about?

Strongman of perversion and lust; depending on the content, homosexual spirits, spiritual adultery, marital infidelity, spirits of guilt and shame.

23. Do members of the opposite sex make uninvited comments to you of a sexual   Yes   No
    nature, tell you "dirty jokes" or behave in a sexually inappropriate manner
    toward you, or "come on" to you in any other way?

Familiar spirits of lust and perversion.

24. How would you describe your sexual relationship with your spouse?

Look for any abnormality in the relationship and cast out spirits involved. Pray that there would be nothing unhealthy between the person and his spouse. Pray for a healthy, happy, mutually satisfying sexual relationship with spouse.

CATEGORY E   BONDAGES AND ADDICTIONS

1. Did any of your family as far back as you know have addictions of any   Yes   No
   kind?
   Who and to what?

   Inherited strongman of bondage.

2. Have you ever been or are you currently addicted to any of the following?

Alcohol	No	Currently addicted	Used to be addicted
Smoking	No	Currently addicted	Used to be addicted
Food	No	Currently addicted	Used to be addicted
Gambling	No	Currently addicted	Used to be addicted
Compulsive exercise	No	Currently addicted	Used to be addicted

Being a spendthrift	No	Currently addicted	Used to be addicted
Watching TV	No	Currently addicted	Used to be addicted
Coffee	No	Currently addicted	Used to be addicted
Marijuana	No	Currently addicted	Used to be addicted
Prescription Drugs	No	Currently addicted	Used to be addicted
Which ones?			
Street Drugs	No	Currently addicted	Used to be addicted
Which ones?			
Any other addictions?			

Strongman of bondage and whoredoms, spirits of dependence, false comfort, escapism, compulsion. The spirit behind obsessive compulsive disorder (OCD) is whoredoms.
(Drugs) The specific name of the addictive drug, deception, control, plus problems drugs cause such as lust, stealing, violence, other addictions, etc.
(Alcohol) Spirits of alcohol dependence, inability to cope, deception, lying, violence.

First determine if the person is truly willing to give up the addiction and exercise the self-discipline needed to keep the demon out. If not, do not cast out the spirit of addiction. Bind the spirit of addiction and any linked spirits, and allow the person to return at a later date when he is ready to give up the addiction and walk out his deliverance.

With some addictions, especially addiction to food, the spirit of bondage may be linked with the spirit of whoredom or idolatry. The spirit of bondage would manifest in a compulsion to eat, eating for false comfort or escapism. The spirit of whoredom would manifest in obsessive thinking about food, "all-or-nothing" dieting, etc. In these cases, renounce both spirits, command them to unlink, and cast them out together.
(Anorexia Nervosa and Bulimia) Hereditary spirits must go first, followed by both the spirits of anorexia and bulimia. Also spirits of death, deception, lies, violence and the deceptive body image. The spirit of the fear of getting fat must go, together with the whole rejection syndromes. When incest, rape or sexual molestation are basic causes, these spirits must also be cast out.

It is recommended that the person seek Christian counseling after deliverance to receive help with the changing of habits and thinking patterns.

CATEGORY F

1. What is your country of birth?

2. Have you lived in other countries?　　　　　　　　　　　　　Yes　　　No
   Which ones?

A general prayer of release is often sufficient, but specific spirits may need to be cast out.

APPENDIX A

SECTION 1

Look for any spirits associated with the geographic area, such as spirits associated with false worship and witchcraft.

3. Where was your mother born? (city, state, nation)
   Where was your father born? (city, state, nation)

4. Where were your grandparents born? (city, state, nation)
   Maternal grandmother?
   Maternal grandfather?
   Paternal grandmother?
   Paternal grandfather?

   When there is obvious resistance from demonic ethnic or cultural spirits during a general prayer of release, identify, and cast out each one.

5. Have you ever been in a counter-culture? (circle all that apply)

Surfers	Hippies	Drug drop-outs	Gangs	Bikers	Skin heads	New Age	Hip Hop

   Others?

   Dominant spirits of idolatry, (be specific) lust, immorality, pride, arrogance, drugs, antisocial aggression, rebellion against authority, astrology, occultism, witchcraft, possibly Satanism, and rejection. Subjection to, and fear of group leaders may also need to be broken and the person being prayed for cleansed. Renounce any oaths taken to the group and dissolve any covenants made. Break any "soul ties" to the other members or leaders of the group.

CATEGORY G

1. Do you suffer from any chronic illness or allergies?   Yes   No
   Which?
   Is it hereditary?   Yes   No

   Strongman of infirmity; family curses may be generational causing hereditary physical impairments such as blindness, deafness, etc. Curses must be broken before deliverance is administered. After familiar spirits have been removed, pray for cleansing and healing. When praying for people with seizures or asthma, first bind "the strongman" very tightly. If symptoms start to manifest while you are praying, remind the spirit it is forbidden to operate.

   After freedom, anoint the person with oil and pray for healing.

APPENDIX A

SECTION 1

2. Have you had any severe accidents or traumas that stand out in your mind not   Yes   No
   already mentioned above? (These can be emotional or physical traumas).
   Explain:
   Who was involved in the trauma with you? (i.e. car wreck, I was with my daughter)

   Break "soul ties" with anyone involved in an accident with a person. The trauma creates a soul tie.

   Pray trauma prayer.

3. Have you ever received a blood transfusion?   Yes   No

4. Have you ever donated blood?   Yes   No

   Break "soul ties" with anyone from whom you have received blood or to whom you have given blood. You will usually not know who the person is even if a family member donated it for you. If the donated blood isn't a match for you, you will be given blood from someone who matches. Simply ask God to break the "soul ties" that were created with the person who received your blood or whose blood you received.

5. Describe yourself in as many one or two word phrases as you can:

   a.   h.
   b.   i
   c.   j.
   d.   k.
   e.   l.
   f.   m.
   g.   n.

6. Do you have any other problems you feel this questionnaire hasn't uncovered? Explain as fully as you can. Try to pinpoint when they began and if they were connected with a trauma of some kind or if you were victimized or if you invited the problem in.

Much of this material is taken from the book *Evicting Demonic Intruders* by Noel and Phyl Gibson, and *Freedom in Christ* by Noel and Phyl Gibson, both published by New Wine Press. Distributed in the USA by Gospel Light, and from *How to Cast Out Demons* by Doris Wagner, published by Regal.

ADOLESCENT QUESTIONNAIRE KEY

Name:		Age:		Sex:	
Current Profession:					
What is the best time to schedule your deliverance?		Weekday	Evening	Weekend	

Please answer the following briefly:

1. What is your church background?

   Religious spirits, legalism, idolatry, worship of saints, pride, critical spirits, judgmental spirits, doubt and unbelief, skepticism.

2. Explain briefly your conversion experience. If you came to Christ as a teenager was you life really changed?

3. Were you baptized or dedicated as a child?   Yes   No

   Were you baptized since you've been born again?   Yes   No

4. In one word who is Jesus Christ to you?

   Savior and Lord are ideal answers. God or Son of God are also satisfactory. Indirect answers such as example, friend, leader and redeemer usually indicate a general belief in the biblical Christ but not close relationship.

5. What does the blood of Jesus mean to you?

   Pray leaders should not accept theological definitions, but only spontaneous declarations of faith in the substitutionary and explainable death, burial and resurrection of Jesus Christ for them personally. If the person is not born again, lead him to the Lord before proceeding with the deliverance.

6. Is repentance part of your Christian life?   Yes   No

   Should the person being prayed for refuse to repent, the deliverance procedure will be a waste of time.

7. What is your prayer life like?

8. Do you have assurance of salvation?   Yes   No

Frequently victims of rejection are 'wobbly' about assurance. After deliverance from rejection, they usually confess assurance. Should doubts still remain, check for:

Hereditary spirits of antichrist, spirits of intellectualism, rationalism, humanism, doubt and unbelief.

After release; cleanse and minister faith to believe God's word. If positive responses are still not given, check the genuineness of their claim to salvation.

9. Do you have a problem with doubt and unbelief in everyday   Yes   No
   Christian living?

Spirits of doubt and unbelief. If there is a blockage of the things of God, look for spirits of antichrist, stupor, error, and lying spirits. Anti-Christ spirits may also come from Freemasonry and witchcraft.

Believers under oppression find faith difficult.

10. Are you satisfied with your Christian Walk?   Yes   No
    If not. How would you like to see it improve?

Whatever is listed here, pray for this improvement at the end of the deliverance.

CATEGORY A   **REJECTION**

1. Is your relationship with your parents: (circle one)   Good   Bad   Indifferent
   Explain:

   a. Is your father (circle)   Passive   Strong   Manipulative   Neither

   Are you friends?   Yes   No   Sort of

   Describe briefly your relationship with your father:

   b. Any special problems with your father?

   Look for issues needing forgiveness. Spirit of rejection. Depending on relationship, look for fear, dread, guilt and shame, control, etc. Patriarchal bondages must be broken, and inherited spirits cast out; apathy, passivity, lack of motivation, anger, laziness, etc.

APPENDIX A

SECTION 2

c. Is your mother: (circle)   Passive   Strong   Manipulative   Neither

Are you friends?   Yes   No   Sort of

Describe briefly your relationship with your mother:

d. Any special problems with your mother?

Look for issues needing forgiveness. Spirits of rejection. Depending on relationship, look for fear, dread, guilt and shame, control, etc. Matriarchal bondages must be broken, and inherited spirits cast out; apathy, passivity, lack of motivation, anger, laziness, etc.

2. a. Were you a planned child?   Yes   No   Don't Know

Spirit of rejection.

b. The "right sex" for your mother?   Yes   No   Don't Know

The "right sex" for your father?   Yes   No   Don't Know

Spirit of rejection. In extreme cases, self-hatred and homosexuality.

c. Do your parents favor one of your siblings over you?   Yes   No   Don't Know
Who and in what way?

Spirit of rejection. Forgiveness issues of parents and the favored sibling.

d. Were you conceived out of wedlock?   Yes   No   Don't Know

Spirits of rejection, lust, fear, guilt and shame.

e. Were you adopted?   Yes   No   Don't Know

Spirits of rejection, abandonment; forgiveness of biological parents.

f. The result of a violent conception (i.e. rape)?   Yes   No   Don't Know

Spirits of fear, anger, rage, violence, lust, rejection.

SECTION 2

g. If adopted, do you know anything about your biological parents?

Pray against any hereditary spirits associated with known characteristics or behaviors of biological parents, (i.e. spirits of addiction, lust, fear, etc.)

h. Do you know if your mother suffered any trauma during her pregnancy with you? Physical trauma? Explain:

Spirits of fear, rejection.

Emotional trauma? Explain:

Spirits of fear, rejection.

i. Was your birth difficult or complicated?   Yes   No
If yes, in what way?

Spirits of fear, death, infirmity.

j. Were you held by your mother shortly after your birth?   Yes   No

If baby was kept in an incubator; spirits of rejection, fear.

A breast-fed baby?   Yes   No

If not breast-fed, look for spirit of rejection.

k. Do you have brothers and sisters?   Yes   No

Name:	Age:

Where do you fall in the sibling line?

Depending on the family, any position in the sibling line can allow in a spirit of rejection.

How is your relationship with them?

Look for forgiveness issues and spirits of rejection, jealousy, guilt and shame.

Any special problems?

Look for forgiveness issues and spirits of rejection, jealousy, guilt and shame.

3. Are your parents living?

Mother		Yes	No
Father		Yes	No

Are they Christians?

Mother		Yes	No
Father		Yes	No

If not Christians, determine if they have rejected the faith of the person being prayed for. If so, spirit of rejection. If parents (or other loved ones) died unsaved, look for spirits of grief and mourning, fear, guilt.

Living together?	Yes	No
Divorced?	Yes	No

Forgiveness issues. Spirits of rejection, fear of abandonment, betrayal, covenant breaking.

Remarried?	Yes	No

Forgiveness issues. Spirits of rejection, betrayal, jealousy.

If parent(s) are deceased, at what age did they die?
Mother
Father

If grandparents are deceased, at what age did they die?
Maternal grandmother
Maternal grandfather
Paternal grandmother
Paternal grandfather

Have any other members of your family died before the age of 60?   Yes   No
If so, who?

Look for premature death; (any death before the age of 60).

4. Who do you live with?

5. Do you have (circle all that apply)

Step-mother   Step-father   Step-siblings

6. Do you currently have a step-parent living in the home?   Yes   No

7. Are there now, or have there been other adults living in the home other   Yes   No
than your parents?

8. How is your relationship with stepparents?

Are they Christians?

Forgiveness issues. Spirits of rejection, control, jealousy, anger, rebellion, self-pity.

9. How is your relationship with   Stepbrothers?   Stepsisters?

Are they Christians?   Yes   No   Yes   No

Forgiveness issues. Spirits of rejection control, anger, rebellion, jealousy, self-pity.

10. Are you a people pleaser (do you jeopardize yourself to   Yes   No   Maybe
please others)?
In what way?

Strongman of pride. Spirits of performance, competitiveness, codependency; commonly born out of rejection.

11. Are you a critical person?   Yes   No   Maybe
Of what activities or characteristics are you most critical?

Do you feel superior to people of whom you are critical?   Yes   No   Maybe

Spirits of criticism and judgment, envy, pride and jealously. May be born out of rejection, pride, fear, control, anger.

12. Do you feel emotionally immature?　　　　　　　　　　Yes　　No　　Maybe
    What is your emotional age?

    May be symptom of rejection.

13. Tell us about yourself-image (circle all that apply):
    Low self-image　　　　　　　Feel insecure
    Condemn myself　　　　　　　Hate myself
    Feel worthless　　　　　　　　Believe I am a failure
    Feel inferior　　　　　　　　　Question my identity
    Punish myself (if so, how?)
        Mentally
        Emotionally
        Physically
        Sexually

    *Low self-image is commonly a symptom of rejection. However, look for spirits of
    hopelessness, depression, despair, self-accusation, self-condemnation or punishment.*

14. Is yours a happy home?　　　　　　　　　　　　　　　Yes　　　　No
    Describe briefly:

    Spirits of rejection. Forgiveness issues.

15. How would you describe your family's financial situation?
    Poor
    Slight financial struggles
    Moderate income
    Affluent

    Spirits of rejection, poverty, fear (of poverty, etc.), pride, shame, greed.

16. Do your parents tithe?　　　　　　　　　　　　　　　Yes　　　No
    Do you tithe?　　　　　　　　　　　　　　　　　　　　Yes　　　No

    Spirits of poverty, fear; God robbing spirits.

    **You don't have the legal ground to pray for prosperity for a person who isn't
    keeping his part of God's covenant concerning sowing and reaping.**

17. Are you lonely as a teenager?　　　　　　　　Sometimes　　Yes　　No
    Explain:

    Forgiveness issues. Spirits of rejection, rebellion, independence, abandonment.

18. Do you experience a mixture of anger, resentment, bitterness, revenge, rage, feelings
    or actions of violence? (circle all that apply)
    Explain:

    Strongman of jealousy, spirits of anger, resentment, bitterness, revenge, rage, rancor, violence; these feelings and actions may allow in a spirit of guilt and shame. Identify entry points and close them.

19. Has lying been a problem to you?　　　　　　　　　　　　Yes　　No
    Is it now?　　　　　　　　　　　　　　　　　　　　　　Yes　　No
    Has stealing been a problem to you?　　　　　　　　　　Yes　　No
    Is it now?　　　　　　　　　　　　　　　　　　　　　　Yes　　No
    Do you exaggerate?　　　　　　　　　　　　　　　　　　Yes　　No

    Strongman of lying, spirits of deception, guilt and shame; possibly spirits of rebellion, lawlessness.

20. Do you have trouble giving or receiving love?　　　　At times　　Yes　　No

    May be symptoms of rejection and fear of rejection. May have allowed in a spirit of fear (fear of being emotionally hurt, fear of abandonment, etc). Look for 'inner wall'.

21. Do you find it easy to communicate with persons close to you?

    I have real difficulty　　　I have problems at times　　　I am unwilling　　　It's easy

    Difficulty may be symptom of rejection. Spirit of stubbornness. Look for 'inner wall'.

22. Are you a perfectionist?　　　　　　　　　　　　　　Yes　　No

    Are your parents perfectionists?　　　　　　　　　　Yes　　No

    Perfectionist spirit. May be born out of rejection, pride, fear, control, anger, obsessions (whoredoms).

SECTION 2

23. Do you come from a proud family?   Yes   No

    Inherited strongman of pride.

24. Do you personally have a problem with pride?   Yes   No

    Strongman of pride; identify entry points and close them.

25. Do you have a history of conflict with those in authority over you,   Yes   No
    i.e. teachers, bosses, pastors, police, etc.
    If so, please describe:

    Strongman of pride, rebellion. If there is a pattern of conflict, spirit of lawlessness.

25. Do you have or have you had problems with (circle all that apply):

    Below are the aggressive reactions to rejection (left side of the tree)

Impatience	Used to	Now	Irritability	Used to	Now
Racial prejudice	Used to	Now	Moodiness	Used to	Now
Violence	Used to	Now	Anger	Used to	Now
Defensiveness	Used to	Now	Rebellion	Used to	Now
Temper	Used to	Now	Stubbornness	Used to	Now
Temptation to murder	Used to	Now			

Strongman of jealousy, spirits of anger, temper, violence, murder

26. Have you been given to: Swearing   Blasphemies   Obscenities
    Do you now?   Swear   Blaspheme   Use Obscenities

    Blaspheming spirits, spirits of obscenity, anger, rebellion, lawlessness.

27. Think over your life and list any times you've been hurt or suffered an injustice. Ask God to
    remind you of specific incidents, large or small. These incidents can involve parents,
    family members, siblings, spouses, children, friends, pastors, bosses, teachers, neighbors,
    or even total strangers. Don't be concerned with *why* they did what they did; if it hurt
    you, please include it. For example, has anyone ever treated you unfairly? Has anyone
    ever done anything that hurt your feelings? Can you remember anytime when you cried or
    felt like crying because of something someone did to you? Did anyone ever embarrass you,

leave you out, abandon you, or frighten you? *(Note: Please take your time with this. If it comes to your mind during this time, it is probably the Holy Spirit reminding you, so include it in the list).*

Pre-school years:
Grade school years:
Middle school and high school years:
Incidents at work:
Incidents at church:
Incidents involving friends:
Incidents involving people you dated of wanted to date:
Recent incidents:
Others:

All of the above must be dealt with in the area of forgiveness. Also look for entry points for the spirits below:

Spirits of rejection, anger, rage, jealously, control, fear.

CATEGORY B   MENTAL AND EMOTIONAL PROBLEMS

1. Are you easily frustrated?   Yes   No

   Do you show it or bury it?   Show   Bury

2. Are you: An anxious person   A worrier   Get depressed

   Strongman of heaviness; spirits of anxiety, doubt and unbelief, depression.

3. Have either of your parents or grandparents suffered from depression?   Yes   No
      Father   Mother   Grandmother   Grandfather

   Inherited spirits of depression, anxiety, nervousness.

4. Have you or has any parent, brother, sister, or grandparent suffered from   Yes   No
   acute nervousness or a mental problem, such as schizophrenia, bipolar
   disorder or obsessive compulsive disorder?

   Who?   Problem?

   Unless the person being prayed for obviously needs professional help, cast out the following:

SECTION 2

Hereditary or personal strongman of heaviness; spirits of anxiety, fear.

5. Have you personally ever had psychiatric counseling?	Yes	No
Hospitalization for psychiatric treatment?	Yes	No
Other hospitalization?	Yes	No
Shock treatment?	Yes	No
Psychoanalysis?	Yes	No
Been under anesthesia?	Yes	No
Been intoxicated (alcohol)?	Yes	No
Used drugs inducing a passive-mind state? (prescription or non-prescription)	Yes	No
Had a fever with delirium?	Yes	No
Been unconscious?	Yes	No
Other?	Yes	No

In people who are medicated, the demons often become sluggish and are slow to respond to deliverance prayer. If possible, it is better to pray after the effects have lessened or when no medication has been taken.

Deaf and dumb spirits, heaviness, depression; cast out any spirits that took advantage of a 'passive mind state' to enter the person's life. Close doors opened to any spirits that entered while in a hypnotic, drugged or unguarded mental state.

6. Have you ever been hypnotized?   Yes   No
   If so, when and why?

Spirits that entered during a 'passive mind state'. Familiar spirits, spirits of deception, mind-control, confusion, spirits of antichrist are common, but any spirit can take advantage of a 'passive mind state'.

7. Are you currently taking any medication for depression, anxiety or pain, or   Yes   No
   an anti-psychotic drug? If so, what are you taking and how often are you
   taking it?

8. Since you have been taking it, do you have difficulty concentrating   Have   It's
   and focusing or is it easier?   Difficulty Easier

During the interview process, you need to find out if the person is taking anything that is mind altering in a way that would cause him to be unable to receive deliverance. Often a person needs to be on a medication in order to focus and receive deliverance. You can often tell by talking with him and determine if he can follow your conversation or if he is spacing out. Never tell anyone to stop his medication. If you feel that he is on so much medication that he can't receive deliverance; ask him to consult his physician to get his medications regulated so he will be able to concentrate and work with you. Then reset the appointment when that is accomplished.

9. Have you, your parents, or grandparents been in any cults (circle all that apply)

Christian Science	Myself	Others	Rosicrucian	Myself	Others
Armstrong Worldwide COG	Myself	Others	Gurus	Myself	Others
Christadelphians	Myself	Others	Unity	Myself	Others
Jehovah's Witnesses	Myself	Others	Mormons	Myself	Others
Children of Love	Myself	Others	Scientology	Myself	Others
Religious Communes	Myself	Others	Bahai	Myself	Others
Unification Church (Moonies)	Myself	Others	Theosophy	Myself	Others
Eastern Religions (specify)	Myself	Others	Anthroposophy	Myself	Others
Native Religions	Myself	Others	Spiritists Church	Myself	Others
Others:					

Spirits of false religion, doubt and unbelief, deception, and spirits with the name of the cult.

10. Have you or has any close family member been a:

Freemason	Odd Fellow	Rainbow Girl	Mormon
Eastern Star	Shriner	Daughter of the Nile	Amaranth
Job's Daughter	Elk	DeMolay	Fraternities
Sororities	Secret organizations or societies		
If so, who?			

Do you suffer from (circle all that apply)

Apathy	Hardness of Emotion	Confusion	Financial Disaster
Skepticism	Comprehension Difficulties	Unbelief	Doubt
Infirmities	Frequent Sickness	Allergies	

Spirits of Freemasonry. If no Freemasonry is identified, look for other causes.

Is there any Masonic regalia or memorabilia in your possession?   Yes   No
If yes, what?

Ensure the person destroys any regalia or memorabilia.

11. Do you feel mentally confused?   Yes   No

Do you have mental blocks?   Yes   No

May be symptoms of Freemasonry; also may be spirits of occultism, witchcraft, Satanism, confusion. If mental blocks center around the things of God, spirits of antichrist, stupor.

12. Do you day-dream? Yes No
   If yes, what is the nature of your day-dreams?

   If day-dreaming is excessive, interferes with daily activities, or is used to escape reality, look for spirits of escapism, fantasy, false comfort, addiction. Other spirits as revealed by the content of the day-dreams. Also may be symptoms of Freemasonry.

13. Do you have mental fantasies Yes No
   If yes, what is the nature of the fantasies?

   If fantasizing is excessive, interferes with daily activities, is used to escape reality, or indicates a loss of grasp on reality, spirits of escapism, fantasy, false comfort, addiction, self-hatred, grandeur. Other spirits as revealed by the content of the fantasies. Also may be symptoms of Freemasonry.

14. Do you suffer from bad dreams? Yes No
   What is the content or nature of the dreams?

   Look for elements of the dreams revealing spirits such as fear, lust, etc. Also, may be symptoms of Freemasonry.

15. Do you suffer from sleeplessness? Yes No

   Symptoms of Freemasonry. Also, depending on the circumstances, spirits of fear, lust, depression, worry.

16. Have you ever been tempted to commit suicide? Yes No
   Have you tried? Yes No
   If yes, what did you do?

   Spirits of death, depression and any other spirits associated with the emotions which prompted the attempt such as self-pity, fear or shame. If the person felt out of control as if something were driving him to try to kill himself, deaf and dumb spirit. If the person was trying to get attention or get his way, spirit of control. Also symptom of Freemasonry.

   Have the person repent.

17. Have you ever wished to die? Yes No

Have you spoken it aloud?   Yes   No

Break "Word Curse" of death. Spirits of death or depression. Look for any spirits associated with the emotions which prompted the death wish such as self-pity, fear, shame. If the person was trying to get attention or get his way, spirit of control. Also may be symptom of Freemasonry.

Have the person repent.

18. Have you had a strong and prolonged fear of any of the following? Please list the first time you remember experiencing fear in each area marked:

Failure	Used to	Now		Inadequacy	Used to	Now
Inability to cope	Used to	Now		Death	Used to	Now
Authority figures	Used to	Now		The dark	Used to	Now
Being alone	Used to	Now		Rape	Used to	Now
Satan and evil spirits	Used to	Now		The future	Used to	Now
Violence	Used to	Now		Women	Used to	Now
Crowds	Used to	Now		Heights	Used to	Now
Men	Used to	Now		Insanity	Used to	Now
Public speaking	Used to	Now		Accident	Used to	Now
The opinion of people	Used to	Now		Old age	Used to	Now
Enclosed places	Used to	Now		Insects	Used to	Now
Terminal illness	Used to	Now		Spiders	Used to	Now
Dogs	Used to	Now		Snakes	Used to	Now
Animals	Used to	Now		Pain	Used to	Now
Flying in an airplane	Used to	Now		Water	Used to	Now
Grocery stores	Used to	Now		Open spaces	Used to	Now
Death or injury of a loved one	Used to	Now		Rodents	Used to	Now
Divorce or marriage Breakup	Used to	Now				

List any other fears not included above:

Name the demons by the particular fear they cause such as: 'a spirit of the fear of failure' 'fear of the opinions of people' 'fear of spiders', etc. Also symptoms of Freemasonry.

To find entry points, look for the first time the person experienced the fear or any times of intense or memorable fear. There may be multiple entry points for any given fear. Treat 'used to' fears the same as if they were current fears so that all entry points can be closed. Look for fears from childhood – specific and generalized. For example, a perfectionist mother may have instilled fear of failure and inadequacy in a child. Living with an alcoholic father may have instilled a generalized dread (or fear) in the child. Divorce of parents may open the door to a fear of the unknown or fear of abandonment. Some fears are simply taught, by parents or others in childhood by example or in an attempt to keep the child safe. For example, children who are constantly advised to watch out for snakes may develop a fear of snakes. If a parent is afraid of something, such as storms or water, children may develop a similar fear. Close these doors as they are recognized.

CATEGORY C   WITCHCRAFT AND THE OCCULT

1. Have you ever made a pact with the devil?   Yes No

   Brings on a curse, the person must repent.

   Was it a blood pact?   Yes No

   Very strong; apply oil representing the blood of Jesus to break the pact. The person must repent.

   What was it?

   When did you make it?
   Why did you make it?

   Are you willing to renounce it?   Yes No

   Have the person specifically renounce the pact, reversing specific words spoken. Familiar spirits, spirits of witchcraft, occult, anti-christ, manipulation, control, and other related spirits such as fear.

2. To your knowledge, has any curse been placed on you or your family?   Yes No
   By whom?
   Explain:

   Look for generational patterns such as: The eldest son of every married descendant is born blind. The first daughter of every family dies in childhood. Suicides take place in families at regular intervals.

   If family histories are unknown, but certain generational problems occur regularly, it would be wise to treat them as curses. Break their power, evict any oppressive demons and pray for healing of victims. All curses must be broken and every oppressive demon that has entered because of the oaths or curses, cast out, before praying for cleansing and healing.

3. To your knowledge, have your parents or any relative as far back as you know   Yes No
   been involved in occultism or witchcraft?
   Whom and doing what?

   To what extent?

   As a child, did any family member dedicate you to Satan or any demonic   Yes No
   worship?

If yes, who, when and why?

Renounce the dedication. Inherited familiar spirits, spirits of divination, witchcraft, antichrist, spiritism, or any spirits associated with the particular activity.

4. Have you ever had involvement with any of the following? (circle all that apply)

Fortunetellers	Tarot cards	Ouija boards		
Astrology	Séances	Mediums		
Palmistry	Color therapy	Levitation		
Astral travel	Horoscopes	Good luck charms		
Black magic	Demon worship	Asked for a spirit guide		
Clairvoyance	Crystals	Done automatic handwriting		
New Age Movement	Reincarnation	Past lives regression		
Psychics	Iridology	Been to a curandero or native healer		
Been involved in any other witchcraft or demonic or Satanic things?			Yes	No
If so, what?				
To your knowledge have your parents, grandparents or other ancestors ever been involved in any of the above?			Yes	No
Which ones?				

Experiences, no matter how innocent they seem, must be taken seriously and the demon dominating each activity cast out.

Familiar spirits, spirits of divination, witchcraft, antichrist, spiritism, or any spirits associated with the particular activity.

5. Have you ever read books on occultism or witchcraft?   Yes   No
   Why?

   Those who read them out of fascination or a desire to learn to practice the craft need cleansing, and books should be destroyed. If the books were read solely for research, demonic entry would be unlikely.

   Spirits of divination and familiar spirits; also, look for spirit of fear.
   Note: The following games, movies, television programs and list of music is not an exhaustive list but is as current as our research was able to determine. These lists should be updated frequently to address the current market.

6. Have you ever played games or played with toys such as: (circle all that apply)

Fable Role Playing Game - X-Box	Used to play	Currently plays
Starcraft Role Playing computer game	Used to play	Currently plays
Everquest Role Playing computer game	Used to play	Currently plays
World of Warcraft Role Playing computer game	Used to play	Currently plays
Dungeons & Dragons	Used to play	Currently plays

Pokemon	Used to play	Currently plays
Magic 8 Ball	Used to play	Currently plays
Magic - the - Gathering	Used to play	Currently plays
Visionaires	Used to play	Currently plays
Moon Dreamers	Used to play	Currently plays
Vampire Role Play Games	Used to play	Currently plays
Sword and Sorcery Battle Gear	Used to play	Currently plays
Starriors	Used to play	Currently plays
Secret Wars	Used to play	Currently plays
Other World	Used to play	Currently plays
Masters of the Universe	Used to play	Currently plays
Snake Mountain	Used to play	Currently plays
Robo Force	Used to play	Currently plays
Super Natural	Used to play	Currently plays
Alien Blood & Monster Flesh	Used to play	Currently plays
Troll Dolls	Used to play	Currently plays
Pegasus	Used to play	Currently plays
Unicorns	Used to play	Currently plays
Gremlins	Used to play	Currently plays
ET	Used to play	Currently plays

Fable role Playing Game – X- Box: Starcraft Role Playing Computer Game; Everquest role Playing Computer Game; World of Warcraft Role Playing Computer Game; *Witchcraft, murder, death, loss of identity.* **Role playing games can result in a person taking on a demonic personality of the character played.**
Many of these toys and games are evidently occult by their name. Some are less obvious.
Dungeons & Dragons: teaches demonology, witchcraft, voodoo, murder, rape, blasphemy, suicide, assassination, insanity, sexual perversion, Satan worship, barbarianism, cannibalism, sadism, demon summoning, necromancy, divination and human sacrifice. Role playing can result in a person taking on a demonic personality of the character played.
Pokemon: Pokemon means pocket monster. These toys and games teach witchcraft and evoke curses.
Visionaries: This toy features Knight of the Magical Light. Extar has a mystical personality with magical holographic power to see the enemy. This figure represents witchcraft and divination.
Ghost Busters: Banshee Ghost Bomber drops Ecto-Plazam on its victim. Ecto-Plazam (ectoplasm) "in spiritism is the vaporous luminous substance supposed to emanate from the medium's body during a trance" (Webster's New Universal Unabridged Dictionary). This is blatantly occult.
Moon Dreamers: Magic dream crystals make wishes come true when given Dream Gazer, the mystical sorceress. This bears a New Age occult concept.
Sword and Sorcery Battle Gear: A fantasy of sorcery, the occult and violence.
Starriors: Warrior robots kill for control of the earth using chain saws, buzz saws, drills, spikes, reams and vibrator chisels. Starriors are extremely violent.
Secret Wars: In this game one fights aliens with "the force", a counterfeit of God. There are wild mutants and hideous creatures.

Other World: This game is similar to Dungeons and Dragons. The player battles with warlords, demons and dragons. It is violent.

Masters of the Universe: Skeletor is an evil lord of destruction, beastmen and evil goddesses. It is based upon sorcery, and witchcraft.

Snake Mountain: The player acts like a snake while working the snake's jaw as it speaks. The child pretends to be a snake.

Robo Force: An evil robot empire. It has a killer instinct and a crusher hand. Robo Force is a dictator and destroyer. It is very violent. Other transformers are Voltron, Robotech, GoBots and Transformers. The evil of such toys is not easily discerned until they are observed in their corresponding cartoons, then their extreme violence is seen along with occult overtones and, in some sexual implications.

Super Naturals: These characters display powers of divination through insight into the future. Other occult powers include snake charming and hypnotism. Witchcraft is brought in through pentagram power released by each toy. Books that accompany the toys carry occult stories.

Alien Blood and Monster Flesh: This is sold in cans!

Troll dolls: Trolls are either giants or dwarf-like creatures which originated in Scandinavian folklore. They inhabit hills, caves or live underground. Webster's New Collegiate Dictionary defines *troll* as a "demon".

Pegasus: A mythical flying horse from the Dungeon & Dragons monster manual. Pegasus originated in Greek mythology, and is said to have been born of the blood of the decapitated Medusa.

Unicorns: These mythical creatures are also monsters listed in the Dungeon & Dragons manual. Medieval kings and popes used amulets supposedly made from its horns. They believed it had magical and healing powers. The unicorn is a long-standing occult beast of a schizophrenic nature - at one time docile and loving, laying its head in the lap of a maiden; then aggressive and violent in goring its enemies to death.

Gremlins: They are violent, grotesque, sadistic and cannibalistic. They also employ transformation which is a New Age concept. Webster defines *gremlin* as: "a creature supposed to interfere with the smoothness of any procedure". Thus, a gremlin represents a curse.

Spirits of divination and familiar spirits as well as spirits of the obvious ones associated with the title of the game; spirits of necromancy, witchcraft, murder and spirit guides; spirits of fear, violence, murder; these will depend on what games were played.

Taken in part from *A Manual For Children's Deliverance* by Frank and Ida Mae Hammond, 1996, Impact Children's Books, Inc. 332 Leffingwell Ave., Kirkwood, MO 63122

APPENDIX A

SECTION 2

7. Have you read books or seen cartoons, movies or TV shows with themes about the occult, supernatural, ghosts, science fiction, Wicca, vampires or werewolves? (circle all that apply)

That's so Raven	Used to watch	Currently watches
Jack Ass	Used to watch	Currently watches
Tales from the Crypt	Used to watch	Currently watches
Digemon	Used to watch	Currently watches
Pokemon	Used to watch	Currently watches
Gremlins	Used to watch	Currently watches
Power Rangers	Used to watch	Currently watches
Masters of the Universe	Used to watch	Currently watches
Ninja Turtles	Used to watch	Currently watches
Ghost Busters	Used to watch	Currently watches
ET	Used to watch	Currently watches
So Weird	Used to watch	Currently watches
Buffy the Vampire Slayer	Used to watch	Currently watches
Sabrina the Teenage Witch	Used to watch	Currently watches
Alex Mac	Used to watch	Currently watches
Angel	Used to watch	Currently watches
Charmed	Used to watch	Currently watches
Harry Potter	Used to watch	Currently watches
Medium	Used to watch	Currently watches
Ghost Whisperer	Used to watch	Currently watches

Others (list by name):

Most of these were addressed above with the toys and games. The problem with Buffy the Vampire Slayer and Sabrina the Teenage Witch is apparent by their titles. Any movie that portrays witches as "good" cause problems because they confuse the young person in his ability to discern good from evil. These programs also deal with necromancy, witchcraft, curses, blood shed, evoking and asking in demons and spirit guides. Angel is a series on prime time television in which the main character is chasing demons. The demons are portrayed as some good and some bad. Again this causes confusion as well as desensitizing the child to evil. Medium and Ghost Whisperer are TV shows in which the lead characters get advise and insight from spirits of the dead.

Spirits of divination and familiar spirits as well as spirits of the obvious ones associated with the title of the books or movies. Spirits of necromancy witchcraft, murder and spirit guides. Filthy spirits that sexually attack or rape people, appearing as gray shapes, but are able to cause physical stimulation. Spirits of fear, violence and murder. These will depend on what games were played, and what films were watched.

8. Do you play video games?   Yes   No
How much time do you spend playing these games?

APPENDIX A

SECTION 2

Have you played any of the following Nintendo Games? (circle all that apply)

Devils	Used to play	Currently plays
Dragons	Used to play	Currently plays
Babylon	Used to play	Currently plays
Mysterious Forces	Used to play	Currently plays
Mythical Beasts	Used to play	Currently plays
Mythical gods	Used to play	Currently plays
Wizards	Used to play	Currently plays
Warriors	Used to play	Currently plays
Magic Power	Used to play	Currently plays
Black Princes	Used to play	Currently plays
Minions of Hell	Used to play	Currently plays
Evil Monsters	Used to play	Currently plays
Magic Items	Used to play	Currently plays
Beelzebub	Used to play	Currently plays
Ectoplasm	Used to play	Currently plays
Curse of Death	Used to play	Currently plays
Evil Spirits	Used to play	Currently plays
Black Magic	Used to play	Currently plays
Magical Scrolls	Used to play	Currently plays
Druids	Used to play	Currently plays
Witchcraft	Used to play	Currently plays
Evil Wizards	Used to play	Currently plays
Sorcery	Used to play	Currently plays
Potions	Used to play	Currently plays
Demons	Used to play	Currently plays
Curses	Used to play	Currently plays
Necromancy	Used to play	Currently plays
Holy Water	Used to play	Currently plays
Buddha	Used to play	Currently plays
Monsters	Used to play	Currently plays
Magical Spells	Used to play	Currently plays
Magical Swords	Used to play	Currently plays
Magical Books	Used to play	Currently plays
Beasts	Used to play	Currently plays
Wands and Witches	Used to play	Currently plays

There has been a marriage of electronics and the occult. It has birthed everything from computerized demonology to seemingly harmless but powerfully seductive video games. These games are as progressively addictive as drugs. Young players usually start out with the less violent ones such as Donkey-Kong, Pac-Man and Smurf. Tiring of these easy games, the children progress on to more challenging ones which often provide increased

emphasis upon violence and occultism. The names of the Nintendo games listed are self explanatory. When praying for the teen, try to determine the effect the games have had on his belief system especially in the realm of reality verses fantasy. It is best to destroy the books, videos, etc. Advise the teen of the importance of this.

Spirits of divination and familiar spirits, spirits of death, murder, violence and control as well as the obvious ones associated with the title of the video.

9. Have you watched films with extremely violent themes or scenes, or with   Yes   No
   scenes portraying graphic violence or injury to human beings or animals?
   If yes, do you now?   Yes   No
   What, when and how often?

Strongman of fear; spirits of divination, occult, familiar spirits, violence, murder.

10. Have you watched professional wrestling?   Yes   No

Strongman of fear, violence, murder, death

11. What music do you listen to?   Secular   Christian
    What groups?
    If secular, do you listen to: (circle all that apply)

Grunge	Nirvana	Pearl Jam	Alice in Chains	Other

Spirits of rebellion, death, witchcraft, Satanism, murder, lust, perversion, violence, bestiality, bondage.

These groups encourage the use of drugs as well as being actively associated with the spirits listed, also hardness of emotion and an unkempt hippy attitude.

R & B	Ludacris	Lil Jon	50 Cent	Snoop Dawg	Other

Spirits of violence, perversion, lust, pornography, murder, rebellion

These groups encourage gang activity, multiple partner sex, the use of pornography and violence.

APPENDIX A

SECTION 2

Pop	Britney Spears	Christine Aguilera	Ryan Cabrera	Other

Spirits of lust, rebellion, perversion

These groups encourage illicit sex and no accountability.

Classic Rock	Led Zeppelin	Leonard Skinnard	Rush	Doors	Jimi Hendrix

Spirits of perversion, rebellion, occultic Satanism, lust, violence, murder, bondage.

These groups encourage the use of drugs and produce hardness of emotion.

Heavy Metal	Mega Death	Slayer	Iron Maiden	Korn	Other

Spirits of lust, rebellion, perversion, occultic Satanism, violence, murder, death.

These groups encourage the use of drugs.

Emo	The Used	The Black Maria	Straylight Run	Senses Fall	Other

Spirits of rejection, depression, guilt, shame, suicide, drugs, homosexuality, rebellion.

A broad title that covers many different styles of emotionally charged punk rock. Some of these kids dress metro sexually (dressing and acting homosexually without being gay).

Alternative / Punk	Weezer	The Donnas	Incubus	Ramones	Goo Goo Dolls

Spirits of rebellion, rejection, death, suicide, anger, hate, isolation.

These kids will dress to stand out and shock people. Wearing chains, dog collars, spikes, dressed in all black, Mohawks and sometimes funky hair colors.

How much time to you spend listening to it?

12. What do you like to do in your spare time?

13. Have you been involved in Transcendental Meditation?   Yes No
    Do you have a mantra?   Yes No

If so, what is it?

Have you ever had acupuncture?   Yes   No

Spirits of false religion, Hinduism, Buddhism, idolatry, antichrist, deception, divination, familiar spirits; the person needs to renounce the mantra; mantras may be demonic names, calling up demon powers. Renounce any spirits that took advantage of the unguarded mental state to enter.

14. Have you been involved in Eastern religions?   Yes   No
    Have you followed a guru?   Yes   No

Spirits of false religion, Hinduism, Buddhism, idolatry, antichrist, deception, divination, familiar spirits.

15. Have you ever visited heathen temples or a Mosk?   Yes   No
    If so when and why?

    Did you make offerings?   Yes   No
    What were they?
    Did you take part in any ceremony?   Yes   No
    Explain:

Look for the reason they visited the temples; if they were just tourists or were there to pray against the false religion and did not participate in any offerings or ceremonies, there may have been no demonic entry. If they were required to remove their shoes or cover their heads in order to pay respect to the premises , this is considered a form of worship and must be renounced.

Spirits associated with the temple or mosk involved, Hinduism, Buddhism, Islam, etc.

16. Have you ever celebrated Halloween or Mardi Gras?   Yes   No
    If so, when and in what way?

These are both celebrations honoring demonic powers.

Spirits of divination, occult, witchcraft, idolatry, familiar spirits, voodoo spirits.

17. Have you ever done any form of yoga?   Yes   No
    Meditation?   Yes   No
    Exercises?   Yes   No

Spirits of false religion, Hinduism, idolatry, antichrist, deception, divination, familiar spirits. If meditation was involved, cast out spirits that took advantage of a ' passive mind state'. Each position of yoga exercises invokes a demon.

APPENDIX A

SECTION 2

Repent and renounce any involvement with yoga and renounce any spirit that may have entered because of the positions taken.

18. Have you ever learned or used any form of mind communication, mind control   Yes   No
or ESP?
Explain:

Familiar spirits, occult, divination.

19. Were your parents or grandparents superstitious?   Yes   No
If so, who?
Were you?   Yes   No
If so, are you now?   Yes   No
Were their lives or your life governed by superstition?   Yes   No
Explain:

Spirits of divination, occult, doubt and unbelief, witchcraft, fear of the unknown.

20. Have you ever worn or kept any of the following:

Signs of the Zodiac	Fetishes	Amulets
Peace Symbols	Ankh	Pyramids
Tai Chi Symbols	Swastika	Caduceus
Good luck charms	Power crystals	Buddha beads
Karma beads	Mood rings	Dream catchers
Wish pouches or jewelry	Other good luck symbols or jewelry	

Do you have any in your possession?   Yes   No

Ensure that the person destroys the item.

Spirits of divination, occult, doubt and unbelief, witchcraft, fear of the unknown; deal with spirits associated with the specific item.

21. Do you have in your possession any symbols of idols or spirit worship such as:

Buddha	Totem Poles	Masks
Carvings	Pagan Symbols	Fetish Objects or Feathers
Gargoyles	Obelisks	Statues or Pictures of Dragons or Snakes
Rosary	Zodiac Symbols	Statues or Pictures of Saints
Native American art or jewelry depicting spiritual subjects or symbols		

If so, what?

Where are they from, and how did you get them?

Ensure that the person destroys the item.

Spirits of divination, occult, doubt and unbelief, witchcraft, fear of the unknown; deal with spirits associated with the specific item.

22. Do you have any witches, such as "good luck witches" in your home? Yes No

Ensure that the person destroys the item.

Spirits of divination, occult, doubt and unbelief, witchcraft.

23. Are you drawn by demonic art, abstract art, or surrealistic art? Yes No
If so, which?

Spirits of idolatry, occult, and spirits associated with the specific art form.

24. Have you ever learned any of the martial arts: Yes No
If so, which?
Do you practice it now? Yes No

Spirits of eastern religions, spirits of each martial art form, plus spirits of anger, violence, murder, idolatry, antichrist, control.

25. Have you ever had premonitions? Yes No
Deja vou? Yes No
Psychic sight? Yes No
If so, how frequently?

Depending on frequency and content, familiar spirits, deception; look for false spiritual gifts, i.e. if the person is called to a prophetic gift, familiar spirits may have perverted it into psychic sight. Close the third eye.

26. Have you ever been involved in: (circle all that apply)
     Firewalking   Voodoo
Any other form of religious pagan ceremony? Yes No
If so, what and when?

Spirits of voodoo, occult, witchcraft; spirits associated with the specific ceremony such as spirits of the sun dance, rainbow serpent fire, Native American vision quests, sweat lodge, etc.

27. Do you have any tattoos?   Yes   No
    If so, what?

    Spirits of rebellion and lawlessness; any spirits associated with the specific tattoo must be cast out and the power of the tattoo broken, i.e. tattoos of dragons symbolize Satan and/or rebellion and the occult, some tattoos have themes of violence, murder, lust. If the subject of the tattoo is demonic, it should be removed if possible.

    Ask the person the reason for getting the tattoo. Was it rebellion, peer pressure, etc. and pray accordingly.

28. Have you ever had a near-death experience?   Yes   No
    If so, when and what happened?

    Spirits of death, fear, dear and dumb spirit.

29. Have you had a loved one who died?   Yes   No
    If so, who and when?
    Did you mourn or grieve for them?   Yes   No
    Explain:
    Do you now?   Yes   No
    Women only: Have you ever had a miscarriage?   Yes   No
                  Have you ever had a stillbirth?   Yes   No
    Did you mourn or grieve for them?   Yes   No
    Do you now?   Yes   No
    Have you ever been with someone when they died?   Yes   No
    Describe your feelings about it:

    Spirits of death, grief and mourning, fear, spirits that transfer as a person dies, especially death.

    Usually normal grieving can last a year; any grieving past that time may open the door to a spirit of grief and mourning.

30. Do you have or have you ever had tendencies toward violent behavior?   Yes   No
    Have you ever acted violently?   Yes   No
    If so, when and towards whom?

    Strongman of jealousy; spirits of violence, rage, anger, rancor, murder, guilt and shame. Look for forgiveness issues.

    The person needs to repent.

SECTION 2

31. Are you or have you been extremely competitive?   I am now   I used to be

    Is it out of control?   Yes   No

    Explain:

    May be born out of rejection, pride, anger, fear. Identify the nature and reason for the competitiveness and deal with the spirit behind it.

32. As a child, did you have an imaginary playmate?   Yes   No
    Explain:

    Determine if the playmate talked to the person or gave him instructions, guidance, or advice. If so, familiar spirit and spirit guide.

33. Have you ever studied or used "visualization" or "inner healing"?   Yes   No
    Explain:

    Look for any technique that did not rely on the name of Jesus or a natural means of healing. If there was any supernatural aspect of the healing that was not based solely and specifically on the power of the Holy Spirit, deal with familiar spirits, new age, sorcery, witchcraft, mind control, and any other spirits associated with the specific technique.

34. Have you ever been in a counter-culture? (circle all that apply)

Surfers	Bikers	Hip Hop	Hippies	Drug drop-outs	New Age	Gangs

Dominant spirits of idolatry (be specific), lust, immorality, pride, arrogance, anti-social aggression, rebellion against authority, astrology, occultism, witchcraft, possibly Satanism, and rejection. Subjection to and fear of group leaders may also need to be broken and the person being prayed for cleansed. Renounce any oaths taken to the group and dissolve any covenants made. Break any "soul ties" to the other members or leaders of the group.

CATEGORY D   SEXUAL SINS, SEXUAL BONDAGES

1. Do you have lustful thoughts?   Fantasy Lust?   Yes   No
   Heterosexual   Homosexual   Pedophilia   Bi-sexual
   Of what?
   Frequency?

   Strongman of perversion and lust, spirits of homosexuality, violence, and any other spirits associated with the content of the thoughts or fantasies.

2. To your knowledge, was there evidence of lust in your parents, grandparents or
   further back?
   If so, explain:

   **Clues: Family history of pre-marital conceptions, marriages following pregnancies,
   incest, extra-marital affairs, pornography.**

   *Inherited strongman of perversion and lust; spirits of guilt and shame, depending on the
   nature of the behavior, homosexuality and violence.*

3. Do you masturbate?   Yes   No
   Frequency?
   Do you know why?
   Do you feel it is a compulsive problem?   Yes   No

   *In children, usually the first evidence of hereditary lust. Strongman of
   perversion and lust; spirits of guilt and shame; if compulsive problem, spirits
   of bondage, whoredoms and addiction.*

4. Were you ever sexually molested by someone outside your family as a child or   Yes   No
   teenager?
   More than once?   Yes   No
   Explain:

   *Strongman of perversion and lust. Forgive the perpetrator and anyone who failed to
   protect the person from the molestation. Also, deal with all spirits allowed in due to the
   emotional response such as anger, hatred of the opposite sex, rejection, fear, guilt and
   shame. Break "soul tie." If pattern exists in the person's life, familiar spirit of lust and
   victim spirit.*

   Were you actually raped?   Yes   No
   By whom?
   More than once?   Yes   No
   Explain:

   Spirits of violence, fear, victim, predator.

5. Have you ever participated in incest (sex with a family member)?   Yes   No
   With whom?
   Was it voluntary on your part?   Yes   No
   If not voluntary, were you actually raped?   Yes   No
   How often?
   Over what period of time?

APPENDIX A

SECTION 2

Strongman of perversion and lust; spirits of guilt and shame; forgive the perpetrator; if the act was voluntary, forgive himself. If a pattern of abuse exists, familiar spirit of lust and victim spirit. Break "soul tie."

6. Boys: Have you ever molested or raped anyone?　　　　　　Yes　　No
　　　First names:

Strongman of perversion and lust; spirits of the predator; behavior may be born out of rejection, spirits of violence, anger, rage, pride, guilt and shame. Break "soul tie."

　　Girls: Have you ever been raped?　　　　　　　　　　　Yes　　No
　　　　By whom?
　　　　Explain:

Strongman of perversion and lust; spirit of violence, victim spirit; also deal with all spirits allowed in due to the emotional response such as anger, male hatred, rejection, fear, guilt and shame. Forgive the perpetrator. If pattern exists in the person's life, familiar spirit of lust and victim spirit. Break "soul tie."

7. Have you ever committed fornication (sex while not married?)　　Yes　　No
   How many partners?
   First names and when:

Strongman of perversion and lust; spirits of guilt and shame; Break "soul tie."

Have the person repent.

8. Have you ever been involved in oral sex?　　　　　　　　Yes　　No
   With whom? (first names)

Strongman of perversion and lust; spirits of guilt and shame; Break "soul tie."

Have the person repent.

　　　　　　　　　　　　　　　　　　　　　　　　　　　　Yes　　No
9. Have you ever had sex with prostitutes?
   How many?
   When?

Strongman of perversion and lust; spirits of guilt and shame; break "soul tie."

Have the person repent.

10. Have you ever committed adultery (at least one partner married)?   Yes   No
First names and when?

Strongman of perversion and lust; spirits of guilt and shame; break "soul tie."

Have the person repent.

11. Are you currently involved in an illicit sexual relationship?   Yes   No
First name:
Are you willing to break it off?   Yes   No

Strongman of perversion and lust; spirits of guilt and shame; break "soul tie."

Have the person repent.

12. Have you ever had homosexual or lesbian desires?   Yes   No
Do you now?   Yes   No
Have you ever had a homosexual or lesbian experience?   Yes   No
With whom and when?
Do you currently participate in homosexual or lesbian activity?   Yes   No
If so, how frequently and with whom?
Are you willing to stop?   Yes   No

Strongman of perversion and lust; spirits of homosexuality, guilt and shame, self-rejection; break "soul ties."

The person must be willing to repent and stop the activity.

13. Have you ever had tendencies toward transvestite behavior?   Yes   No
Have you ever acted on transvestite tendencies?   Yes   No
If so, when and how often?
Do you now?   Yes   No
Are you willing to stop?   Yes   No

Strongman of perversion; spirits of self-rejection, self-hatred, guilt and shame.

Have the person repent and the person must be willing to stop the activity.

14. Have you ever sexually fantasized about an animal?   Yes   No
Have you committed a sex act with an animal   Yes   No
Name all animals involved:
How often and when?

Very often hereditary. Strongman of perversion and lust; spirits of bestiality, fantasy, rejection, guilt and shame; name the spirit of the animal, and evict it; (i.e. a dog would have a canine spirit, a cow would have a bovine spirit, etc.). Break "soul tie."

Have the person repent.

15. Has pornography ever attracted you?   Yes   No
    How did you become involved?
    Name of persons involved:

If material was given to him, have him forgive the person who got him involved.

To what extent have you viewed pornography?
How frequently?
When?

Have you seen pornographic movies, videos or DVDs?	Yes	No
When and where?		
Have you viewed pornographic magazines or photos?	Yes	No
Have you viewed live sex shows?	Yes	No
When and where?		
Have you viewed pornographic material on the Internet?	Yes	No
Have you participated in sexually oriented "chat rooms" or discussion groups on the Internet?	Yes	No
Have you had a sexual fetish?	Yes	No
What is it?		
Do you still view pornographic material?	Yes	No
What, when and how often?		
Do you currently purchase or rent pornographic movies, videos or DVDs or have such a channel on your home TV?	Yes	No
How frequently?		
Are you willing to discontinue any use of pornography?	Yes	No

Strongman of perversion and lust; spirits of guilt and shame; depending on the content of the material, any spirits involved such as homosexual spirits, violence, pedophilia, etc. If sexual partner encouraged use of pornography during sex, spirit of rejection, forgiveness issues.

The person must be willing to repent and stop the activity. Pray for cleansing; pray for purging of the memories of what he saw and heard.

16. Have you ever been involved in anal sex?   Yes   No
    With whom?

Strongman of perversion and lust; spirits of sodomy, control; if a homosexual experience, spirits of homosexuality. For women, common entry point for spirits of rejection, control, guilt and shame. Close all channels that were opened to demonic entry during anal sex.

In all cases of sexual perversion, self-forgiveness, and forgiveness of the other party involved need to be emphasized, cleansing ministered and inner healing prayed for. They also need to receive love, and be encouraged to share it without shame or fear.

17. Girls: Have you ever had an abortion? Yes No
    How many?
    Give dates and father's first name(s)

Spirits of death, murder, grief, guilt and shame. Forgive father of the child and anyone who pressured her into having the abortion. Break "soul ties" with the baby.

Repent and forgive herself. Causes a hostile environment in the womb for future pregnancies. Pray for cleansing and healing of the womb.

18. Boys: Have you ever fathered a child that was forcefully aborted? Yes No
    How many?
    Give dates and mother's first name(s):

Pray to forgive the mother.

    Were you in favor of the abortion? Yes No

If no, forgive the mother. If yes, repent, pray for forgiveness and forgive himself.

If the father knew of the abortion, and especially if he was in favor of it, spirits of death, murder, grief, guilt and shame.

19. Have you been plagued with desires of having sex with a child? Yes No
    Have you actually done so? Yes No
    If yes, how many times and when?

Strongman of perversion and lust; spirits of pedophilia, control, guilt and shame.

Repent and pray for forgiveness. May need to apologize to all concerned. May need to turn himself in to the authorities.

20. Have you ever had inner sexual stimulation and climax out of your control, Yes No
    especially at night? (By this I mean, do you have dreams of a personage approaching and asking to have sex with you, or just doing it, and you "feel" a presence in bed with you, then wake up with a sexual climax? This is something other that a normal nocturnal emission).

If yes, when and how frequently?

Spirit of incubus (manifests as a male) or succubus (manifests as a female); these may be familiar spirits, or gain access through witchcraft ceremonies or satanic worship.

21. Have you ever gone to a massage parlor and been sexually stimulated?   Yes   No

Strongman of perversion and lust; spirits of guilt and shame; if there was genital contact, break "soul ties."

22. Have you had sexual fantasies?   Yes   No
    Do you now?   Yes   No
    How frequently?
    What are they about?

Strongman of perversion and lust; depending on the content, homosexual spirits, spiritual adultery, marital infidelity, spirits of guilt and shame.

23. Do members of the opposite sex make uninvited comments to you of a sexual   Yes   No
    nature, tell you "dirty jokes" or behave in a sexually inappropriate manner
    toward you, or "come on" to you in any other way?

Familiar spirits of lust and perversion.

CATEGORY E   **BONDAGES AND ADDICTIONS**

1. Did any of your family as far back as you know have addictions of any   Yes   No
   kind?
   Who and to what?

Inherited Strongman of bondage.

Have you ever been or are you currently addicted to any of the following?

Alcohol	No	Currently addicted	Used to be addicted
Smoking	No	Currently addicted	Used to be addicted
Food	No	Currently addicted	Used to be addicted
Gambling	No	Currently addicted	Used to be addicted
Compulsive exercise	No	Currently addicted	Used to be addicted
Being a spendthrift	No	Currently addicted	Used to be addicted
Watching TV	No	Currently addicted	Used to be addicted
Coffee	No	Currently addicted	Used to be addicted

Marijuana	No	Currently addicted	Used to be addicted
Prescription Drugs	No	Currently addicted	Used to be addicted
Which ones?			
Street Drugs	No	Currently addicted	Used to be addicted
Which ones?			

Any other addictions?

Strongman of bondage and whoredoms, spirits of dependence, false comfort, escapism, compulsion. The spirit behind obsessive compulsive disorder (OCD) is whoredoms.
(Drugs) The specific name of the addictive drug, deception, control, plus problems drugs cause such as lust, stealing, violence, other addictions, etc.
(Alcohol) Spirits of alcohol dependence, inability to cope, deception, lying, violence.

First determine if the person is truly willing to give up the addiction and exercise the self-discipline needed to keep the demon out. If not, do not cast out the spirit of addiction. Bind the spirit of addiction and any linked spirits, and allow the person to return at a later date when he is ready to give up the addiction and walk out his deliverance.

With some addictions, especially addiction to food, the spirit of bondage may be linked with the spirit of whoredom or idolatry. The spirit of bondage would manifest in compulsion to eat, eating for false comfort or escapism. The spirit of whoredom would manifest in obsessive thinking about food, "all-or-nothing" dieting, etc. In these cases, renounce both spirits, command them to unlink, and cast them out together.
(Anorexia Nervosa and Bulimia) Hereditary spirits must go first, followed by both the spirits of anorexia and bulimia. Also spirits of death, deception, lies, violence and the deceptive body image. The spirit of the fear of getting fat must go, together with the whole rejection syndromes. When incest, rape or sexual molestation are basic causes, these spirits must also be cast out.

It is recommended that the person seek Christian counseling after deliverance to receive help with the changing of habits and thinking patterns.

CATEGORY F

1. What is your country of birth?

2. Have you lived in other countries?   Yes   No
   Which ones?

A general prayer of release is often sufficient, but specific spirits may need to be cast out.

Look for any spirits associated with the geographic area, such as spirits associated with false worship and witchcraft.

3. Where was your mother born? (city, state, nation)
   Where was your father born? (city, state, nation)

4. Where were your grandparents born? (city, state, nation)
   Maternal grandmother?
   Maternal grandfather?
   Paternal grandmother?
   Paternal grandfather?

   When there is obvious resistance from demonic ethnic or cultural spirits during a general prayer of release, identify, and cast out each one.

CATEGORY G

1. Do you suffer from any chronic illness or allergies?   Yes   No
   Which?
   Is it hereditary?   Yes   No

   Strongman of infirmity; family curses may be generational causing hereditary physical impairments such as blindness, deafness, etc. Curses must be broken before deliverance is administered. After familiar spirits have been removed, pray for cleansing and healing. When praying for people with seizures or asthma, first bind "the strongman" very tightly. If symptoms start to manifest while you are praying, remind the spirit it is forbidden to operate.

   After freedom, anoint the person with oil and pray for healing.

2. Have you had any severe accidents or traumas that stand out in your mind not   Yes   No
   already mentioned above? (These can be emotional or physical traumas).
   Explain:
   Who was involved in the trauma with you? (i.e. car wreck, I was with my mother)

   Break "soul ties" with anyone involved in an accident with a person. The trauma creates a soul tie.

   Pray trauma prayer.

3. Have you ever received a blood transfusion?   Yes   No
4. Have you ever donated blood?   Yes   No

   Break "soul ties" with anyone from whom you have received blood or to whom you have given blood. You will usually not know who the person is even if a family member

donated it for you. If the donated blood isn't a match for you, you will be given blood from someone who matches. Simply ask God to break the "soul ties" that were created with the person who received your blood or whose blood you received.

5. Describe yourself in as many one or two word phrases as you can:
a.	h.
b.	i
c.	j.
d.	k.
e.	l.
f.	m.
g.	n.

6. Do you have any other problems you feel this questionnaire hasn't uncovered? Explain as fully as you can. Try to pinpoint when they began and if they were connected with a trauma of some kind or if you were victimized or if you invited the problem in.

Much of this material is taken from the book *Evicting Demonic Intruders* and *Freedom in Christ* both by Noel and Phyl Gibson, published by New Wine Press. Distributed in the USA by Gospel Light, and from *How to Cast Out Demons* by Doris Wagner, published by Regal.

APPENDIX A

SECTION 3

CHILD QUESTIONNAIRE KEY

Name:		Age:	Sex:	
Name of parent completing this questionnaire:				
What is the best time to schedule your deliverance?	Weekday		Evening	Weekend

1. Who does this child live with?

2. Mother's Name   Father's Name

3. Is the mother a Christian?   Yes   No

4. Has the mother gone through deliverance at this church?   Yes   No
   If yes, when?

   What were some of the generational spirits and/or special problems she dealt with in her deliverance that we may need to deal with while praying for your child?

   Pray against appropriate spirits named.

5. Is the father a Christian?   Yes   No

6. Has the father gone through deliverance at this church?   Yes   No
   If yes, when?

   What were some of the generational spirits and/or special problems he dealt with in his deliverance that we may need to deal with while praying for your child?

   Pray against appropriate spirits named.

7. If either parent has not gone through deliverance, what special problems or generational spirits do you feel we may need to deal with while praying for your child?

   Pray against appropriate spirits named.

8. Is this child born again?   Yes   No
   If yes at what age?

9. Has this child been baptized?   Yes   No

10. Has this child been filled with the Holy Spirit?   Yes   No
    If yes, at what age?

11. Does this child attend children's church?   Yes   No
   If yes, for how long?

12. Does this child pray?   Yes   No
   If yes, how often?

13. At the time of this child's birth, were his/her parents (circle one)

   Married to each other   Married to others   Not married

   Generational covenant breaking spirit, spirit of rejection

14. Are the parents currently (circle one)

   Married to each other   Divorced   Never married to each other

   Generational covenant breaking spirit, spirit of rejection

15. If this child's parents are divorced, what age was this child when the divorce
   took place?
   How did the child deal with the divorce?

   *Generational covenant breaking spirit, spirit of rejection, fear of abandonment, spirits of
   abandonment, rebellion, anger, resentment, self pity, manipulative spirits*

16. Does this child have (circle all that apply)

   Step-mother   Step-father   Step-siblings

   Spirit of rejection, spirit of rebellion

17. Does this child currently have a step-parent living in the home?   Yes   No
   Who?

   *Spirit of rejection, self rejection, fear of rejection, spirits of rebellion, anger
   resentment, self pity, manipulative spirit, spirit of control*

APPENDIX A

SECTION 3

18. Are there now or have there been other adults living in the home with this child?   Yes   No

    Who and when?

    Spirit of rejection, spirit of rebellion

19. Describe this child's relationship with his/her:

    Mother:

    Father:

    Step-mother:

    Step-father:

    Maternal grandmother:

    Maternal grandfather:

    Paternal grandmother:

    Paternal grandfather:

    Look for areas of forgiveness

    Spirit of rejection, spirit of rebellion

20. Does this child have siblings?

Name	Age
Name	Age
Name	Age
Name	Age

21. Where does this child fall in the sibling line?

    Depending on the family, any position in the sibling line can allow in a spirit of rejection.

22. What is this child's relationship with siblings?

SECTION 3

Look for forgiveness issues and spirits of rejection, jealousy, guilt and shame

CATEGORY A

1. Did the biological mother contemplate an abortion or have an abortion, or have a miscarriage before this child was conceived?   Yes   No

   If yes, spirit of murder, spirit of death, spirit of fear

2. Did the biological mother contemplate an abortion with this child?   Yes   No

   Spirit of rejection

3. Was this child planned?   Yes   No
   a. If not, what was the parent's initial reaction to the pregnancy?

   After the initial reaction, were the parents happy about the baby?   Yes   No

   If no, spirit of rejection

   b. Was this child conceived out of wedlock?   Yes   No

   Spirit of rejection, spirit of lust

   c. Was this child the result of a violent conception (i.e. rape)?   Yes   No

   Spirits of fear, anger, rage, violence, lust, spirit of rejection

   d. Was this child adopted   Yes   No

   If yes, do you know anything about the biological parents? (list all you can recall):   Yes   No

   Spirit of rejection, spirit of abandonment, any hereditary spirits associated with known characteristics of behaviors in biological parents, i.e. spirits of addiction, spirits of lust

   Have the child forgive the biological parents.

e. Was this child the right sex for the mother?   Yes   No

f. Was this child the right sex for the father?   Yes   No

   Spirits of rejection, self hatred, homosexuality

4. What was the mother's physical and emotional condition during the pregnancy?
   (circle all that apply)

Calm	Headaches	Depressed
Peaceful	Nervous	Worried
Happy	Fearful	Anxious
Physically ill	Angry	Fighting
Smoking	Alcohol use	Drug use
Listened to loud music	Loving environment	Strong emotional support
Little emotional support		

5. Did the mother or child suffer complications or difficulties during the   Yes   No
   birth?

   Spirits of bondage, addiction, heaviness, fear, spirit of whoredoms

a. Was the labor induced?   Yes   No

b. Was labor extremely fast?   Yes   No

   If the birth was very fast, the baby may suffer from shock, fear & insecurity. Pray trauma prayer.

   Spirit of fear, spirit of death, spirit of infirmity

c. Was pain medication used during labor?   Yes   No

d. Was the labor protracted or extremely long?   Yes   No

   Babies born after protracted labor are often drowsy.

   Spirit of apathy

e. Was the child delivered by cesarean section?   Yes   No

f. Were forceps used during delivery?   Yes   No

   Spirit of trauma, spirit of fear

g. Was the mother put to sleep during delivery?   Yes   No

   Spirit of apathy, any spirit that took advantage of an unguarded mind

h. Did the child suffer from birth defects or complications after birth? Yes   No

   Children who have had difficulties at birth need release for the individual trauma and other problems mentioned.

   Spirit of fear, spirit of rejection

i. Other: (explain in detail)   Yes   No

CATEGORY B

1. How soon after this child's birth was a parent allowed to hold him/her?

   Spirit of rejection, spirit of abandonment

2. Where was the child placed after birth? (circle all that apply)

   Incubator (how long)?   In room with mother

   ICU (how long)?   Hospital nursery

   Spirits of rejection, abandonment, death, spirit of infirmity

3. Was the child breast fed or bottle fed?

a. Was the child unable to be breast fed?   Yes   No
   If yes, explain:

   Spirit of rejection, spirit of abandonment

b. Did the child have problems with allergies to formula or keeping formula down? Yes No

Look for eating disorders and food allergies.

4. Did the child have good eye contact with the parent during feeding and when the parent spoke to the child? Yes No

Spirit of rejection, spirit of abandonment

CATEGORY C

1. What habits does this child exhibit? (circle all that apply)

Sucking thumb or fingers	No	Used to be a problem	Currently a problem
Nail biting	No	Used to be a problem	Currently a problem
Attachment to object (blanket or toy; what was the object?)	No	Used to be a problem	Currently a problem

The above three habits might tell us that bonding with parent and child may be disturbed and bonding has been replaced with the object. Break that bond and release a passion and drawing of parent and child to one another with healing of the relationship. The child may exhibit defensiveness along with distrust and disrespect of authority.

Spirits of rejection, insecurity, self pity, hopelessness, rebellion, bitterness, various fears

Hair twisting	No	Used to be a problem	Currently a problem

This may indicate nervousness.

Spirit of fear, spirit of rejection

Clinging to caregiver (more than age appropriate)	No	Used to be a problem	Currently a problem

Spirits of fear, abandonment, rejection

Increased amount of crying (for no apparent cause)	No	Used to be a problem	Currently a problem

Consider an inherited spirit of grief

Cursing or bad words	No	Used to be a problem	Currently a problem

Generational or personal spirit of obscenity, blaspheming spirits

Lying	No	Used to be a problem	Currently a problem

Spirit of lying, spirit of deception

Stealing	No	Used to be a problem	Currently a problem

Spirit of lying, spirit of deception

Cheating (games, school work, etc.	No	Used to be a problem	Currently a problem
Cover-up/excessive excuses	No	Used to be a problem	Currently a problem
Exaggeration	No	Used to be a problem	Currently a problem
Evasiveness	No	Used to be a problem	Currently a problem

Spirits of lying, of deception, rejection, spirit of fear

Withdrawing	No	Used to be a problem	Currently a problem
Pouting	No	Used to be a problem	Currently a problem

Spirits of rejection, fear, self pity; if used to get his/her own way or punish others, spirit of control

Unfairness	No	Used to be a problem	Currently a problem

Spirits of self pity, rejection

Bed wetting	No	Used to be a problem	Currently a problem

Was there a trauma around that time?   Yes   No

If so, what was it?

Make sure you are not dealing with a medical problem. If not, bedwetting may indicate insecurity and fear. It can also be a child's method of showing displeasure for a real or imagined hurt or wrong. In the event of some trauma, pray for release from the dominating spirit involved together with those listed below. If rejection has caused the problem, release the fear of rejection. Also break the habit and pray for cleansing and healing.

Spirits of insecurity, fear, spirits of rejection, self-rejection, fear of rejection

List any other habits not mentioned:

CATEGORY D

1. Has this child suffered from any of the following? (Mark all that apply and describe what happened and/or who was involved. (Example: mother, father, playmate, etc.):

Excessive physical punishment (even one time)

Spirits of fear, rebellion, rejection

Over reaction or harsh verbal reprimand

Spirits of fear, rebellion, rejection

Accidents (falls, car accident, hit while playing, etc.)

Spirits of death, fear, infirmity, rejection

Surgeries or illness requiring hospitalization

Spirits of abandonment, infirmity, death, fear, rejection

Extended time away from parents

Spirits of abandonment, fear, rejection

Anesthesia

High fever with delirium

The above two produce an unguarded mind state. Come against any spirits that took advantage.

CATEGORY E

1. How is this child most often disciplined in the home? (circle all that apply and number in the order of frequency)

Time out	Spanking	Grounded	Raised voice
Shamed	Threats	Fear	Reasoned with
Called names	Other		

Depending on the discipline, look for spirits that would be associated with that type of punishment.

APPENDIX A

SECTION 3

Spirits of shame, fear, rebellion

2. What type of discipline works best with this child? (circle all that apply and number in the order of frequency)

Time Out	Spanking	Grounded	Raised voice
Shamed	Threats	Fear	Reasoned with
Called names	Other		

3. Who is the main disciplinarian in the home?

Mother   Father   Other

4. How does this child respond to authority? (Teachers, Church leaders, parents, etc).

Gets along well	Is often in trouble	Is passive
Gets angry easily	Is eager to please	Is the teacher's pet
Disobeys most of the time	Temper tantrums	Is afraid of authority figures

Spirits of rebellion, control, performance, people pleasing spirit

5. How does this child get along with his/her siblings? (circle all that apply)

Is a leader	Is a follower	Fights a lot
Instigates trouble	Is selfish	Is bossy
Gets along well with siblings	Demands attention	Is jealous
Gets picked on by others	Other	

Spirits of control, victimization, predator spirit, spirits of rejection, jealousy, rebellion

6. How does this child get along with other children? (circle all that apply)

Has one or two close friends	Has no friends	Has lots of friends
Is a leader	Is a follower	Fights a lot
Is bossy	Instigates trouble	Gets picked on by others
Gets along well with other Children	Other	

7. Which of the following would best describe this child? (circle all that apply)

Happy	Easy going	Serious
Carefree	Sad	Quiet
Easily excited	Lots of interests	Active
Sedentary	Talkative	Questioning
Easily frustrated	Outgoing	Playful
Shy	Hyperactive	Over-eager to please
Selfish	Rebellious	Angry
Fearful	Bossy	Whines
Unforgiving	Forgiving	Other

Look for spirits associated with problem behavior.

8. How does this child spend most of his/her leisure time? (circle all that apply)

Playing outside	Reading	Watching TV
Playing with other children	Playing alone	In his room
Demanding parents attention	Listening to music	Playing a sport
Talking on the phone	Coloring	Computer/Internet
Studying school work	Other:	

Look for spirits of rejection, self rejection, escapism, etc.

9. How does this child take care of his/her belongings? (circle all that apply)

Keeps room tidy	Keeps room messy	Takes care of toys
Breaks or neglects care of toys		

Spirits of rebellion, self rejection, anger

10. Does this child have a pet?   Yes   No
    If yes, does he/she take care of the pet, feed & play with it?   Yes   No

Spirits of rebellion, possibly a "soul tie."

11. Does this child enjoy school?   Yes   No

SECTION 3

Are his/her grades acceptable to this child?   Yes   No
Are his/her grades acceptable to the mother?   Yes   No
Are his/her grades acceptable to the father?   Yes   No
Does he/she have any problems with schoolwork?   Yes   No

Question carefully; the child may have a learning disability, or be hyperactive and need medication. Don't give medical advice, but try to ascertain if this is a demonic problem, disinterest in school, poor teachers or a condition requiring medical care. It is alright to ask if the child has been tested or seen by a doctor, if there is a problem with learning, but don't recommend that the child be put on medication.

12. Has or does this child suffer from any of the following? (circle all that apply)

Fear of teacher	Used to be a problem	Currently a problem
Fear of tests	Used to be a problem	Currently a problem
Fear of failure	Used to be a problem	Currently a problem
Fear of punishment	Used to be a problem	Currently a problem
Learning difficulties	Used to be a problem	Currently a problem
Public embarrassment at school	Used to be a problem	Currently a problem
Insecurity / inferiority	Used to be a problem	Currently a problem
Competition / must be first	Used to be a problem	Currently a problem
Peer pressure	Used to be a problem	Currently a problem
Persecution from peers or teachers	Used to be a problem	Currently a problem
Hates to go to school	Used to be a problem	Currently a problem
Told he/she was stupid or wouldn't be successful academically	Used to be a problem	Currently a problem
Singled out and/or picked on by peers	Used to be a problem	Currently a problem

These issues may represent the effects of spirits of rejection, fear and shame or may be door openers for them.

Look for the time the door was opened to each occurrence circled and pray against the spirits that came in at that time. For instance, if a teacher embarrassed or unfairly punished the child, a spirit of shame, rejection, unforgiveness, rebellion or fear of authority might have entered. If a teacher or a friend persecuted the child, a spirit of shame or rejection might have entered, etc.

CATEGORY F

1. Has this child's parents or grandparents been in any cults (circle all that apply)

Christian Science	Myself	Others		Rosicrucian	Myself	Others
Armstrong Worldwide COG	Myself	Others		Gurus	Myself	Others

Christadelphians	Myself	Others	Unity	Myself	Others
Jehovah's Witnesses	Myself	Others	Mormons	Myself	Others
Children of Love	Myself	Others	Scientology	Myself	Others
Religious Communes	Myself	Others	Bahai	Myself	Others
Unification Church (Moonies)	Myself	Others	Theosophy	Myself	Others
Eastern Religions (specify)	Myself	Others	Anthroposophy	Myself	Others
Native Religions	Myself	Others	Spiritists Church	Myself	Others
Others:	Myself	Others			

Spirits of a false religion, deception, doubt and unbelief; you can address spirits by the name of the cult.

2. To your knowledge, has any close family member been a member of:

Freemason	Odd Fellow	Rainbow Girl	Mormon
Eastern Star	Shriner	Daughter of the Nile	Amaranth
Job's Daughter	Elk	DeMolay	Fraternities
Sororities	Secret Organizations or Societies		
If so who?			

Does this child suffer from (circle all that apply)

Hardness of Emotion	Apathy	Confusion	Financial Disaster
Comprehension Difficulties	Skepticism	Unbelief	Doubt
Infirmities	Frequent Sickness	Allergies	

Is there any Masonic regalia or memorabilia in your possession?   Yes   No
If yes, what?

Spirits of idolatry, occultism and witchcraft, spirits of mockery, antichrist, spirits of confusion, doubt and unbelief, infirmity, financial disaster, spirit of false religion, deception; pray to close the third eye.

Have the parent pray the Freemasonry prayer. Ensure that the parents destroy any regalia or memorabilia.

3. Does this child seem mentally confused?   Don't know   Yes   No
   Have mental blocks?   Don't know   Yes   No

Spirit of antichrist from Freemasonry, spirits of occultism, witchcraft or Satanism, spirits of confusion, heaviness

4. Does this child day dream?   Don't know   Yes   No

*All spirits which dominate fantasy must be cast out, and the mind thoroughly
cleansed and renewed. Symptom of Freemasonry, look for elements of the day
dream revealing other spirits.*

**Determine the extent, frequency and, if known, nature of day dreams; depending on the
results you may be dealing with escapism.**

5. Does this child have bad dreams, or night terrors?   Don't know   Yes   No
   If yes, what is the nature of the dreams?

   Spirit of fear, symptom of Freemasonry; look for elements revealing other spirits.

6. Does this child suffer from sleeplessness   Yes   No

   Spirit of fear, symptom of Freemasonry, also fear of death

7. Does this child sleep walk?   Yes   No

   Spirit of fear

8. Has this child ever exhibited any suicidal tendencies?   Yes   No

   Has he/she tried?   Yes   No

   Spirit of death, spirit of heaviness

9. Has this child ever spoken a death wish, i.e. "I'd be better off dead",   Yes   No
   "I wish I were dead', etc.?

   Have child repent; break word curse.

   *Spirits of heaviness, death, self-pity, grief and mourning, deaf and dumb spirit, also
   symptom of Freemasonry; if the child was trying to get attention, spirit of rejection.
   If the child was trying to get his/her way, spirit of control.*

10. Has this child exhibited any fear of any of the following? (circle all that apply)

Failure	Inadequacy
Authority Figures	The dark

Violence	Death
Being alone	Satan and evil spirits
Crowds	Women
Men	Heights
Enclosed places	Accident
Insects	Dogs
Spiders	Snakes
Water	Loud noises
Animals	Open places
Pain	Flying in an airplane
Storms	Lightening
Being left alone (abandoned)	Other (specify)

Strongman of fear; name the demons by the particular fear they cause such as: "a spirit of the fear of the dark," "fear of violence," "fear of failure," etc. Also symptoms of Freemasonry may be entry points or symptoms of other spirits.

CATEGORY G

1. To you knowledge has any curse been placed on your child or your family?   Yes   No
   By whom?
   Why?

   Explain:

   Always break any curses identified before praying for anything else. Look for generational patterns such as: The eldest son of every married descendant is born blind. The first daughter of every family dies in childhood. Suicides take place in families at regular intervals. Break the power of the curse, evict any oppressive demons and pray for the healing of victims. All curses must be broken and every oppressive demon that has entered because of the oaths or curses cast out before praying for cleansing and healing.

2. To your knowledge, have any relatives of this child as far back as you know,   Yes   No
   been involved in occultism or witchcraft?
   Who and doing what?

   To what extent?

   Was this child ever dedicated to Satan or any demonic worship?   Yes   No
   Has that dedication been renounced?   Yes   No

   Strongman of divination, spirit of witchcraft, familiar spirits, antichrist

3. To your knowledge, has this child ever had any involvement with any of the following? (circle all that apply):

Fortunetellers	Tarot cards	Ouija boards
Astrology	Séances	Mediums
Palmistry	Color therapy	Levitation
Astral travel	Horoscopes	Good luck charms
Black magic	Demon worship	Asked for a spirit guide
Clairvoyance	Crystals	Done automatic handwriting
New Age Movement	Reincarnation	Past lives regression
Psychics	Iridology	Been to a curandero or native healer
Been involved in any other witchcraft or demonic or Satanic things?		Yes No

If so, what?

To your knowledge have you or any of this child's ancestors ever been   Yes   No
involved in any of the above?
Which ones?

No matter how innocent the involvement, this is an open door. Cast out any spirits involved.

Spirits of divination, false religion

Note: the following games, movies, television programs and music are not an exhaustive list, but it is as current as our research was able to determine at the time. These lists should be updated frequently to address the current market.

4. Has this child played games or played with toys such as: (circle all that apply)

Fable Role Playing Game – X-Box	Used to play	Currently plays
Starcraft Role Playing computer game	Used to play	Currently plays
Everquest Role Playing computer game	Used to play	Currently plays
World of Warcraft Role Playing computer game	Used to play	Currently plays
Dungeons & Dragons	Used to play	Currently plays
Pokemon	Used to play	Currently plays
Magic 8 Ball	Used to play	Currently plays
Magic – the – Gathering	Used to play	Currently plays
Visionaires	Used to play	Currently plays
Moon Dreamers	Used to play	Currently plays
Vampire Role Play Games	Used to play	Currently plays

Sword and Sorcery Battle Gear	Used to play	Currently plays
Starriors	Used to play	Currently plays
Secret Wars	Used to play	Currently plays
Other World	Used to play	Currently plays
Masters of the Universe	Used to play	Currently plays
Snake Mountain	Used to play	Currently plays
Robo Force	Used to play	Currently plays
Super Natural	Used to play	Currently plays
Alien Blood & Monster Flesh	Used to play	Currently plays
Troll Dolls	Used to play	Currently plays
Pegasus	Used to play	Currently plays
Unicorns	Used to play	Currently plays
Gremlins	Used to play	Currently plays
ET	Used to play	Currently plays

Fable role Playing Game – X- Box: Starcraft Role Playing Computer Game; Everquest role Playing Computer Game; World of Warcraft Role Playing Computer Game; *Witchcraft, murder, death, loss of identity.* Role playing games can result in a person taking on a demonic personality of the character played.

Many of these toys and games are evidently occult by their name. Some are less obvious. Dungeons & Dragons: teaches demonology, witchcraft, voodoo, murder, rape, blasphemy, suicide, assassination, insanity, sexual perversion, Satan worship, barbarianism, cannibalism, sadism, demon summoning, necromancy, divination and human sacrifice. Role playing can result in a person taking on a demonic personality of the character played.

Pokemon: Pokemon means pocket monster. These toys and games teach witchcraft and evoke curses.

Visionaries: This toy features Knight of the Magical Light. Extar has a mystical personality with magical holographic power to see the enemy. This figure represents witchcraft and divination.

Ghost Busters: Banshee Ghost Bomber drops Ecto-Plazam on its victim. Ecto-Plazam (ectoplasm) "in spiritism is the vaporous luminous substance supposed to emanate from the medium's body during a trance" (Webster's New Universal Unabridged Dictionary). This is blatantly occult.

Moon Dreamers: Magic dream crystals make wishes come true when given Dream Gazer, the mystical sorceress. This bears a New Age occult concept.

Sword and Sorcery Battle Gear: A fantasy of sorcery, the occult and violence.

Starriors: Warrior robots kill for control of the earth using chain saws, buzz saws, drills, spikes, reams and vibrator chisels. Starriors are extremely violent.

Secret Wars: In this game one fights aliens with "the force", a counterfeit of God. There are wild mutants and hideous creatures.

Other World: This game is similar to Dungeons and Dragons. The player battles with warlords, demons and dragons. It is violent.

Masters of the Universe: Skeletor is an evil lord of destruction, beastmen and evil goddesses. It is based upon sorcery, and witchcraft.

Snake Mountain: The player acts like a snake while working the snake's jaw as it speaks. The child pretends to be a snake.

Robo Force: An evil robot empire. It has a killer instinct and a crusher hand. Robo Force is a dictator and destroyer. It is very violent. Other transformers are Voltron, Robotech, GoBots and Transformers. The evil of such toys is not easily discerned until they are observed in their corresponding cartoons, then their extreme violence is seen along with occult overtones and, in some sexual implications.

Super Naturals: These characters display powers of divination through insight into the future. Other occult powers include snake charming and hypnotism. Witchcraft is brought in through pentagram power released by each toy. Books that accompany the toys carry occult stories.

Alien Blood and Monster Flesh: This is sold in cans!

Troll dolls: Trolls are either giants or dwarf-like creatures which originated in Scandinavian folklore. They inhabit hills, caves or live underground. Webster's New Collegiate Dictionary defines *troll* as a "demon".

Pegasus: A mythical flying horse from the Dungeon & Dragons monster manual. Pegasus originated in Greek mythology, and is said to have been born of the blood of the decapitated Medusa.

Unicorns: These mythical creatures are also monsters listed in the Dungeon & Dragons manual. Medieval kings and popes used amulets supposedly made from its horns. They believed it had magical and healing powers. The unicorn is a long-standing occult beast of a schizophrenic nature - at one time docile and loving, laying its head in the lap of a maiden; then aggressive and violent in goring its enemies to death.

Gremlins: They are violent, grotesque, sadistic and cannibalistic. They also employ transformation which is a New Age concept. Webster defines *gremlin* as: "a creature supposed to interfere with the smoothness of any procedure". Thus, a gremlin represents a curse.

Spirits of divination and familiar spirits as well as spirits of the obvious ones associated with the title of the game; spirits of necromancy, witchcraft, murder and spirit guides; spirits of fear, violence, murder; these will depend on what games were played.

Taken in part from *A Manual For Children's Deliverance* by Frank and Ida Mae Hammond, 1996, Impact Children's Books, Inc. 332 Leffingwell Ave., Kirkwood, MO 63122

5. Has this child read books or seen cartoons, movies or TV shows with themes about the occult, supernatural, ghosts, science fiction, Wicca, vampires or werewolves? (circle all that apply)

That's so Raven	Used to watch	Currently watches
Jack Ass	Used to watch	Currently watches
Tales from the Crypt	Used to watch	Currently watches
Digemon	Used to watch	Currently watches
Pokemon	Used to watch	Currently watches

Gremlins	Used to watch	Currently watches
Power Rangers	Used to watch	Currently watches
Masters of the Universe	Used to watch	Currently watches
Ninja Turtles	Used to watch	Currently watches
Ghost Busters	Used to watch	Currently watches
ET	Used to watch	Currently watches
So Weird	Used to watch	Currently watches
Buffy the Vampire Slayer	Used to watch	Currently watches
Sabrina the Teenage Witch	Used to watch	Currently watches
Alex Mac	Used to watch	Currently watches
Angel	Used to watch	Currently watches
Charmed	Used to watch	Currently watches
Harry Potter	Used to watch	Currently watches
Medium	Used to watch	Currently watches
Ghost Whisperer	Used to watch	Currently watches
Others (list by name):		

What were the child's reaction?

Most of these were addressed above with the toys and games. The problem with Buffy the Vampire Slayer and Sabrina the Teenage Witch is apparent by their titles. Any movie that portrays witches as "good" cause problems because they confuse the child in his ability to discern good from evil. These programs also deal with necromancy, witchcraft, curses, blood shed, evoking and asking in demons and spirit guides. Angel is a series on prime time television in which the main character is chasing demons. The demons are portrayed as some good and some bad. Again this causes confusion as well as desensitizing the child to evil. Medium and Ghost Whisperer are TV shows in which the lead characters get advise and insight from spirits of the dead.

Spirits of divination and familiar spirits as well as spirits of the obvious ones associated with the title of the books or movies. Spirits of necromancy witchcraft, murder and spirit guides. Filthy spirits that sexually attack or rape people, appearing as gray shapes, but are able to cause physical stimulation. Spirits of fear, violence and murder. These will depend on what games were played, and what films were watched.

6. Does this child play video games?   Yes   No
    How much time does he/she spend playing these games?
    Has he/she played any of the following Nintendo Games? (circle all that apply)

Devils	Used to play	Currently plays
Dragons	Used to play	Currently plays
Babylon	Used to play	Currently plays
Mysterious Forces	Used to play	Currently plays
Mythical Beasts	Used to play	Currently plays

Mythical gods	Used to play	Currently plays
Wizards	Used to play	Currently plays
Warriors	Used to play	Currently plays
Magic Power	Used to play	Currently plays
Black Princes	Used to play	Currently plays
Minions of Hell	Used to play	Currently plays
Evil Monsters	Used to play	Currently plays
Magic Items	Used to play	Currently plays
Beelzebub	Used to play	Currently plays
Ectoplasm	Used to play	Currently plays
Curse of Death	Used to play	Currently plays
Evil Spirits	Used to play	Currently plays
Black Magic	Used to play	Currently plays
Magical Scrolls	Used to play	Currently plays
Druids	Used to play	Currently plays
Witchcraft	Used to play	Currently plays
Evil Wizards	Used to play	Currently plays
Sorcery	Used to play	Currently plays
Potions	Used to play	Currently plays
Demons	Used to play	Currently plays
Curses	Used to play	Currently plays
Necromancy	Used to play	Currently plays
Holy Water	Used to play	Currently plays
Buddha	Used to play	Currently plays
Monsters	Used to play	Currently plays
Magical Spells	Used to play	Currently plays
Magical Swords	Used to play	Currently plays
Magical Books	Used to play	Currently plays
Beasts	Used to play	Currently plays
Wands and Witches	Used to play	Currently plays

There has been a marriage of electronics and the occult. It has birthed everything from computerized demonology to seemingly harmless but powerfully seductive video games. These games are as progressively addictive as drugs. Young players usually start out with the less violent ones such as Donkey-Kong, Pac-Man and Smurf. Tiring of these easy games, the children progress on to more challenging ones which often provide increased emphasis upon violence and occultism. The names of the Nintendo games listed are self explanatory. When praying for the teen, try to determine the effect the games have had on his belief system especially in the realm of reality verses fantasy. It is best to destroy the books, videos, etc. Advise the teen of the importance of this.

Spirits of divination and familiar spirits, spirits of death, murder, violence and control as well as the obvious ones associated with the title of the video.

APPENDIX A

SECTION 3

7. Has this child watched films with extremely violent themes or scenes, or   Yes   No
    with scenes portraying graphic violence or injury to human beings or animals?

    Strongman of fear, spirits of violence, divination, occult, familiar spirits,
    spirit of murder

    What when and how often?
    If yes, what were the child's reactions?

8. Has he/she watched professional wrestling?

                                                          Yes   No
    Depending on the person's devotion to and reaction to the sport; spirits of fear,
    violence, murder, death

9. What music does this child listen to?   Secular   Christian
    What groups?
    If Secular, do you listen to: (circle all that apply)

Grunge	Nirvana	Pearl Jam	Alice in Chains	Other

Spirits of rebellion, death, witchcraft, Satanism, murder, lust, perversion, violence,
bestiality, bondage

**These groups encourage the use of drugs as well as activity associated with the spirits
listed, also hardness of emotion and an unkempt hippy attitude.**

R & B	Ludacris	Lil Jon	50 Cent	Snoop Dawg	Other

Spirits of violence, perversion, lust, pornography, murder, rebellion

**These groups encourage gang activity, multiple partner sex, the use of pornography and
violence.**

Pop	Britany Spears	Christina Aguilera	Ryan Cabrera	Other

Spirits of lust, rebellion, perversion

These groups encourage illicit sex and no accountability.

Classic Rock	Led Zeppelin	Leonard Skinnard	Rush	Door	Jimi Hendricks

Spirits of perversion, rebellion, occultic Satanism, lust, violence, murder, bondage.

These groups encourage the use of drugs and produce hardness of emotion.

Heavy Metal	Mega Death	Slayer	Iron Maiden	Korn	Other

Spirits of lust, rebellion, perversion, occultic Satanism, violence, murder, death.

These groups encourage the use of drugs.

Emo	The Used	The Black Maria	Straylight Run	Senses Fall	Other

Spirits of rejection, depression, guilt, shame, suicide, drugs, homosexuality, rebellion.

A broad title that covers many different styles of emotionally charged punk rock. Some of these kids dress metro sexually (dressing and acting homosexually without being gay).

Alternative/Punk	Weezer	The Donnas	Incubus	Ramones	Goo Goo Dolls

Spirits of rebellion, rejection, death, suicide, anger, hate, isolation.

These kids will dress to stand out and shock people. Wearing chains, dog collars, spikes, dressed in all black, Mohawks and sometimes funky hair colors.

How much time does he/she spend listening to it?

10. Has this child ever celebrated Halloween?   Yes   No

This is a celebrations honoring demonic powers.

Spirits of divination, occult, witchcraft, idolatry, familiar spirits

11. Are you or your parents superstitious?   Yes   No
12. Is this child superstitious?   Yes   No

Spirits of divination, occult, doubt and unbelief, witchcraft, fear of the unknown

13. Has this child ever worn or kept any of the following? (circle all that apply):

Lucky charms	Fetishes	Amulets
Peace Symbols	Ankh	Pyramids
Tai Chi Symbols	Swastika	Caduceus
Power crystals	Yin / Yang	Buddha beads
Signs of the zodiac		

Does he/she have any in his/her possession?

Yes   No

Ensure that the item is destroyed.

Spirits of divination, occult, doubt and unbelief, witchcraft, fear of the unknown; deal with spirits associated with the specific item.

14. Does this child have in his/her possession any symbols of idols or spirit worship such as? (circle all that apply):

Buddha	Totem Poles	Masks
Carvings	Pagan Symbols	Fetish Objects or Feathers
Gargoyles	Obelisks	Statues or Pictures of Dragons or Snakes
Rosary	Zodiac Symbols	Statues or Pictures of Saints
Native American art or jewelry depicting spiritual subjects or symbols		

If so, what?

Ensure that the person destroys the item.

Spirits of divination, occult, doubt and unbelief, witchcraft, fear of the unknown; deal with spirits associated with the specific item.

15. Does this child have any pictures or posters of a demonic theme, such as   Yes   No
music groups, etc?

Depending on the subject and content of the picture, deal with spirits associated with the item.

Ensure that the item is destroyed. Be sure to encourage the parent to talk with the child and help him/her to make the decision to destroy anything that belongs to him/her.

16. Has this child ever learned any of the martial arts?   Yes   No

If so, which?
Does he/she practice it now?   Yes   No

Spirits of eastern religions, spirits of each martial art form, plus spirits of anger, violence, murder, idolatry, antichrist, control.

17. Does this child have any tattoos?   Yes   No
    If so, of what?

    Spirits of rebellion and lawlessness; any spirits associated with the specific tattoo must be cast out and the power of the tattoo broken, i.e. tattoos of dragons symbolize Satan and/or rebellion and the occult, some tattoos have themes of violence, murder, lust. If the subject of the tattoo is demonic, it should be removed if possible.

    Ask the person the reason for getting the tattoo. Was it rebellion, peer pressure, etc. and pray accordingly.

18. Has this child ever had a loved one who died?   Yes   No

    If so, who and when?
    Did he/she mourn or grieve for them?   Yes   No
    Does he/she now?   Yes   No

    Spirits of death, grief and mourning, fear, spirits that transfer as a person dies, especially Death

19. Is this child extremely competitive?   Yes   No

    May be born out of rejection, pride, anger, fear. Identify the nature and reason for the competitiveness and deal with the spirit behind it.

20. Does this child have an imaginary playmate?   Yes   No
    Does this playmate speak to the child or give instructions? (explain):

    At what age did this begin?
    Was there any significant event prior to this?   Yes   No
    What was it?

    Determine if the playmate talked to the person or gave him/her instructions, guidance, or advice. If so, familiar spirit and spirit guide.

21. Has this child exhibited any significant changes in behavior such as (circle all that apply)

Drop in school grades	Loss of interest in school, church, friends or activities	Rebelliousness
Lack of interest in appearance or hygiene	Drastic change in friends	Increased interest in things of a sexual nature

Did anything significant happen to this child prior to these changes?   Yes   No

What was it?

Try to find out if there was some sort of trauma surrounding the behavior change. Look for doors that might have allowed in demonic influence.

Depending on the behavior and any identified cause, cast out any related spirits such as spirits of rejection, rebellion, fear, lust (whatever fits)

22. Does this child display any signs of drug or alcohol use?   Don't know   Yes   No

    Has this child ever experimented with drugs or alcohol?   Don't know   Yes   No

    Spirits of rebellion, bondage, rejection, depression, fear, self-rejection

CATEGORY H

1. To your knowledge has this child ever been sexually molested?   Yes   No

    Strongman of perversion and lust. Forgive the perpetrator and anyone who failed to protect the child from the molestation. Also, deal with all spirits allowed in due to the emotional response such as anger, hatred of the opposite sex, rejection, fear, guilt and shame. Break "soul tie." If pattern exists in the person's life, familiar spirit of lust and victim spirit.

2. Has this child ever committed a sex act with an animal?   Yes   No

    Very often hereditary. Strongman of perversion and lust; spirits of bestiality, fantasy, rejection, guilt and shame; name the spirit of the animal, and evict it; (i.e. a dog would have a canine spirit, a cow would have a bovine spirit, etc.). Break "soul tie."

    Have the child repent.

3. Has this child ever been involved with inappropriate touching with another child?   Yes   No

Was it a mutual experimentation (like playing doctor)?	Yes	No
Was the other child the opposite sex?	Yes	No
Was this child a victim of this act?	Yes	No

Spirits of lust and perversion, spirit of homosexuality if the other child was the same sex. Victim spirit, predator spirit, spirits of guilt and shame. Break "soul ties."

4. Does this child masturbate?   Yes   No

   In children, usually the first evidence of hereditary lust. Strongman of perversion and lust; spirits of guilt and shame; if compulsive problem, spirits of bondage, whoredoms and addiction.

5. To your knowledge has this child ever viewed any pornographic material?

   If material was given to the child have him/her forgive the person who got him involved.

   Spirits of perversion and lust, guilt and shame; depending on the content of the material, any spirits involved such as homosexual spirits, violence, etc.

6. To your knowledge has this child ever viewed any explicit sexual scenes, for   Yes   No
   instance, watching something on HBO, etc?

   Spirits of lust and perversion, spirits of guilt and shame

7. Does this child exhibit an unusual level of interest in things of a sexual nature?   Yes   No

   A positive answer to this or any of the questions in Category H could be signs of molestation. Pray accordingly.

CATEGORY I

1. Are there any generational areas of bondage and addiction that have not been   Yes   No
   dealt with in this packet?

   Any addictions in either parent or any grandparents? List all.

   Issues dealing with bondage and whoredoms are scattered throughout the questionnaire. This question is to make sure we haven't missed anything generational.

CATEGORY J

1. Does this child suffer from any chronic illness or allergies?
   Which?

   Is it hereditary?

   Strongman of infirmity; family curses may be generational causing hereditary physical impairments such as blindness, deafness, etc. Curses must be broken before deliverance is administered. After familiar spirits have been removed, pray for cleansing and healing. When praying for people with seizures or asthma, first bind "the strongman" very tightly. If symptoms start to manifest while you are praying, remind the spirit it is forbidden to operate.

   After freedom, anoint the child with oil and pray for healing.

2. Has this child had any severe accidents or traumas that stand out in your mind (not already mentioned above)? Describe:

   Break "soul ties" with anyone involved in an accident with a person. The trauma creates a soul tie.

   Pray trauma prayer.

3. Has this child ever received a blood transfusion?

   Break "soul ties" with anyone from whom you have received blood or to whom you have given blood. You will usually not know who the person is even if a family member donated it for you. If the donated blood isn't a match for you, you will be given blood from someone who matches. Simply ask God to break the "soul ties" that were created with the person who received you blood or whose blood you received.

4. Does this child take any medication for ADD, ADHD, depression, psychosis, or anxiety?
   Explain:

   Unless the child being prayed for obviously needs professional help, cast out the following:

   Hereditary or personal strongman of heaviness; spirits of anxiety, fear.

APPENDIX A

SECTION 3

CATEGORY K

1. What is this child's country of birth?

2. Has this child lived in other countries?   Yes   No

   Which ones?

   A general prayer of release is often sufficient, but specific spirits may need to be cast out.

   Look for any spirits associated with the geographic area, such as spirits associated with false worship and witchcraft.

3. Where was the biological mother born? (city, state, nation)
4. Where was the biological father born? (city, state, nation)

5. Where were the grandparents born?   (city, state, nation)
   Maternal grandmother?
   Maternal grandfather?

   Paternal grandmother?
   Paternal grandfather?

   When there is obvious resistance from demonic ethnic or cultural spirits during a general prayer of release, identify, and cast out each one.

Do you have any concerns about this child you feel this questionnaire hasn't uncovered? Explain as fully as you can. Try to pinpoint when they began and if it was connected with trauma, if the child was victimized, or the child invited the problem in.

Much of this material is taken from the book *How to Cast out Demons, A Beginner's Guide* by Doris Wagner, published by Regal; *Deliver Our Children from the Evil One* by Noel and Phyl Gibson, published by Sovereign world Ltd. and *A Manual for Children's Deliverance* by Frank and Ida Mae Hammond, published by Impact Christian Books.

BATTLE PLAN TEMPLATE

PRAYER FOR THE RELEASE OF FREEMASONRY

Soul Ties

Word Curses

Forgiveness

    Names of Individuals

        Notes of specific incidents

    Names of Individuals

        Notes of specific incidents

    Names of Individuals

        Notes of specific incidents

    Names of Individuals

        Notes of specific incidents

Unforgiveness, Resentment, etc.

    Cut off root of bitterness, if necessary

    Repent and Renounce

Rejection – Inherited, Self, Perceived, and Fear of Rejection

    List Inherited Rejection Entry Points

        Forgive ancestors

List Personal Rejection Entry Points

Notes of specific incidents

Notes of specific incidents

Notes of specific incidents

Prayer for Trauma

Try to list the traumas in a chronological order from the earliest age to present

Fear

Generational & Personal

List Entry Points

Lust and Perversion

Generational & Personal

List Entry Points

Covenant Breaking Spirit

Generational & Personal

List Entry Points

Jealousy, Anger, Rage, Rancor, Murder, etc.

Generational & Personal

List Entry Points

Occult, witchcraft, Control, etc.

Generational & Personal

List Entry Points

Etc., etc., etc.

EXAMPLE BATTLE PLAN

Example   *Example*   *Example*   *Example*

PRAYER FOR THE RELEASE OF FREEMASONRY

Have person read the prayer and do the prophetic acts.

SOUL TIES

Break Soul Ties with Tom, Dick and Harry.

WORD CURSES

Witch in college placed spell for illness.

Father said she'd never make it in business.

Father said she was stupid and bad.

Math teacher said she cheated on a test.

Harry said she was too stupid to figure out the checkbook.

Mother–didn't make her feel loved and special, didn't hold her and hug her when she needed it, didn't protect her from her father's punishment and abuse, made her quit cheerleading, told her she wasn't very pretty, didn't comfort her when she came home sick from school, didn't believe her about stealing the coat, punished her for breaking the vase when she didn't do it, didn't stand up for her with math teacher, didn't appreciate how hard she tried to keep the house clean.

Father–never talked to her or listened to her, was gone most of the time and when he was home he was angry and mean, spanked her when she hadn't done anything wrong, took his anger out on her, yelled at her in front of her friends, told her she was stupid and bad and that it was her fault he was always angry, made her afraid to say anything to him, hit her in the face for changing the TV channel, yelled at her for spilling her orange juice, not showing up for her school program, for not saying he was proud of her science project, disappearing for days and making her afraid they would be kicked out of their house, saying she wouldn't be able to make it in business.

Math teacher–accusing her of cheating on her test.

Sister (Beth)–stealing Mom's coat and blaming it on her, being jealous of any attention Mom gave her, lying to kids at school to make them like Beth instead of her, not listening to her when she tried to tell her about Jesus.

Mr. Jones–not giving her a promotion when she deserved it instead of Gladys.

Gladys–for getting the promotion she should have had.

Pastor Smith–telling her she was in sin if she didn't pray every day.

Witch–for placing a curse on her in college.

Ex-husband (Harry)–talking her into having sex before they were married, getting her pregnant, not listening to her when she wanted to talk about how she felt, refusing to go to marriage counseling, being cold and indifferent to her feelings, telling her their marriage would be fine if she would change, telling her he was no longer attracted to her, threatening to hit her with the phone when she tried to call her mother, leaving for three days after they fought about her job, for making her feel unsafe and afraid he would leave her, for blaming her for the dent in the fender of the car when it wasn't her fault, for telling her she was too stupid to figure out the checkbook, divorcing her.

Self—for having sex before marriage and getting pregnant out of wedlock.

God—repent for blaming God

REJECTION
INHERITED, SELF, PERCEIVED, FEAR OF

Not a planned child.

Not the right sex for either parent.

Mother almost miscarried twice while pregnant with her

Delivered by C-Section.

Every forgiveness issue is also a rejection issue. Hit each issue again as you have her renounce the rejection, closing the door that was opened with each hurt.

PRAYER FOR TRAUMA

Mother almost miscarried her, delivered by C-section

Car wreck with mother age 4, broke her arm

Almost drowned in river at camp age 10

Father left

Pregnant before marriage

Divorce

FEAR

GENERATIONAL & PERSONAL

Water–almost drowned in river at camp.

Snakes–neighbor boy scared her with snake

Abandonment–Father left, ex-husband left and divorced her

Poverty–father left and she was afraid they'd get kicked out of house

Demons and evil spirits–demonic films, especially The Exorcist

LUST AND PERVERSION
GENERATIONAL & PERSONAL

Fornication–Tom, Dick and Harry

Pornography–video in 8th grade, magazines with ex-husband
Forgive ex-husband and friend who showed her video

COVENANT BREAKING SPIRIT

GENERATIONAL & PERSONAL

Divorce

JEALOUSY

GENERATIONAL & PERSONAL

Father was an angry man

Anger at father for punishing, yelling, hitting, spanking; at ex-husband for yelling, blaming, leaving and divorcing her, boss for not promoting her.

Mixture of feelings of anger, rage, rancor, resentment

Jealous of sister for getting more attention from mother and stealing friends

Gladys for getting the promotion instead of her

OCCULT, WITCHCRAFT, CONTROL, ETC.

GENERATIONAL & PERSONAL

Horoscope, Halloween, Ouija, reading books about occult, hanging out with witch in college, wearing good luck symbols, being superstitious, trying to manipulate and control ex-husband

PASSIVE MIND

Anesthesia

Intoxicated

Etc., etc., etc . . .

PRAYERS FOR SPECIFIC PURPOSES

OPENING PRAYER TO BIND MUZZLE AND GAG

I bind, muzzle and gag every evil spirit at work here in the name of Jesus Christ. You will not affect anyone here. In the name of Jesus Christ, I command every evil spirit to be silent and subject to the name of Jesus. You will not manifest in any way or interfere with this deliverance. You will leave when you are commanded. In the name of Jesus, I bind fear from attacking (*the person being prayed for*).

Father, I pray your Holy Spirit will come in great measure now and that He will touch the one needing freedom today (*or say the name of the person being prayed for*). Because of his willingness to come today, I pray that you would honor that and bring freedom where it is needed in the name of Jesus. Holy Spirit, come in and illuminate his mind and heart. Give him insight into entry points and people he needs to forgive. We ask you to come and act upon our faith and that you will work with great power now. We ask you to fill him with your peace, the peace that passes all understanding.

BREAKING SOUL TIES

THE PERSON PRAYS:

In the name of the Father, the Son, and the Holy Spirit, I break all ungodly spirit, soul, and body ties that have been established between myself and (*speak out here the name of the individual(s) involved*). I sever that linking supernaturally and ask God to remove from me all influence of the other person(s) *(name the person(s) again here if you prefer),* and draw back to myself every part which has been wrongfully tied in bondage to that person(s) *(again name the person(s) here if you prefer).*

I cast out from myself every demon that entered through that ungodly tie(s), in the name of Jesus.

THE MINISTER PRAYS:

I now speak directly to every evil spirit that has taken advantage of this ungodly soul tie.

You no longer have any rights here, and I order you to leave now without hurting or harming *(name here the individual being prayed for),* or any other person, and without going into any other member of the family. I order you to leave now and never come back. In Jesus' name. Amen.

BREAKING WORD CURSES

In the name of Jesus, I cancel every word I have spoken or that was spoken over me or about me by *(name the person or person's known to have spoken the word curse)* when he said *(repeat the word curse).*

I say, in the name of Jesus, that those words are of no effect in my life. I cancel their effect on me and I break the power of those words over my life, now, in the name of Jesus. Those words spoken over me have no power over my present or my future. I call them null and void, in the name of Jesus.

(As the Spirit leads, you may wish to pray the opposite of the word curse over the person.)

BREAKING PACTS, VEXES, HEXES AND INCANTATIONS

In the name of Jesus, I sever every spiritual bond, break every covenant that has been made by me or on my behalf, knowingly or unknowingly. I also break all word curses, hexes, vexes and incantations I have spoken over myself or that have been spoken over me. Satan, I declare that you have no hold over me. Jesus is my Lord, and I sever every spiritual tie, every spiritual covenant that I have ever had with you, in the name of Jesus. I specifically bind and break the power of the spirits of *(name the specific spirits involved, i.e. spirits of divination, sorcery, witchcraft, spiritism, magic, necromancy)* from operating in my life or the lives of my family. I cancel your assignment against me in the name of Jesus Christ.

PRAYER FOR DELIVERANCE FROM REJECTION

RENOUNCE INHERITED REJECTION:
THE PERSON PRAYS:

In the name of Jesus, I renounce the inherited spirit of rejection that has been passed down to me by my ancestors. I forgive my ancestors for passing that spirit down to me, but I renounce it and reject it from my life.

RENOUNCE ALL FORMS OF REJECTION (FEAR OF REJECTION, SELF REJECTION, PERCEIVED REJECTION):

THE PERSON PRAYS:

In the name of Jesus, I renounce every spirit of rejection. I renounce the spirits of fear of rejection, self rejection, and perceived rejection that may have entered my life when *(list all identified entry points for rejection)* or that entered at any other time.

In the name of Jesus, I renounce and repudiate the spirit of rejection. I close every door against the spirit of rejection and cancel every legal right that rejection has had to operate in my life. I command the spirit of inherited rejection, fear of rejection, self rejection and perceived rejection to loose their hold on me now in the name of Jesus.

CASTING OUT THE SPIRITS:

THE MINISTER PRAYS:

In the name of Jesus, I address the spirit of rejection. I address the spirit of inherited rejection, fear of rejection, self rejection, and perceived rejection and I cast you out of *(name the person being prayed for)*'s life and command you to leave him now. Your legal right to operate in his life has been taken away and you must leave now, in the name of Jesus, and never come back. Spirit of rejection, I expel you now, in the name of Jesus, and forbid you to ever operate in his life again.

(*As the Spirit leads, you may wish to speak God's acceptance and favor on the person [see Freedom Scriptures section.)*

PRAYER OF DELIVERANCE FROM GENERATIONAL AND PERSONAL SPIRITS

RENOUNCE AND REPENT OF GENERATIONAL SPIRITS:
THE PERSON PRAYS:

In the name of Jesus, I repent because of the sins of my ancestors that allowed the spirit(s) of *(name spirit(s) being cast out at this time)* to be passed down to me through my generations. I forgive my ancestors for passing this/these spirit(s) down to me, but I renounce the spirit(s) of *(repeat names of spirit(s))* and forbid it/them to operate in my life.

RENOUNCE AND REPENT OF PERSONAL SPIRITS:

THE PERSON PRAYS:
I renounce the spirit(s) of *(name spirit(s) being cast out at this time)* that may have entered my life when *(list each identified entry point for the spirit(s)* or that entered at any other time.

IF THE ENTRY POINTS INVOLVED SIN ON THE PART OF THE PERSON BEING PRAYED FOR:

THE PERSON PRAYS:
I call these acts sin and I repent of them. I ask you to forgive me for these sins and I thank you, Lord, that you do forgive me.

In the name of Jesus, I renounce and repudiate the spirit(s) of *(name spirit(s) being cast out at this time).*

I close every door against this/these spirit(s) and cancel every legal right that it/they has/have had to operate in my life. I command the spirit(s) of *(name spirit(s) being cast out at this time)* to loose its/their hold on me now, in the name of Jesus.

CASTING OUT THE SPIRIT:

THE MINISTER PRAYS:

In the name of Jesus, I address the generational and personal spirit(s) of (*name spirit(s) being cast out at this time*). I cast you out of (*name the person being prayed for*)'s life and command you to leave him now. Your legal right to operate in his life has been taken away and you must leave now, in the name of Jesus, and never come back. Spirit(s) of (*name spirit(s) being cast out at this time*), I expel you now, in the name of Jesus, and forbid you to ever operate in his life again.

PRAYER FOR TRAUMA

1. Lord, I ask that you bring to (*the person's name*) remembrance or to his conscious level any part of the trauma that needs to be healed.

2. I cast out the spirit(s) of (*name the spirits the Lord shows you*) that entered at the time of the trauma.

3. Lord, I ask You to heal the spirit and the soul that were broken, crushed, or damaged in any way during the trauma.

4. Lord, I ask You to show (*the person's name*) where you were when this trauma happened and what you thought about it.

5. Lord, I ask that You bring that healed spirit and soul through the years to the present day and mature that part which was damaged to the level of maturity of today.

6. Lord, I ask that You bring the body in line with the healed spirit and soul and heal the body as well.

7. Lord, I ask that You bring the body, soul, and spirit together into an integrity of strength and healing.

PRAYER FOR A PASSIVE MIND STATE

THE PERSON PRAYS:

In the name of Jesus, I renounce any demonic spirits that took advantage of a Passive Mind State to enter my life. I renounce every spirit that entered when:

(list each identified entry point, i.e. "I was under anesthesia," "I was intoxicated," "I was hypnotized," etc.) or that entered at any other time when my mind was unguarded or defenseless. I renounce those spirits and I break their power over my life now, in the name of Jesus.

THE MINISTER PRAYS:

In the name of Jesus, I address every spirit that took advantage of a passive mind state to enter *(name of the person being prayed for)*'s life. Your legal right to operate in his/her life has been taken away and I cast you out now, in the name of Jesus. I command you to leave now and I forbid you to ever operate in his/her life again.

PRAYER OF RELEASE FOR FREE MASONS AND THEIR DESCENDANTS

This Prayer Last Updated With Some New Material
On July 26th, 2005

If you were once a member of a Masonic organisation or are a descendant of someone who was, we recommend that you pray through this prayer from your heart. Please don't be like the Masons who are given their obligations and oaths one line at a time and without prior knowledge of the requirements. Please read it through first so you know what is involved.

It is best to pray this aloud with a Christian witness present. We suggest a brief pause following each paragraph to allow the Holy Spirit to show any related issues which may require attention.

A significant number of people also reported having experienced physical and spiritual healings as diverse as long-term headaches and epilepsy as the result of praying through this prayer. Christian counsellors and pastors in many countries have been using this prayer in counselling situations and seminars for several years, with real and significant results.

Some language could be described as 'quaint Old English' and are the real terms used in the Masonic ritual. The legal renunciation opens the way for spiritual, emotional and physical healing to take place.

There are differences between British Commonwealth Masonry and American & Prince Hall Masonry in the higher degrees. Degrees unique to Americans are marked with this sign "★" at the commencement of each paragraph. Those of British Commonwealth decent shouldn't need to pray through those paragraphs.

THE PRAYER OF RELEASE

"Father God, creator of heaven and earth, I come to you in the name of Jesus Christ your Son. I come as a believer seeking forgiveness and cleansing from all sins committed against you, and others made in your image. I honour my earthly father and mother and all of my ancestors of flesh and blood, and of the spirit by adoption and godparents, but I utterly turn away from and renounce all their sins. I forgive all my ancestors for the effects of their sins on me and my children. I confess and renounce all of my own sins, known and unknown. I renounce and rebuke Satan and every spiritual power of his affecting me and my family, in the name of Jesus Christ.

True Holy Creator God, in the name of the True Lord Jesus Christ, in accordance with Jude 8–10; Psalm 82:1 and 2 Chronicles 18, I request you to move aside all Celestial Beings, including Principalities, Powers and Rulers, and to forbid them to harass, intimidate or retaliate against me and all participants in this ministry today.

I also ask that you prevent these beings of whatever rank, to not be permitted to send any level of spiritual evil as retaliation against any of those here, or our families, our ministries, or possessions.

I renounce and annul every covenant made with Death by my ancestors or myself, including every agreement made with Sheol, and I renounce the refuge of lies and falsehoods which have been hidden behind.

In the name of the Lord Jesus Christ, I renounce and forsake all involvement in Freemasonry or any other lodge, craft or occultism by my ancestors and myself. I also renounce and break the code of silence enforced by Freemasonry and the Occult on my family and myself. I renounce and repent of all pride and arrogance which opened the door for the slavery and bondage of Freemasonry to afflict my family and me. I now shut every door of witchcraft and deception operating in my life and seal it closed with the blood of the Lord Jesus Christ. I renounce every covenant, every blood covenant and every alliance with Freemasonry or the spiritual powers behind it made by my family or me.

In the name of Jesus Christ, I rebuke, renounce and bind Witchcraft, the principal spirit behind Freemasonry, and I renounce and rebuke Baphomet, the Spirit of Antichrist and the spirits of Death, and Deception.

I renounce and rebuke the Spirit of Fides, the Roman goddess of Fidelity that seeks to hold all Masonic and occultic participants and their descendants in bondage, and I ask the One True Holy Creator God to give me the gift of Faith to believe in the True Lord Jesus Christ as described in the Word of God.

I also renounce and rebuke the Spirit of Prostitution which the Word of God says has led members of Masonic and other Occultic organisations astray, and caused them to become unfaithful to the One True and Holy God. I now choose to return and become faithful to the God of the Bible, the God of Abraham, Isaac and Jacob, the Father of Jesus Christ, who I now declare is my Lord and Saviour.

I renounce the insecurity, the love of position and power, the love of money, avarice or greed, and the pride which would have led my ancestors into Masonry. I renounce all the fears which held them in Masonry, especially the fears of death, fears of men, and fears of trusting, in the name of Jesus Christ.

I renounce every position held in the lodge by any of my ancestors or myself, including "Master," "Worshipful Master," or any other occultic title. I renounce the calling of any man "Master," for Jesus Christ is my only master and Lord, and He forbids anyone else having that title. I renounce the entrapping of others into Masonry, and observing the helplessness of others during the rituals. I renounce the effects of Masonry passed on to me through any female ancestor who felt distrusted and rejected by her husband as he entered and attended any lodge and refused to tell her of his secret activities. I also renounce all obligations, oaths and curses enacted by every female member of my family through any direct membership of all Women's Orders of Freemasonry, the Order of the Eastern Star, or any other Masonic or occultic organisation.

ALL PARTICIPANTS SHOULD NOW BE INVITED TO SINCERELY CARRY OUT IN FAITH THE FOLLOWING ACTIONS:

1. Symbolically remove the blindfold (hoodwink) and give it to the Lord for disposal;

2. In the same way, symbolically remove the veil of mourning, to make way to receive the Joy of the Lord:

3. Symbolically cut and remove the noose from around the neck, gather it up with the cabletow running down the body and give it all to the Lord for His disposal;

4. Renounce the false Freemasonry marriage covenant, removing from the 4th finger of the right hand the ring of this false marriage covenant, giving it to the Lord to dispose of it;

5. Symbolically remove the chains and bondages of Freemasonry from your body;

6. Symbolically remove all Freemasonry regalia, including collars, gauntlets and armour, especially the Apron with its snake clasp, to make way for the Belt of Truth;

7. Remove the slipshod slippers, to make way for the shoes of the Gospel of Peace;

8. Symbolically remove the ball and chain from the ankles.

9. Invite participants to repent of and seek forgiveness for having walked on all unholy ground, including Freemasonry lodges and temples, including any Mormon or any other occultic/Masonic organisations.

10. Proclaim that Satan and his demons no longer have any legal rights to mislead and manipulate the person seeking help.

33RD & SUPREME DEGREE

In the name of Jesus Christ I renounce the oaths taken and the curses and iniquities involved in the supreme Thirty-Third Degree of Freemasonry, the Grand Sovereign Inspector General. I renounce the secret passwords, DEMOLAY-HIRUM ABIFF, FREDERICK OF PRUSSIA, MICHA, MACHA, BEALIM, AND ADONAI, and all their occultic and Masonic meanings. I renounce all of the obligations of every Masonic degree, and all penalties invoked.

I renounce and utterly forsake The Great Architect Of The Universe, who is revealed in the this degree as Lucifer, and his false claim to be the universal fatherhood of God. I reject the Masonic view of deity because it does not square with the revelation of the One True and Holy Creator God of the Bible.

I renounce the cable-tow around the neck. I renounce the death wish that the wine drunk from a human skull should turn to poison and the skeleton whose cold arms are invited if the oath of this degree is violated. I renounce the three infamous assassins of their grand master, law, property and religion, and the greed and witchcraft involved in the attempt to manipulate and control the rest of mankind.

In the name of God the Father, Jesus Christ the Son, and the Holy Spirit, I renounce and break the curses and iniquities involved in the idolatry, blasphemy, secrecy and deception of Freemasonry at every level, and I appropriate the Blood of Jesus Christ to cleanse all the consequences of these from my life. I now revoke all previous consent given by any of my ancestors or myself to be deceived.

BLUE LODGE

In the name of Jesus Christ I renounce the oaths taken and the curses and iniquities involved in the First or Entered Apprentice Degree, especially their effects on the throat and tongue. I renounce the Hoodwink blindfold and its effects on spirit, emotions and eyes, including all confusion, fear of the dark, fear of the light, and fear of sudden noises. I renounce the blinding of spiritual truth, the darkness of the soul, the false imagination, condescension and the spirit of poverty caused by the ritual of this degree. I also renounce the usurping of the marriage covenant by the removal of the wedding ring. I renounce the secret word, BOAZ, and it's Masonic meaning. I renounce the serpent clasp on the apron, and the spirit of Python which it brought to squeeze the spiritual life out of me.

I renounce the ancient pagan teaching from Babylon and Egypt and the symbolism of the First Tracing Board. I renounce the mixing and mingling of truth and error, the mythology, fabrications and lies taught as truth, and the dishonesty by leaders as to the true understanding of the ritual, and the blasphemy of this degree of Freemasonry.

I renounce the breaking of five of God's Ten Commandments during participation in the rituals of the Blue Lodge degrees. I renounce the presentation to every compass direction, for all the Earth is the Lord's, and everything in it. I renounce the cabletow noose around the neck, the fear of choking and also every spirit causing asthma, hayfever, emphysema or any other breathing difficulty. I renounce the ritual dagger, or the compass point, sword or spear held against the breast, the fear of death by stabbing pain, and the fear of heart attack from this degree, and the absolute secrecy demanded under a witchcraft oath and sealed by kissing the Volume of the Sacred Law. I also renounce kneeling to the false deity known as the Great Architect of the Universe, and humbly ask the One True God to forgive me for this idolatry, in the name of Jesus Christ.

I renounce the pride of proven character and good standing required prior to joining Freemasonry, and the resulting self-righteousness of being good enough to stand before God without the need of a saviour. I now pray for healing of . . . (throat, vocal cords, nasal passages, sinus, bronchial tubes etc.) for healing of the speech area, and the release of the Word of God to me and through me and my family.

SECOND OR FELLOW CRAFT DEGREE OF MASONRY

In the name of Jesus Christ I renounce the oaths taken and the curses and iniquities involved in the Second or Fellow Craft Degree of Masonry, especially the curses on the heart and chest. I renounce the secret words SHIBBOLETH and JACHIN, and all their Masonic meaning. I renounce

the ancient pagan teaching and symbolism of the Second Tracing Board.
I renounce the Sign of Reverence to the Generative Principle. I cut off
emotional hardness, apathy, indifference, unbelief, and deep anger from
me and my family. In the name of Jesus' Christ I pray for the healing of
. . . (the chest/lung/heart area) and also for the healing of my emotions,
and ask to be made sensitive to the Holy Spirit of God.

THIRD OR MASTER MASON DEGREE

In the name of Jesus Christ I renounce the oaths taken and the curses
and iniquities involved in the Third or Master Mason Degree, especially
the curses on the stomach and womb area. I renounce the secret words
TUBAL CAIN and MAHA BONE, and all their Masonic meaning. I renounce
the ancient pagan teaching and symbolism of the Third Tracing Board
used in the ritual. I renounce the Spirit of Death from the blows to the
head enacted as ritual murder, the fear of death, false martyrdom, fear of
violent gang attack, assault, or rape, and the helplessness of this degree.
I renounce the falling into the coffin or stretcher involved in the ritual
of murder.

In the name of Jesus Christ I renounce Hiram Abiff, the false saviour
of Freemasons revealed in this degree. I renounce the false resurrection
of this degree, because only Jesus Christ is the Resurrection and the
Life!

I renounce the pagan ritual of the "Point within a Circle" with all its
bondages and phallus worship. I renounce the symbol "G" and its veiled
pagan symbolism and bondages. I renounce the occultic mysticism of the
black and white mosaic chequered floor with the tessellated boarder and
five-pointed blazing star.

I renounce the All-Seeing Third Eye of Freemasonry or Horus in
the forehead and its pagan and occult symbolism. I rebuke and reject
every spirit of divination which allowed this occult ability to operate.
Action: Put your hand over your forehead.) I now close that Third eye
and all occult ability to see into the spiritual realm, in the name of the
Lord Jesus Christ, and put my trust in the Holy Spirit sent by Jesus Christ
for all I need to know on spiritual matters. I renounce all false commu-

nions taken, all mockery of the redemptive work of Jesus Christ on the cross of Calvary, all unbelief, confusion and depression. I renounce and forsake the lie of Freemasonry that man is not sinful, but merely imperfect, and so can redeem himself through good works. I rejoice that the Bible states that I cannot do a single thing to earn my salvation, but that I can only be saved by grace through faith in Jesus Christ and what He accomplished on the Cross of Calvary.

I renounce all fear of insanity, anguish, death wishes, suicide and death in the name of Jesus Christ. Death was conquered by Jesus Christ, and He alone holds the keys of death and hell, and I rejoice that He holds my life in His hands now. He came to give me life abundantly and eternally, and I believe His promises.

I renounce all anger, hatred, murderous thoughts, revenge, retaliation, spiritual apathy, false religion, all unbelief, especially unbelief in the Holy Bible as God's Word, and all compromise of God's Word. I renounce all spiritual searching into false religions, and all striving to please God. I rest in the knowledge that I have found my Lord and Saviour Jesus Christ, and that He has found me.

In the name of Jesus Christ I pray for the healing of . . . (the stomach, gall bladder, womb, liver, and any other organs of my body affected by Masonry), and I ask for a release of compassion and understanding for me and my family.

YORK RITE

I renounce and forsake the oaths taken and the curses and iniquities involved in the York Rite Degrees of Masonry. I renounce the Mark Lodge, and the mark in the form of squares and angles which marks the person for life. I also reject the jewel or occult talisman which may have been made from this mark sign and worn at lodge meetings; the Mark Master Degree with its secret word JOPPA, and its penalty of having the right ear smote off and the curse of permanent deafness, as well as the right hand being chopped off for being an imposter.

I also renounce and forsake the oaths taken and the curses and iniquities involved in the other York Rite Degrees, including Past Master, with the penalty of having my tongue split from tip to root; and of the Most Excellent Master Degree, in which the penalty is to have my breast torn open and my heart and vital organs removed and exposed to rot on the dung hill.

HOLY ROYAL ARCH DEGREE

In the name of Jesus Christ, I renounce and forsake the oaths taken and the curses and iniquities involved in the Holy Royal Arch Degree especially the oath regarding the removal of the head from the body and the exposing of the brains to the hot sun. I renounce the false secret name of God, JAHBULON, and declare total rejection of all worship of the false pagan gods, Bul or Baal, and On or Osiris. I also renounce the password, AMMI RUHAMAH and all it's Masonic meaning. I renounce the false communion or Eucharist taken in this degree, and all the mockery, scepticism and unbelief about the redemptive work of Jesus Christ on the cross of Calvary. I cut off all these curses and their effects on me and my family in the name of Jesus Christ, and I pray for . . . (healing of the brain, the mind etc.)

I renounce and forsake the oaths taken and the curses and iniquities involved in the Royal Master Degree of the York Rite; the Select Master Degree with its penalty to have my hands chopped off to the stumps, to have my eyes plucked out from their sockets, and to have my body quartered and thrown among the rubbish of the Temple.

I renounce and forsake the oaths taken and the curses and iniquities involved in the Super Excellent Master Degree along with the penalty of having my thumbs cut off, my eyes put out, my body bound in fetters and brass, and conveyed captive to a strange land; and also of the Knights or Illustrious Order of the Red Cross, along with the penalty of having my house torn down and my being hanged on the exposed timbers.

I renounce the Knights Templar Degree and the secret words of KEB RAIOTH, and also Knights of Malta Degree and the secret words MAHER-SHALAL-HASH-BAZ.

I renounce the vows taken on a human skull, the crossed swords, and the curse and death wish of Judas of having the head cut off and placed on top of a church spire. I renounce the unholy communion and especially of drinking from a human skull in many Rites.

ANCIENT & ACCEPTED OR SCOTTISH RITE

(ONLY THE 18TH, 30TH, 31ST 32ND & 33RD DEGREE ARE OPERATED IN BRITISH COMMONWEALTH COUNTRIES.)

★ I renounce the oaths taken and the curses, iniquities and penalties involved in the American and Grand Orient Lodges, including of the Secret Master Degree, its secret passwords of ADONAI and ZIZA, and their occult meanings. I reject and renounce the worship of the pagan sun god as the Great Source of Light, and the crowning with laurel – sacred to Apollo, and the sign of secrecy in obedience to Horus;

★ of the Perfect Master Degree, its secret password of MAH-HAH-BONE, and its penalty of being smitten to the Earth with a setting maul;

★ of the Intimate Secretary Degree, its secret passwords of YEVA and JOABERT, and its penalties of having my body dissected, and of having my vital organs cut into pieces and thrown to the beasts of the field, and of the use of the nine-pointed star from the Kabbala and the worship of Phallic energy;

★ of the Provost and Judge Degree, its secret password of HIRUM-TITO-CIVI-KY, and the penalty of having my nose cut off;

★ of the Intendant of the Building Degree, of its secret password AKAR-JAI-JAH, and the penalty of having my eyes put out, my body cut in two and exposing my bowels;

★ of the Elected Knights of the Nine Degree, its secret password NEKAM NAKAH, and its penalty of having my head cut off and stuck on the highest pole in the East;

★ of the Illustrious Elect of Fifteen Degree, with its secret password ELIGNAM, and its penalties of having my body opened perpendicularly and horizontally, the entrails exposed to the air for eight hours so that flies may prey on them, and for my head to be cut off and placed on a high pinnacle;

★ of the Sublime Knights elect of the Twelve Degree, its secret password STOLKIN-ADONAI, and its penalty of having my hand cut in twain;

★ of the Grand Master Architect Degree, its secret password RABBANAIM, and its penalties;

★ of the Knight of the Ninth Arch of Solomon or Enoch Degree, its secret password JEHOVAH, it's blasphemous use, its penalty of having my body given to the beasts of the forest as prey, and I also renounce the revelations from the Kabbala in this and subsequent degrees;

★ of the Grand Elect, Perfect and Sublime Mason or Elu Degree, its secret password MARAH-MAUR-ABREK and IHUH, the penalty of having my body cut open and my bowels given to vultures for food, and I reject the Great Unknowable deity of this degree;

COUNCIL OF PRINCES OF JERUSALEM

★ of the Knights of the East Degree, its secret password RAPH-O-DOM, and its penalties;

★ of the Prince of Jerusalem Degree, its secret password TEBET-ADAR, and its penalty of being stripped naked and having my heart pierced with a ritual dagger;

CHAPTER OF THE ROSE CROIX

★ of the Knight of the East and West Degree, its secret password ABADDON, and its penalty of incurring the severe wrath of the Almighty Creator of Heaven and Earth. I also reject the Tetractys and its representation of the Sephiroth from the Kabbala and its false tree of life. I also reject the false anointing with oil and the proclamation that anyone so anointed is now worthy to open the Book of Seven Seals, because only the Lord Jesus Christ is worthy;

18TH DEGREE

I renounce the oaths taken and the curses, iniquities and penalties involved in the Eighteenth Degree of Freemasonry, the Most Wise Sovereign Knight of the Pelican and the Eagle and Sovereign Prince Rose Croix of Heredom. I renounce and reject the false Jesus revealed in this degree because He doesn't point to the light or the truth since the True Lord Jesus Christ is the Light of the World and the Truth. I renounce and reject the Pelican witchcraft spirit, as well as the occultic influence of the Rosicrucians and the Kabbala in this degree.

I renounce the claim that the death of Jesus Christ was a "dire calamity," and also the deliberate mockery and twisting of the Christian doctrine of the Atonement. I renounce the blasphemy and rejection of the deity of Jesus Christ, and the secret words IGNE NATURA RENOVATUR INTEGRA and its burning. I renounce the mockery of the communion taken in this degree, including a biscuit, salt and white wine.

COUNCIL OF KADOSH

★ I renounce the inappropriate use of the title "Kadosh" used in these council degrees because it means "Holy" and it is here used in a unholy way.

I renounce the oaths taken and the curses, iniquities and penalties involved in the Grand Pontiff Degree, its secret password EMMANUEL, and its penalties;

★ of the Grand Master of Symbolic Lodges or Ad Vitum Degree, its secret passwords JEKSON and STOLKIN, and the penalties invoked, and I also reject the pagan Phoenecian and Hindu deities revealed in this degree;

★ of the Patriarch Noachite or Prussian Knight Degree, its secret password PELEG, and its penalties;

★ of the Knight of the Royal Axe or Prince of Libanus Degree, its secret password NOAH-BEZALEEL-SODONIAS, and its penalties;

★ of the Chief of the Tabernacle Degree, its secret password URIEL-JEHOVAH, and its penalty that I agree the Earth should open up and engulf me up to my neck so I perish, and I also reject the false title of becoming a "Son of Light" in this degree;

★ of the Prince of the Tabernacle Degree, and its penalty to be stoned to death and have my body left above ground to rot. I also reject the claimed revelation of the mysteries of the Hebrew faith from the Kabbala, and the occultic and pagan Egyptian, Hindu, Mithraic, Dionysian and Orphic mysteries revealed and worshipped in this degree;

★ of the Knight of the Brazen Serpent Degree, its secret password MOSES-JOHANNES, and its penalty to have my heart eaten by venomous serpents. I also reject the claimed revelation of the mysteries of the Islamic faith, I reject the insulting misquotations from the Koran, and the gift of a white turban in this degree;

★ of the Prince of Mercy Degree, its secret password GOMEL, JEHOVAH- JACHIN, and its penalty of condemnation and spite by the entire universe. I also reject the claimed revelation of the mysteries of the Christian religion because there are no such mysteries. I reject the Druid trinity of Odin, Frea and Thor revealed in this degree. I also reject the false baptism claimed for the purification of my soul to allow my soul to rejoin the universal soul of Buddhism, as taught in this degree;

★ of the Knight Commander of the Temple Degree, its secret password SOLOMON, and its penalty of receiving the severest wrath of Almighty God inflicted upon me. I also reject the claimed revelation of the mysteries of Numerology, Astrology and Alchemy and other occult sciences taught in this degree;

★ of the Knight Commander of the Sun, or Prince Adept Degree, its secret password STIBIUM, and its penalties of having my tongue thrust through with a red-hot iron, of my eyes being plucked out, of my senses of smelling and hearing being removed, of having my hands cut off and in that condition to be left for voracious animals to devour me, or executed by lightening from heaven;

★ of the Grand Scottish Knight of Saint Andrew or Patriarch of the Crusades Degree, its secret password NEKAMAH-FURLAC, and its penalties;

THIRTIETH DEGREE

I renounce the oaths taken and the curses and iniquities involved in the Thirtieth Degree of Masonry, the Grand Knight Kadosh and Knight of the Black and White Eagle. I renounce the secret passwords, STIBIUM ALKABAR, PHARASH-KOH and all they mean.

SUBLIME PRINCES OF THE ROYAL SECRET

THIRTY-FIRST DEGREE OF MASONRY

I renounce the oaths taken and the curses and iniquities involved in the Thirty-First Degree of Masonry, the Grand Inspector Inquisitor Commander. I renounce all the gods and goddesses of Egypt which are honoured in this degree, including Anubis with the jackel's head, Osiris the Sun god, Isis the sister and wife of Osiris and also the moon goddess. I renounce the Soul of Cheres, the false symbol of immortality, the Chamber of the dead and the false teaching of reincarnation.

THIRTY-SECOND DEGREE OF MASONRY

I renounce the oaths taken and the curses and iniquities involved in the Thirty-Second Degree of Masonry, the Sublime Prince of the Royal Secret. I renounce the secret passwords, PHAAL/PHARASH-KOL and all they mean. I renounce Masonry's false trinitarian deity AUM, and its parts; Brahma the creator, Vishnu the preserver and Shiva the destroyer. I renounce the deity of AHURA-MAZDA, the claimed spirit or source of all light, and the worship with fire, which is an abomination to God, and also the drinking from a human skull in many Rites.

SHRINERS (APPLIES ONLY IN NORTH AMERICA)

★ I renounce the oaths taken and the curses, iniquities and penalties involved in the Ancient Arabic Order of the Nobles of the Mystic Shrine. I renounce the piercing of the eyeballs with a three-edged blade, the flaying of the feet, the madness, and the worship of the false god Allah as the god of our fathers. I renounce the hoodwink, the mock hanging, the mock beheading, the mock drinking of the blood of the victim, the mock dog urinating on the initiate, and the offering of urine as a commemoration.

ALL OTHER DEGREES

I renounce all the other oaths taken, the rituals of every other degree and the curses and iniquities invoked. These include the Acacia, Allied Degrees, The Red Cross of Constantine, the Order of the Secret Monitor, and the Masonic Royal Order of Scotland.

I renounce all other lodges and secret societies including Prince Hall Freemasonry, Grand Orient Lodges, Mormonism, the Ancient Toltec Rite, The Order of Amaranth, the Royal Order of Jesters, the Manchester Unity Order of Oddfellows and its women's Order of Rebekah lodges, the Royal Antediluvian Order of Buffaloes, Druids, Foresters, the Loyal Order of Orange, including the Purple and Black Lodges within it, Elks, Moose and Eagles Lodges, the Ku Klux Klan, The Grange, the Woodmen of the World, Riders of the Red Robe, the Knights of Pythias, the Order of the Builders, The Rite of Memphiz and Mitzraim, Ordo Templi Orientis (OTO), Aleister Crowley's Palladium Masonry, the Order of the Golden Key, the Order of Desoms, the Mystic Order of the Veiled Prophets of the Enchanted Realm, the women's Orders of the Eastern Star, of the Ladies Oriental Shrine, and of the White Shrine of Jerusalem, the girls' order of the Daughters of the Eastern Star, the International Orders of Job's Daughters, and of the Rainbow, the boys' Order of De Molay, and the Order of the Constellation of Junior Stars, and every university or college Fraternity or Sorority with Greek and Masonic connections, and their effects on me and all my family.

Lord Jesus, because you want me to be totally free from all occult bondages, I will burn all objects in my possession which connect me with all lodges and occultic organisations, including Masonry, Witchcraft, the Occult and Mormonism, and all regalia, aprons, books of rituals, rings and other jewellery. I renounce the effects these or other objects of Masonry, including the compass and the square, have had on me or my family, in the name of Jesus Christ.

In the name and authority of Jesus Christ, I break every curse of Freemasonry in my life, including the curses of barrenness, sickness, mind-blinding and poverty, and I rebuke every evil spirit which empowered these curses.

I also renounce, cut off and dissolve in the blood of Jesus Christ every ungodly Soul-Tie I or my ancestors have created with other lodge members or participants in occultic groups and actions, and I ask you to send out ministering angels to gather together all portions of my fragmented soul, to free them from all bondages and to wash them clean in the Blood of Jesus Christ, and then to restore them to wholeness to their rightful place within me. I also ask that You remove from me any parts of any other person's soul which has been deposited within my humanity. Thank you Lord for restoring my soul and sanctifying my spirit.

I renounce and rebuke every evil spirit associated with Freemasonry, Witchcraft, the Occult and all other sins and iniquities. Lord Jesus, I ask you to now set me free from all spiritual and other bondages, in accordance with the many promises of the Bible.

In the name of the Lord Jesus Christ, I now take the delegated authority given to me and bind every spirit of sickness, infirmity, curse, affliction, addiction, disease or allergy associated with these sins I have confessed and renounced, including every spirit empowering all iniquities inherited from my family. I exercise the delegated authority from the Risen Lord Jesus Christ over all lower levels of evil spirits and demons which have been assigned to me, and I command that all such demonic beings are to be bound up into one, to be separated from every part of my humanity, whether perceived to be in the body or trapped in the dimensions, and they are not permitted to transfer power to any other spirits or to call for reinforcements.

I command, in the name of Jesus Christ, for every evil spirit to leave me now, touching or harming no-one, and go to the dry place appointed for you by the Lord Jesus Christ, never to return to me or my family, and I command that you now take all your memories, roots, scars, works, nests and habits with you. I surrender to God's Holy Spirit and to no other spirit all the places in my life where these sins and iniquities have been.

CONCLUSION

Holy Spirit, I ask that you show me anything else which I need to do or to pray so that I and my family may be totally free from the consequences of the sins of Masonry, Witchcraft, Mormonism and all related Paganism and Occultism.

(Pause, while listening to God, and pray as the Holy Spirit leads you.)

Now, dear Father God, I ask humbly for the blood of Jesus Christ, your Son and my Saviour, to cleanse me from all these sins I have confessed and renounced, to cleanse my spirit, my soul, my mind, my emotions and every part of my body which has been affected by these sins, in the name of Jesus Christ. I also command every cell in my body to come into divine order now, and to be healed and made whole as they were designed to by my loving Creator, including restoring all chemical imbalances and neurological functions, controlling all cancerous cells, reversing all degenerative diseases, and I sever the DNA and RNA of any mental or physical diseases or afflictions that came down through my family blood lines. I also ask to receive the perfect love of God which casts out all fear, in the name of the Lord Jesus Christ.

I ask you, Lord, to fill me with your Holy Spirit now according to the promises in your Word. I take to myself the whole armour of God in accordance with Ephesians Chapter Six, and rejoice in its protection as Jesus surrounds me and fills me with His Holy Spirit. I enthrone you, Lord Jesus, in my heart, for you are my Lord and my Saviour, the source of eternal life. Thank you, Father God, for your mercy, your forgiveness and your love, in the name of Jesus Christ, Amen."

SINCE THE ABOVE IS WHAT NEEDS TO BE RENOUNCED, WHY WOULD ANYONE WANT TO JOIN?

This information is taken from *"Unmasking Freemasonry - Removing the Hoodwink,"* by Dr. Selwyn Stevens published by Jubilee Resources, PO Box 36–044, Wellington 6330, New Zealand.(ISBN 1877203–48–3) To obtain copies of this book, please click Web Shop.

NOTICE

Copying of this prayer is both permitted and encouraged provided reference is made to Book title, Author, Publisher & web address - www.jubilee-resources.com or www.jubilee.org.nz. This and other similar prayers are available to download freely from our website. Resources on other subjects are also available to educate and equip Christians on a wide range of spiritual deceptions. These prayers will also be in Spanish, Brazilian Portuguese, French, German and Italian, and other languages as can be arranged.

Written testimonies of changed lives also are welcome.

If additional prayer and ministry is required, or information is required about other spiritual deceptions, please contact us by clicking on Jubilee Resources Enquiry Page. For reasons of distance, we may refer you to someone based closer to you. We have counselling referrals available in many countries particularly in North America, Australia and Europe.

FREEDOM SCRIPTURES

All of the following scriptures are from the King James Version except as otherwise noted.

DELIVERANCE MINISTRY:

Second Corinthians 1:10–11

He has delivered us from such a deadly peril, and he will deliver us. On him we have set our hope that he will continue to deliver us, as you help us by your prayers. Then many will give thanks on our behalf for the gracious favor granted us in answer to the prayers of many. (NIV)

AUTHORITY:

Matthew 18:18–19

I tell you the truth, whatever you bind on earth will be bound in heaven, and whatever you loose on earth will be loosed in heaven. Again, I tell you that if two of you on earth agree about anything you ask for, it will be done for you by my Father in heaven. (NIV)

Mark 16:17–18

And these signs will accompany those who believe: in my name they will drive out demons; they will speak in new tongues, they will pick up snakes with their hands; and when they drink deadly poison, it will not hurt them at all; they will place their hands on sick people, and they will get well. (NIV)

Luke 10:17
. . . Lord, even the demons submit to us in your name.

Luke 10:19
I have given you authority to trample on snakes and scorpions and overcome all the power of the enemy; nothing will harm you. (NIV)

First John 4:4
. . . and have overcome them (spirits); because greater is he that is in you than he that is in the world.

Ephesians 1:20–22
. . . set him at his own right hand in heavenly places, far above all principality, and power, and might, and dominion, and every name that is named . . . and hath put all things under his feet . . .

James 4:7
. . . Resist the devil, and he will flee from you.

Second Corinthians 10:4
The weapons we fight with are not the weapons of the world. On the contrary, they have divine power to demolish strongholds (NIV)

Ephesians 6:12
For our struggle is not against flesh and blood, but against the rulers, against the authorities, against the powers of this dark world and against the spiritual forces of evil in the heavenly realms (NIV)

Philippians 2:9–10
. . . and given Him a name which is above every name; that at the name of Jesus every knee shall bow, of things in heaven, and things in earth, and things under the earth.

Proverbs 11:9

. . . through knowledge shall the just be delivered.

Galatians 3:13

. . . Christ hath redeemed us from the curse of the law . . .

Matthew 6:13

. . . deliver us from evil . . .

Galatians 1:4

Who gave himself for our sins, that he might deliver us from this present evil world . . .

Colossians 1:13

Who hath delivered us from the power of darkness, and translated us into the Kingdom of his dear Son.

Colossians 2:10

And we are complete in him, which is the head of all principality and power.

Colossians 2:15

And having spoiled principalities and powers, he made a show of them openly, triumphing over them in it.

Revelation 12:11

And they overcame him by the blood of the Lamb, and by the word of their testimony . . .

Second Corinthians 5:21

God made him who had no sin to be sin for us, so that in him we might become the righteousness of God. (NIV)

Galatians 5:1

It is for freedom that Christ has set us free. Stand firm, then, and do not let yourselves be burdened again by a yoke of slavery. (NIV)

Hebrews 9:14
How much more, then, will the blood of Christ, who through the eternal Spirit offered himself unblemished to God, cleanse our consciences from acts that lead to death, so that we may serve the living God (NIV)

First Corinthians 6:11
And that is what some of you were. But you were washed, you were sanctified, you were justified in the name of the Lord Jesus Christ and by the Spirit of our God

Psalm 124:7
Our soul is escaped as a bird out of the snare of the fowlers; the snare is broken, and we are escaped

Romans 16:20
The God of peace will crush Satan under your feet shortly.

Psalm 60:12
With God we will gain the victory, and he will trample down our enemies. (NIV)

Isaiah 10:27
And it shall come to pass in that day, that his burden shall be taken away from off his shoulder, and his yoke from off thy neck, and the yoke shall be destroyed because of the anointing.

PREPARATION OF THE DELIVERANCE MINISTER:

Exodus 4: 12, 15
Now therefore go, and I will be with thy mouth, and teach thee what thou shalt say.

. . . I will be with thy mouth, and with his mouth, and will teach you what ye shall do.

Psalm 19: 14
Let the words of my mouth, and the meditation of my heart, be acceptable in thy sight, O Lord, my strength, and my redeemer

Psalm 140: 7
O God the Lord, the strength of my salvation, thou hast covered my head in the day of battle

Psalm 144:1
Blessed be the Lord my strength, which teacheth my hands to war and my fingers to fight

BONDAGE:

Isaiah 14:3
And it shall come to pass in the day that the Lord shall give thee rest from thy sorrow, and from thy fear, and from the hard bondage wherein thou wast made to serve ...

Galatians 5:1
It is for freedom that Christ has set us free. Stand firm, then, and do not let yourselves be burdened again by a yoke of slavery. (NIV)

CLEANSING:

First John 1:9
If we confess our sins, he is faithful and just to forgive us our sins, and to cleanse us from all unrighteousness.

Hebrews 9:14
How much more, then, will the blood of Christ, who through the eternal Spirit offered himself unblemished to God, cleanse our consciences from acts that lead to death, so that we may serve the living God (NIV)

Second Corinthians 6:11

And that is what some of you were. But you were washed, you were sanctified, you were justified in the name of the Lord Jesus Christ and by the Spirit of our God (NIV)

CONFUSION:

Psalm 71:1

In thee, O Lord, do I put my trust; let me never be put to confusion.

First Corinthians 14:33

For God is not the author of confusion, but of peace, as in all churches of the saints.

FEAR:

Psalm 34:4

I sought the Lord, and He heard me, and delivered me from all my fears.

Second Timothy 1:7

God has not given me a spirit of fear, but of power and of love and of a sound mind. (NIV)

Psalm 56:3–4

When I am afraid, I will trust in you. In God, whose word I praise, in God I trust; I will not be afraid. What can mortal man do to me? (NIV)

Zephaniah 3:15

The Lord has taken away your punishment, he has turned back your enemy. The Lord, the King of Israel, is with you, never again will you fear any harm (NIV)

Isaiah 14:3
And it shall come to pass in the day that the Lord shall give thee rest from thy sorrow, and from thy fear, and from the hard bondage wherein thou wast made to serve ...

GUILT/SHAME:

Isaiah 53:6
... and the Lord hath laid on him the iniquity of us all.

Isaiah 54:4
Fear not; for thou shalt not be ashamed; neither be thou confounded; for thou shalt not be put to shame; for thou shalt forget the shame of thy youth ...

Isaiah 61:7
Instead of their shame my people will receive a double portion, and instead of disgrace they will rejoice in their inheritance; and so they will inherit a double portion in their land, and everlasting joy will be theirs. (NIV)

Psalm 71:1
In thee, O Lord, do I put my trust; let me never be put to confusion.

GRIEF/MOURNING:

Isaiah 61:2–3
... to comfort all that mourn; to appoint unto them that mourn in Zion, to give unto them beauty for ashes, the oil of joy for mourning, the garment of praise for the spirit of heaviness (NIV)

Psalm 30:11
Thou hast turned for me my mourning into dancing; thou hast put off my sackcloth, and girded me with gladness (joy-NIV)

Isaiah 51:11

... and everlasting joy shall be upon their head: they shall obtain gladness and joy; and sorrow and mourning shall flee away.

Jeremiah 31:13

... for I will turn their mourning into joy, and will comfort them, and make them rejoice from their sorrow

Isaiah 66:13

As one whom his mother comforts, so will I comfort you; and you shall be comforted in Jerusalem.

Matthew 5:4

Blessed are they that mourn; for they shall be comforted.

Isaiah 53:4

Surely he hath borne our griefs, and carried our sorrows

Isaiah 14:3

And it shall come to pass in the day that the Lord shall give thee rest from thy sorrow, and from thy fear, and from the hard bondage wherein thou wast made to serve ...

Second Samuel 12:21–23

.... thou didst fast and weep for the child, while it was alive; but when the child was dead, thou didst rise and eat bread. And he said, While the child was yet alive, I fasted and wept; for I said, Who can tell whether God will be gracious to me, that the child may live? But now he is dead, wherefore should I fast? Can I bring him back again? I shall go to him, but he shall not return to me.

HEAVINESS/DEPRESSION/DESPAIR (JOY, PRAISE):

Isaiah 61:3
. . . to bestow on them a crown of beauty instead of ashes, the oil of gladness instead of mourning, and a garment of praise instead of a spirit of despair (NIV). (heaviness-KJ)

Psalm 5:11
But let all those that put their trust in thee rejoice; let them ever shout for joy, because thou defendest them; let them also that love thy name be joyful in thee.

Psalm 89:16
In thy name shall they rejoice all the day; and in thy righteousness shall they be exalted.

Psalm 149:5
Let the saints be joyful in glory; let them sing aloud upon their beds.

Psalm 150:6
Let everything that has breath praise the Lord. Praise ye the Lord.

Isaiah 61:10
I will greatly rejoice in the Lord, my soul shall be joyful in my God; for he hath clothed me with the garments of salvation, he hath covered me with the robe of righteousness, as a bridegroom decketh himself with ornaments, and as a bride adorneth herself with her jewels.

REJECTION (FAVOR):

First Samuel 2:26
And the child Samuel grew on, and was in favour both with the Lord, and also with men.

Job 10:12
Thou hast granted me life and favour, and thy visitation hath preserved my spirit

Psalm 5:12
For thou, Lord, wilt bless the righteous; with favour wilt thou compass him as with a shield

Psalm 41:11
By this I know that thou favourest me, because mine enemy doth not triumph over me

Proverbs 3:4
So shalt thou find favour and good understanding in the sight of God and man

Genesis 39:6
. . . And Joseph was a goodly person, and well favoured.

Zephaniah 3:17,19,20
The Lord our God is with you, he is mighty to save. He will take great delight in you, he will quiet you with his love, he will rejoice over you with singing . . . I will rescue the lame and gather those who have been scattered. I will give them praise and honor in every land where they were put to shame . . . I will give you honor and praise among all the peoples of the earth when I restore your fortunes before your very eyes, says the Lord. (NIV)

Isaiah 62:5
. . . as a bridegroom rejoices over his bride, so will your God rejoice over you. (NIV)

Jeremiah 31:3–4
The Lord appeared to us in the past, saying: 'I have loved you with an everlasting love; I have drawn you with loving-kindness. I will

build you up again and you will be rebuilt, O Virgin Israel. Again you will take up your tambourines and go out to dance with the joyful.' (NIV)

Isaiah 62:4
Thou shalt no more be termed Forsaken; neither shall thy land any more be termed Desolate . . . for the Lord will take delight in you, and your land will be married.

WITCHCRAFT:

Micah 5:12
And I will cut off witchcrafts out of thine hand; and thou shalt have no more soothsayers

Ezekiel 13:20,21,23
Therefore this is what the Sovereign Lord says: I am against your magic charms with which you ensnare people like birds and I will tear them from your arms; I will set free the people that you ensnare like birds. I will tear off your veils and save my people from your hands, and they will no longer fall prey to your power. Then you will know that I am the Lord . . . therefore you will no longer see false visions or practice divination. I will save my people from your hands. And then you will know that I am the Lord. (NIV)

HEALING OF MEMORIES:

Isaiah 65:17
Behold, I will create new heavens and a new earth. The former things will not be remembered, nor will they come to mind (NIV)

Isaiah 54:4
. . . You will forget the shame of your youth and remember no more the reproach of your widowhood. (NIV)

Philippians 3:13,14

Brethren, I do not count myself to have apprehended; but one thing I do, forgetting those things which are behind and reaching forward to those things which are ahead, I press toward the goal for the prize of the upward call of God in Christ Jesus.

RIGHTEOUSNESS:

Second Corinthians 5:21

God made him who had no sin to be sin for us, so that in him we might become the righteousness of God. (NIV)

Galatians 5:1

It is for freedom that Christ has set us free. Stand firm, then, and do not let yourselves be burdened again by a yoke of slavery. (NIV)

Hebrews 9:14

How much more, then, will the blood of Christ, who through the eternal Spirit offered himself unblemished to God, cleanse our consciences from acts that lead to death, so that we may serve the living God. (NIV)

First Corinthians 6:11

And that is what some of you were. But you were washed, you were sanctified, you were justified in the name of the Lord Jesus Christ and by the Spirit of our God (NIV)

HEALING:

Isaiah 61:1–3

The Spirit of the Sovereign Lord is on me, Because the Lord has anointed me to preach good news to the poor. He has sent me to bind up the brokenhearted, to proclaim freedom for the captives and release from darkness for the prisoners, to proclaim the year of the Lord's favor and the day of vengeance of our God, to comfort all who mourn, and provide for those who grieve in Zion - to bestow on them a crown of beauty instead of ashes, the oil of gladness instead of mourning, and a garment of praise instead of a spirit of despair. They will be called oaks of righteousness, a planting of the Lord for the display of his splendor. (NIV)

APPENDIX C

SECTION 1

INTRODUCTION LETTER AND SCRIPT FOR TAPE

PRAYER MINISTRY QUESTIONNAIRE

Name: _____ *Appointment time:* _____

Address: _____ Phone: _____

Reasons for requesting ministry: _____

Instructions:

1. (*Insert the name of your church or ministry*) prayer team members are neither psychological nor medical professionals. They do not charge for their time. This is a prayer ministry only. The process may take as long as six hours or more. Be prepared for an appointment of this length.

2. Pray before you begin to fill out this questionnaire. Ask the Holy Spirit to help and guide you, and bring key things to your mind. Please add any information concerning background or problems that may provide additional pertinent information. Be sure to note incidents that produced trauma, great disappointment or hurt that come to mind. When names are requested, it is only for prayer purposes - first names only, please. Since forgiveness of those who sinned against us is our greatest weapon in deliverance, we ask that you be willing to pray to forgive such persons when necessary. You must be willing to do this for good results.

3. Full disclosure and complete honesty are required. If you are unwilling to comply for any reason, or to pray to forgive where necessary, please cancel your appointment, pray and wait until you feel you are ready, and reschedule at that time. Results will not be satisfactory and may even be hurtful in the long run if we are unable to deal with situations in depth and with complete honesty. There may be at least one other person present to pray and assist. Be prepared for this. Confidentiality will be maintained. Be assured that "we have heard it all" and nothing shocks or angers us. We are here to aid in a healing process.

4. The exceptions to confidentially include the following: If you report a crime to us and name a victim; i.e. sexual abuse to a child, elder abuse, or assault, we must, by law, report it to the authorities. We will also notify the head pastor of our church. We must also call the authorities if you tell us you are planning to commit suicide and are unable to resolve not to do it before leaving your deliverance session. *(This is the law in Oklahoma; check the laws in your jurisdiction and reword the above accordingly.)*

5. To protect your privacy, your completed questionnaire will be destroyed at the completion of your prayer session. No copies are kept on file for any reason.

6. If you are physically able, and you sense the Lord leading you, please add fasting to your pray before your appointment. If you have mature Christian friends who know you have an appointment, ask them to fast and pray if you feel comfortable doing this- it usually adds strength, guidance and rapidity to the process. Our team will have fasted and prayed also.

7. As a general rule, we do not pray with a person more than once. If your problem has to do with sin, past or present, we will pray with you only if you are willing to come to the place where you will forsake such action and promise to cut it off. Be warned that after deliverance, if a person invites the problem back, the latter state of the person may be far worse than the original, and much

effort, energy and time will have been wasted. You must agree to this or please cancel you appointment.

8. Before we begin our session, you will be asked to pray the following prayer aloud (it may be read): "I confess Jesus Christ to be my personal Savior. I renounce any oppression from the evil one in my life because of iniquity, transgression and sin of my parents, ancestors or myself and humbly ask God for release and cleansing through the blood of Jesus Christ. I repent from every sinful attitude, action or habit of mine which does not glorify Jesus Christ and ask forgiveness, release, cleansing and wholeness. I renounce the devil and all demonic influences, bondages, dominations, and infirmities in my life. I ask you, Lord, for the release and freedom promised by Jesus Christ so that He may be Lord of my total personality and be glorified in all I say and do . In His name I pray. Amen." This must be your honest and sincere desire, or we will need to postpone ministry until a later time.

9. Please return this questionnaire to *(insert the name of your church or ministry)* at least one week before your appointment. If you are unable to keep your appointment or plan to cancel, please call us as soon as possible.

10. I have read the above instructions and agree to comply fully.

_____   _____

Signature   Date

INSTRUCTIONS TO THE PERSON COMING FOR DELIVERANCE

We recommend that someone on your team read this into a tape recorder and the tape be included with each deliverance packet.

You have just taken the first step toward freedom. Freedom in Christ from demonic powers and influences in your life. And we are here to help you. You have been given some paperwork that's required before we can schedule a session to pray for you. Like I said, we are here to help you, but you'll be doing a lot of the work, too.

You have been given a form called a Voluntary Release. Please read it over, sign it and return it to us with the rest of your paperwork. Basically, it says that you agree not to sue us for praying for you. It's a strange world we live in that makes it necessary to do this, but we have to protect the ministry.

You have also been given an Instruction Sheet. We need you to read it, too, and sign it along the bottom. This tape will expand a little on the Instruction Sheet.

Then you can turn to the Questionnaire. Please pray before you begin to fill out this survey. Ask the Holy Spirit to help you with it, to bring things to your mind and memory that will help us to know how to pray. The survey is a little lengthy and will require some soul searching on your part. It may make you think about things you'd rather not think about and it may bring up some painful memories. I told you you'd be doing a lot of the work, remember? But the freedom you can receive makes it more than worth it.

Be completely honest when answering the questions. This will require revealing some very personal information and probably some information that will be embarrassing. First of all, we want you to understand that no one is going to see your questionnaire except the people directly involved in prayer for your deliverance and possibly your senior pastor. It will be kept completely confidential. The exceptions to confidentially include the following: If you report a crime to us and name a victim; i.e. sexual abuse to a child, elder abuse, or assault, we must, by law, report it to the authorities. We will also notify the head pastor of our church. We must also call the authorities if you tell us you are planning to commit suicide and are unable to resolve not to do it before leaving your deliverance session. *(This is the law in Oklahoma; check the laws in your jurisdiction and reword the above accordingly).* And the questionnaire will be destroyed as soon as your deliverance session is finished. In fact, we will tear it up right in front of you before you ever leave the session. You can tear it up yourself, if you want to. Sometimes, there's a lot of satisfaction in doing that.

Our purpose is not to pry into your personal life or to embarrass you. Our only purpose is to identify demonic problems and to know how to pray about them. And to know how to break them. There is a reason for each question on the survey. Your answers will help us to identify problems and how they got started. We are not shocked by what we read or what you tell us. We've almost certainly heard it before. In fact, no matter how bad you think things are on your survey, probably the last person we prayed for had things just as bad. We have all been through deliverance and we may have had things on our survey that were even worse. I think it's important for you to know that we are all human. You don't need to be embarrassed. Our only desire in this is to see you set free.

Don't skip over any of the questions. If you are sure the answer is 'no', write 'no' on the survey. But don't dismiss any of the questions without searching your heart to see if there is anything there that needs to be dealt with. We're not trying to dredge up something where there's nothing, but we don't want to leave anything behind that should have been gotten rid of. There's no sense in going to all this trouble if you're going to leave some garbage behind. Let's get it all cleared out once and for all, if we can. Each of the questions has a definite purpose. You don't have to know what it is at this point; that's what we're here for. We just need you to answer each question fully and honestly. We always let the Holy Spirit direct and guide a deliverance session, but it is very helpful to have this information as a place to start.

Now, your answers to some of the questions will involve another person. You may be concerned that you will be embarrassing him or betraying his confidence in some way. We need only enough information to identify the event that opened the door to demons. We don't have any interest in knowing who the people involved were. We don't need last names of these people. Just tell us enough so that you are clear in your mind who you are talking about and so that God knows who you mean. First names and a time and place are enough. You won't be gossiping about anyone or embarrassing someone else.

When you have completed the questionnaire, ask the Holy Spirit to show you anything else that you have not included. It is possible that there is some demonic influence or an event that opened the door to demons that escaped the prompting of the questions. If so, be sure to put it down. You can use the back of a page or add a separate page if you need to. Don't be concerned on any of the questions about being too lengthy or detailed. And don't edit out things that come to your mind that may seem trivial or minor. If it came to your mind, there's probably a reason.

We're not concerned about your responses to the questionnaire being too long, so include as much information as you feel you need to. We need to use our time during the session wisely, and the more information that is on the questionnaire, the less time we have to spend gathering information during the session.

There are a couple of things you must be willing to do in order to receive deliverance. For some people they may not be easy things to do. Please pray and search your heart and decide if you are truly willing to do these things. If you aren't, you'll need to postpone scheduling your session until you are more prepared to deal with these things the way God would have you deal with them. If there are some areas that you are especially struggling with, let us know. We may be able to recommend some tapes or books that would help you get a handle on it.

*Salvation

I am assuming you have accepted Jesus Christ as your Lord and Savior. If you haven't, you need to do that before we can even talk about deliverance. If you need help with this, have questions, or want someone to pray with you, let us know. We are always glad to help.

*Forgiveness

By the time you have completed the survey, you will have had to recall people who have hurt you in some way in your life. Some in small ways and some in really big ways. You must be willing to forgive each and every one of these people. Forgiveness is absolutely essential and deliverance cannot take place until you have forgiven them. You can't hold anything back, you can't forgive with conditions or reservations. You can't do it grudgingly. You just have to make the decision that you will forgive them, now and forever. And you have to be willing to pray for them, to pray blessings on them. If you can't do that, you'll need to postpone scheduling your deliverance session and WORK on forgiving them.

Forgiveness the way God defines it is a new concept to a lot of us and if you don't know about it or understand it, let us recommend some books or tapes that will help you understand it. Forgiveness does not mean that you think what the person did was right, and it is not "letting him get away with it." It doesn't mean you weren't hurt. It is simply a decision you make in obedience to God. While Jesus was dying a horrible, painful, humiliating death on the cross, he asked God to 'forgive them for they know not what they do'. I heard it taught one time that even though he forgave them, he still felt the pain. That's the way forgiveness is. But forgiving someone is the first step toward making that pain stop.

Forgiveness is one of our greatest weapons against demonic forces. You must be willing to forgive each and every one before you come for deliverance or our hands are tied. If you want to forgive but you're not sure you can do it, the good news is you don't have to do it alone. Pray and ask God to help you with it. He never expects us to do things in our own power, just to be obedient to Him. If you ask, he'll help you get to a point of forgiveness. Study the word, get some teaching on it, and eventually, if you want to be free, you will be able to forgive. That's the time to schedule your deliverance session.

*Willing to give up habits and deliberate sin

Next you must be willing to give up your old bad habits, behaviors, addictions, and deliberate sin. You must be willing to discipline your flesh in regard to these things. These are really two different issues.

First, you must be willing to give up these old, bad habits. For a lot of people, bad habits and bad thought patterns are comfortable and familiar and you may not really want to give them up. You may have gotten pleasure from some of them. You may have used them to avoid difficult situations or to escape from things you find unpleasant. They may seem like the 'easy way' to do things.

For example, with forgiveness, it may be easier to hold a grudge than to have to deal with the problem. You may have developed unforgiveness as a way to protect yourself from having to feel the hurt. The same may be true with alcohol or drugs. You may have used it to dull emotional pain or to avoid having to deal with the realities of life. It may *seem* to be the easiest way. It is at least familiar and comfortable to you.

You know in your heart that it is not the easiest way, or you wouldn't have requested deliverance. But you must be willing to let go of those things entirely in order to receive freedom from them. You will be asked to repent of and renounce those things. If you aren't completely willing, again, ask God to help you to get in position to receive deliverance.

Along with this goes the willingness to destroy or at least get rid of permanently, any objects that you possess of a demonic nature. You will see some of these mentioned on the questionnaire. They may include objects of art, jewelry, clothing, games and the like. You must be willing to be rid of these things.

*Self discipline of your flesh

After renouncing bad habits and behaviors, addictions and deliberate sins, you must be willing to discipline your flesh to keep them out. This can be hard work and if you are not committed to it up front, we would not be doing you any favor to pray for deliverance for you. You can end up worse off than you are now. If you don't understand all that, read in Matthew 12 starting in verse 43. But we would be doing you a disservice if we prayed for you before you are ready to make the commitment to forsake the action and promise to resist going back to it.

This should be easier after deliverance, but it still requires self-discipline on your part. You must understand going in that deliverance is not a 'quick fix'. With successful deliverance, the demonic power is broken that may have been driving a certain behavior, feeling, thought process, habit or addiction. You may or may not feel a change after deliverance. We rely on faith and not feelings, remember? With the release from demonic power, freedom from the behavior may be immediate and permanent. But you must continue to discipline your flesh on a daily basis. You will have to exercise your will to keep from slipping back into old, bad habits.

The demonic powers will not be happy that you escaped them and will probably come back and try to talk you into going back to your old ways. Resisting should be easier after deliverance because the demon spirit has lost its power to *make* you do something. Now it can just try to trick you or talk you into it. You have the free will to refuse to indulge in the old behavior or habit. If you sense the old habit resurfacing, you must discipline yourself to resist it. Again, ask God to help you. You don't have to do it alone, but you do have to do it.

Deliverance cannot take the place of discipline, and discipline cannot take the place of deliverance. Both are needed and you must be willing to promise to do your part. If you're not yet ready, please postpone scheduling your session until you are.

*Faithful to attend church, home fellowship group. Stay in the word and in prayer. Live a holy life.

Another commitment you must make before undergoing deliverance is to stay connected to your church and the Word. This goes right along with what we were just talking about as far as keeping your deliverance and not letting the demons back in. It is absolutely essential that after deliverance you stay in the Word and in prayer. You must live as holy a life as you possibly can.

The best, and I believe possibly the only, way to do that is be in church regularly and we must have your promise that you will be faithful to attend church services and to stay closely connected to your church. I would also like to know that you are a faithful member of a home fellowship group. If I could require you to be a member of a home fellowship group I would, but at the very least I *strongly* recommend it. You *must* have a close system of support of mature Christians who can pray for you and help you walk out your deliverance. You need more personal care and support than you can get in a regular service. You need someone who knows you and with whom you can share your heart. That is the best way to head off problems at the pass, before they can take hold of your life again.

So we are asking for a commitment from you that you will stay in the Word and in prayer, that you will be faithful to attend church, and that you will have a support system of mature Christians.

Examine your heart and if you are willing to commit to these things, its time to schedule your session. I would ask right now that you get out your questionnaire and write on the upper right hand corner of the first page "yes" and today's date. Just write the word "yes" followed by today's date. Then we'll know you have listened to this tape and are in agreement and are ready to receive your deliverance. Then contact us to schedule your session.

We do ask that you spend time praying before your session. If you feel lead by God and are physically able, you will want to fast, too. Fasting can be a great help in disciplining the flesh and hearing what God has to say. Your deliverance team will be praying, too, to be ready to pray with you.

It's a good idea to spend some time beforehand meditating on the Word, especially the scriptures promising us freedom from demonic powers. This is helpful in building up you own faith level prior to being prayed for. The stronger your faith that God will answer your prayers, the stronger your faith when you pray those prayers. I would suggest these scriptures–Galatians 5:1, Hebrews 9:14, Matthew 18:18–19, First Corinthians 6:11, Luke 10:19, Ephesians 6:12 and Second Corinthians 10:4. There are many others, so just let the Lord lead you.

If you don't really understand what you're doing, I'd suggest you listen to some tapes or read some books on deliverance. I don't mean that you need to understand the whole process and how to do it. That's what we're here for. The Holy Spirit will direct the session and do the work, and your prayer team will facilitate His work. You don't need to learn the process, but you do need to have an understanding that deliverance was purchased for you by the Blood of Jesus and that it belongs to you as a believer. You also need to have an understanding of our authority in the name of Jesus, so that you will have confidence that our prayers have power and effect. If you need to learn more before your session, let us know and we will recommend some materials to help you.

Your session will probably take at least three hours and may take six hours or more. Please allow sufficient time in your personal schedule for the deliverance to be completed without rushing. Because of limited time of the deliverance teams, we will probably not be able to reschedule you for a second session because you ran out of time, and we don't want to leave anything undone. So you need to allow plenty of time.

You'll need to arrange for child care if you have children. The session must be uninterrupted and free from any distractions. You should come to the session alone. Please don't bring anyone with you without getting an okay from your deliverance team. Again, the session must be free of any distractions.

Your deliverance team will consist of at least two people. These people are carefully chosen and trained and anointed by the Holy Spirit to be doing the work they are doing. Don't be shy with them. People who work in the deliverance ministry truly love God's children and have only a desire to do His work by helping you get freedom and healing. They will guide you through the process gently and kindly. If you have heard things about deliverance in the past that may have concerned or even scared you, I can assure you that you have nothing to be scared about. No one is going to yell at you or do anything to frighten or harm you. Every team member has his own personality, of course, and so each session will be a little different. But it is the Holy Spirit doing the work and He is gentle and loving. So as your deliverance team submits themselves to the Holy Spirit, you can expect them to be gentle and loving as well.

If you have any real concerns or fears, call a member of your deliverance team ahead of time and discuss it. We want you to be able to come into the prayer session full of the hope and optimism and joy that God brings us. And we fully expect you to walk out full of freedom and victory in Jesus Christ.

WAIVERS

VOLUNTARY RELEASE, ASSUMPTION OF RISK AND INDEMNITY AGREEMENT

In consideration for being permitted to participate in voluntary prayer ministry, herein referred to as the "Prayer Ministry," the undersigned, _____ _____herein referred to as the "Releaser," agrees as follows:

1. *Release, Waiver, Discharge and Covenant not to Sue.* Releaser and Releaser's personal representatives, assigns, insurer, heirs, executors, administrators, spouse and next of kin, hereby releases, waives, discharges and covenants not to sue, (*Insert the name and address of your church or ministry*) and its directors, officers, employees, agents, volunteers as well as it successors, assigns, affiliates, subordinates, and subsidiaries, all herein referred to as the "Releasees," from any and all liability to Releaser, and to Releaser's personal representatives, assigns, insurer, heirs, executors, administrators, spouses and next of kin for any and all loss, damage, or cost on account of injury to the person or property or resulting in the death of Releaser, whether caused by the negligence of Releasees or otherwise while Releaser is participating in the Prayer Ministry and any other activities in connection with the Prayer Ministry.

2. *Assumption of Risk.* Releaser understands, is aware of, and assumes all risks inherent in participating in the Prayer Ministry. These risks include, but are not limited to, physical and emotional responses and reactions as a result of this prayer ministry.

3. *Indemnity.* Releaser agrees to indemnify Releasees from any liability, loss, damage or cost Releasees may incur due to the participation by Releaser in the Prayer Ministry whether caused by the negligence of Releasees or otherwise. Releaser assumes full responsibility for and risk of bodily injury, death or property damage due to negligence of Releasees or otherwise while participating in the Prayer Ministry.

Releaser expressly agrees that this Voluntary Release, Assumption of Risk and Indemnity agreement, herein referred to as "Agreement," is intended to be as broad and inclusive as permitted by the laws of the State of *(Insert name of your state)* and that, if any portion of this Agreement is held invalid, it is agreed that the balance, notwithstanding, continue in full legal force and effect. This Agreement contains the entire agreement between the parties in regard to the Prayer Ministry.

Releaser Represents That:

I have carefully read this agreement. I understand it is a release of all claims, including the negligence of releasees.

I understand that I assume all risks inherent in the prayer ministry set forth in this Agreement.

I understand that I am indemnifying the releasees.

I voluntarily sign my name evidencing my understanding and acceptance of the provisions of this agreement.

Dated: _____

_____   _____

Signature of Releaser   Printed Name of Releaser

_____

Witness

LIABILITY RELEASE
(MINOR'S)

I, the undersigned Parent or Guardian of: _____,
(a minor) jointly referred to as "Participant," state that I freely and voluntarily am requesting the prayers and spiritual guidance for my child by
(*Insert name and address of your church or ministry*) and its directors, officers,
employees, agents, volunteers as well as its successors, assigns, affiliates,
subordinates, and all persons associated with (*Insert name of your church or
ministry*) referred to herein as "(*Insert name of your church or ministry*) " I
state that I clearly understand that the Staff and volunteers of (*Insert name
of your church or ministry*) are not professional Psychologists, Psychiatrists,
Counselors, Medical Doctors, or Medical Experts but are Spirit-filled
believers, trained in God's word. With this understanding, it is my desire
to request spiritual assistance including but not limited to Deliverance,
physical and/or mental healing, and any other situation or condition
which I request prayer and help with or which prayer and guidance
are given to my child at or from (*Insert name of your church or ministry*)
("Prayer Ministry"), I do hereby waive forever on behalf of myself and
my child all liability and responsibility on the part of (*Insert name of your
church or ministry*) and all functions and organizations connected thereto
(either directly or indirectly), including but not limited to the Directors,
Officials, Officers, Staff, Employees, and all Personnel (both paid and
volunteer), regarding any and all aid, assistance, direction, or guidance
given or rendered to me and/or my child at my request by (*Insert name of
your church or ministry*), its staff, volunteers, parishioners, home care group
leaders, deliverance ministers, etc. The undersigned understands, is aware
of, and assumes all risks inherent in participating in the Prayer Ministry. These risks include, but are not limited to, physical and emotional
responses and reactions as a result of this Prayer Ministry. This Release of
Liability is binding upon the undersigned Participant's and their child's
heirs, successors, assigns, and personal representatives.

Participant Represents That:

I have carefully read this agreement. I understand it is a full, final and complete release of any and all claims, including negligence by *(enter the name of your church or ministry here)*.

I understand that I assume all risks inherent in the prayer ministry.

I understand that I am voluntarily signing my name on behalf of myself and my child evidencing my understanding and acceptance of the provisions of this agreement.

Dated: _____

_____
Signature of Parent/Guardian-Participant

_____   _____
Witness   Printed Name of Parent/Guardian

_____   _____
Signature of Minor   Printed Name of Minor

**LIABILITY RELEASE
(CHILDREN'S)**

I, the undersigned Parent or Guardian of: _____
(a minor) jointly referred to as "Participant," state that I freely and voluntarily am requesting the prayers and spiritual guidance for my child by *(Insert name of your church or ministry)* and its directors, officers, employees, agents, volunteers as well as its successors, assigns, affiliates, subordinates, and all persons associated with *(Insert name of your church or ministry)* referred to herein as "*(Insert name of your church or ministry)*." I state that I clearly understand that the Staff and volunteers of *(Insert name of your church or ministry)* are not professional Psychologists, Psychiatrists, Counselors, Medical Doctors, or Medical Experts but are Spirit-filled believers, trained in God's word. With this understanding, it is my desire to request spiritual assistance including but not limited to Deliverance, physical and/or mental healing, and any other situation or condition which I request prayer and help with or which prayer and guidance are given to my child at or from *(Insert name*

of your church or ministry) ("Prayer Ministry"), I do hereby waive forever on behalf of myself and my child all liability and responsibility on the part of *(Insert name of your church or ministry)* and all functions and organizations connected thereto (either directly or indirectly), including but not limited to the Directors, Officials, Officers, Staff, Employees, and all Personnel (both paid and volunteer), regarding any and all aid, assistance, direction, or guidance given or rendered to me and/or my child at my request by *(Insert name of your church or ministry),* its staff, volunteers, parishioners, home care group leaders, deliverance ministers, etc. The undersigned understands, is aware of, and assumes all risks inherent in participating in the Prayer Ministry. These risks include, but are not limited to, physical and emotional responses and reactions as a result of this Prayer Ministry. This Release of Liability is binding upon the undersigned Participant's and their child's heirs, successors, assigns, and personal representatives.

Participant Represents That:

I have carefully read this agreement. I understand it is a full, final and complete release of any and all claims, including negligence by *(enter the name of your church or ministry here).*

I understand that I assume all risks inherent in the prayer ministry.

I understand that I am voluntarily signing my name on behalf of myself and my child evidencing my understanding and acceptance of the provisions of this agreement.

Dated: _____

_____

Signature of Parent/Guardian-Participant

_____   _____

Witness   Printed Name of Parent/Guardian

_____   _____

Signature of Minor   Printed Name of Minor

Printed Name of First Child _____

Printed Name of Second Child _____

SUGGESTED READING AND TAPE LIST

(many of these resources may be ordered from The Arsenal –
www.arsenalbooks.com)

BOOKS:

Evicting Demonic Intruders, Noel & Phyl Gibson
New Wine Press
How to Cast Out Demons, A Guide to the Basics, Doris Wagner
Regal
They Shall Expel Demons, Derek Prince
Chosen Books
The Little Skunk, Sue Banks
Impact Christian Books

TAPES:

Doris Wagner, *Basic Issues in Deliverance* (1 tape)
Joseph Thompson, *Deliverance to Occult Members* (1 tape)
John Eckhardt, *How to Break Curses: The Demon Hit List* (1 tape)
Cindy Jacobs, *Witchcraft and Generational Iniquity* (1 tape)
Alice Smith, *Spiritual House Cleansing* (1 tape)
Frank Hammond, *Deliverance of Children* (1 tape)
Che Ahn, *How to Minister Physical Healing Through Deliverance* (1 tape)
Kimberly Daniels, *Deliverance Ministry in the Inner City* (2 tapes)
Doris Wagner, *Deliverance Seminar* (2 tapes)

ADDITIONAL STUDY:

BOOKS:

Strongman's His Name... What's His Game? Drs. Jerry & Carol Robeson
  Shiloh Publishing House
Strongman's His Name... II, Drs. Jerry & Carol Robeson
  Shiloh Publishing House

TAPES:

Pablo Bottari, *Facing the Enemy* (5 tapes)
Pablo Deiros, *Equipping the Soldiers* (4 tapes)
          Bible Study (4 tapes)
Ron Campbell, *Cursed No Longer-Freemasonry* (1 tape)
          Freemasonry (1 tape)
Carlos Mraida, *Healing the Army* (5 tapes)
          Bible Study (1 tape)
Randy Clark, *Renewal Service* (5 tapes)
Kimberly Daniels, *Who is the Strongman?* (2 tapes)
          Renewing the Mind (2 tapes)

INDEX

A

Abortion, 48, 83, 178, 201

Abuse, 58, 59, 60, 73, 82, 83, 89, 91, 124, 127, 128, 132, 163, 168, 170, 187, 199, 206, 225, 228

Addictions, 57, 61, 114, 116, 156, 217, 225

Adopted children, 49, 79, 113, 184

Adultery, 59, 78, 112, 153, 154, 155, 200, 242

Alcoholism, 57, 60, 62, 82, 168, 199, 217

Anal sex, 156

Anesthesia, 190

Angels, worship of, 131

Anger, 45, 52, 56, 58, 59, 62, 70, 75, 78, 134, 171, 175, 187, 188, 189, 190, 197, 198, 199, 212, 218, 230, 233, 234, 246

Ankhs, 120

Anoint, anointing, 121, 155, 193, 219

Anorexia, bulimia, 114, 227

Antichrist, spirit of antichrist, 92, 144, 146, 165, 183, 192

Authority to cast out demons, 23

B

Battle Plan, 184, 205, 206, 207, 214, 218, 222

Bestiality, 153, 155, 163

Binding demons, 45, 46, 48, 150, 177, 210, 211, 218, 227, 247

Bitterness, 59, 67, 187, 242

Blasphemies, swearing, obscenities, 84, 190

Blockages to Deliverance. *See Deliverance, blockages*

Blood pacts, 121, 193

Blood transfusion, 178

Bondage versus whoredoms, 115
Bondage, defined, 114
Bondage, spirit of bondage, 48, 113, 114, 116, 217
Broken spirit, 152, 174
Brokenhearted, 177
Bulimia, anorexia, 114, 227

C

Charmers, 119
Church background, 183
Closing doors, 193, 204, 216, 218
Combat, 198
Compulsions, 114, 116
Conceived out of wedlock, 78, 184
Confusion, 95, 114, 162, 169, 192, 206
Contention, 108, 133, 242
Controlling demons during deliverance, 44, 45, 131, 212
Controlling spirits, 122, 124, 125, 126, 156, 228
Conversing with demons, 131
Counter cultures, 202
Critical spirit, 163, 164, 185, 190, 214, 236
Curses, Buddhist, 199
Curses, generational (family), 89
Curses, witchcraft, 170, 193
Curses, word, 90, 124, 169, 170, 171, 176, 192, 193, 199, 206

D

Daydreams, 192
Deaf and dumb spirit, 148
Death, 177, 192, 199, 201, 218, 226, 227, 228
Death, spirit of death, 151
Delirium, fever, 94, 150, 190
Deliverance session, basics, 215

Deliverance session, instructions to individual, 212

Deliverance session, method, 209

Deliverance session, setting, 207

Deliverance team, function, 204

Deliverance team, training, 39

Deliverance, blockages, 47

Deliverance, blockages - bad habits, 48

Deliverance, blockages - fear, 48

Deliverance, blockages - inner walls, 48

Deliverance, blockages - unforgiveness, 47

Deliverance, blockages - unrepented sin, 48

Depression, spirit of, 83, 135, 149, 171, 190, 192

Devil defined, 51

Disciplining demons, 61

Disciplining Demons, 135

Divination, spirit of divination., 59

Doctrinal error, 166

Doubt, unbelief, 183, 189, 196

Dread. See Fear, See Spirit of Fear

Dream Catchers, 167

Dungeons and Dragons, 131, 194

E

Eagles, Moose Lodges, 95

Eastern Star, 96

Education, 85, 111, 126, 162, 189

Emotional manipulation, 122

Emotional Manipulation, 124

Entry Points, 55, *See Open doors,*

Epilepsy. See Deaf and dumb spirit

Error, Spirit of error, 143, 145

Escapism, 114, 192

ESP, 130

Exaggerate, exaggeration, 188

F

False religion, spirit of false religion, 59

Familiar spirits, 128

Fasting, 34, 40, 150, 205

Fear, spirit of, 54, 55, 58, 62, 83, 84, 94, 101, 113, 138, 141, 171, 175, 176, 177, 178, 184, 190, 193, 194, 196, 198, 199, 207, 212, 218, 225, 227, 228, 230, 232, 234, 243

Fever, delirium, 94, 150, 190

Forgiveness, 66, 68, 73, 80, 214

Forgiveness - empathy, 74

Forgiveness - forgiving God, 74

Forgiveness and cleaning out the closet, 67

Forgiveness from the heart, 68

Forgiveness, blockages – denial, 69

Forgiveness, blockages – guilt, 73

Forgiveness, blockages – prayer, 72

Fornication, 153, 188, 242

Freemasonry, 66, 90, 92, 100, 150, 183, 189, 191, 192, 206

Frustration, 134, 190

G

Garden of Eden, 15, 16, 18

Generational spirits, sins, 31, 58, 77, 86, 150, 177

God's eyes, 167

Good luck charms, 120

Grief, sorrow, 100, 101, 103, 136, 168, 200, 225, 228

Guilt, shame, 73, 83, 160, 162, 163, 175, 178, 198, 199, 201, 225, 232, 239

H

Halloween, 59
Handwriting- analysis, automatic, 119
Homosexual, Homosexuality, 153, 154, 163, 200
Hoodwinked, 27
How demons behave, 42, 44, 45, 47, 120
How demons enter, 58
Hypnotists, hypnosis, 131

I

Identifying demons, 53
Idleness, 106
Imaginary playmates, 130
Impatience, 189
Incest, 78, 153, 154, 225
Incubus, 201
Independence, 110
Infirmity, spirit of infirmity, 150, 177, 192
Iniquity, 87
Inner Walls, 48, 70, 72, 85, 189
Inner wounds, 175, 178
Intercessors, 40, 203
Intoxication, 190

J

Judgmentalism, 164, 166, 185

K

Ku Klux Klan, 96

L

Languages of love, 80
Lawlessness, spirit of lawlessness, 164

Legalism, 145
Legalism, legalistic, 166
Leper, 161
Love languages, 80
Lucifer, 14, 16, 31, 94, 106, 196
Lying, stealing, 145, 188, 233

M

Magicians, 119
Manipulation, 122, 127
Manipulation, intimidation, 84
Marriage, 48, 99, 153, 170, 179, 187
    Masons, *See Freemasonry*

Martial Arts, 197
Mediums, 100, 129
Mental illness, 149
Military, 198
Miscarriage, 178
Mocking spirits, 107
Moose, Eagles Lodges, 95
Mormonism, 96
Music, 114, 196

N

Names, 171
Names of demons, 53
Native Americans, 167, 169
Necromancy, 128

O

Obscenities, swearing, blasphemies, 84, 190
Obstinacy, 107

Occultism, 194

Oddfellows, 96, 191

Oklahoma Concert of Prayer, 50, 203

Open doors, 58, 162

Open Doors, 55

Organ transplant, 102, 178

Ouija boards, 59, 118, 129, 131, 216, 217

P

Pacts with the devil, 121

Passive mind states, 119

Past life regressions, 131

Paul hindered by Satan, 23

Pedophilia, Pedophile, 38, 153, 156

People pleaser, 184, 185, 227

Perfectionism, 84, 185

Performance, 84, 185

Perversion, spirit of perversion, 152, 153

Pornography, 114, 153, 155, 156

Possession, possessed, afflicted, oppressed, 25, 28, 196, 226

Praise, 31

Prayerlessness, 146, 242

Praying to the dead, 132

Prejudice, 84, 95, 111, 167, 189

Premature death, 151, 184

Pride, spirit of pride, 95, 106, 108, 109, 110, 111, 166, 167, 189, 202

Prince Hall Freemasonry, 95

Psychic powers, 129

Psychoanalysis, 190

Q

Questionnaire, understanding and using, 182

R

Rabshekeh, 53

Racial prejudice, 84, 95, 111, 167, 189

Rape, 59, 78, 94, 132, 163, 233

Rebellion, spirit of rebellion, 83, 109, 120, 146, 165, 189, 197, 198, 224, 225

Receiving deliverance, 30

Redeemed from the curse, 29

Rejection, defined, 76

Rejection, spirit of rejection, 43, 59, 62, 83, 84, 107, 108, 109, 140, 160, 164, 168, 175, 178, 184, 185, 186, 187, 188, 189, 202, 207, 218, 225, 227, 228

Rejection, types, 77

Religious spirit, 110, 145, 164, 166, 183, 185, 231

Reprobate mind, 153

Role of the pastor, 34

S

Satan's beginnings, Nature of Satan, 15, 16

Séances, 128

Seducing spirit, 144, 145, 146

Self-deception, 108

Self-Image, 83, 185, 202

Self-mutilation, 227, 228

Self-Righteousness, 109

Sexual sin, 98, 99, 111, 113, 153, 188, 200, 242

Shamanism, 167

Shame, guilt, 73, 83, 160, 162, 163, 175, 178, 198, 199, 201, 225, 232, 239

Shock, trauma, 175, 177

Shriners, Freemasonry, 95

Smoking, 48, 61, 62, 115

Sorrow, grief, 137, 168, 175, 228

Soul Ties, animals, 101, 113, 114

Soul Ties, breaking, 103

Soul Ties, demonic, 66, 98, 99, 100, 176

Soul Ties, sexual, 98

Spirit guides, 60, 130

Spirit of antichrist, 92, 144, 146, 165, 183, 192

Spirit of bondage, 48, 113, 114, 116, 217

Spirit of death, 151, 177, 192, 199, 201, 218, 226, 227, 228

Spirit of divination, 59, 118, 119, 120, 226

Spirit of error, 43, 143, 144, 145, 146, 152

Spirit of false religion, 59, 144, 145, 167, 168, 194, 195, 196

Spirit of fear, 54, 55, 58, 62, 83, 84, 94, 101, 113, 138, 141, 171, 175, 176, 177, 178, 184, 190, 193, 194, 196, 198, 199, 207, 212, 218, 225, 227, 228, 230, 232, 234, 243

Spirit of heaviness, depression, 83, 135, 149, 171, 190, 192

Spirit of infirmity, 150, 177, 192

Spirit of jealousy, 84, 102, 133, 189

Spirit of lawlessness, 146, 164, 189

Spirit of lust, 48, 54, 59, 128, 132, 153, 154, 156, 200

Spirit of perversion, 113, 152, 153, 154, 156

Spirit of pride, 45, 54, 84, 95, 107, 108, 110, 111, 166, 167, 185, 189, 200, 202

Spirit of rebellion, 83, 109, 120, 146, 165, 189, 197, 198, 224, 225

Spirit of rejection, 43, 62, 84, 168, 175, 184, 218

Spirit of sorrow, grief, 100, 101, 103, 136, 168, 175, 200, 225, 228

Spirit of whoredoms, 112, 113, 115, 116, 117, 200

Spirits of guilt and shame, 73, 83, 160, 162, 163, 175, 178, 198, 199, 201, 225, 232, 239

Spiritual manipulation, 124

Stealing, lying, 145, 188, 233

Strife, 52, 107, 133

Strongholds, 52, 168, 190, 227

Strongman, Strongmen, 51, 53, 106, 107, 112, 133, 135, 138, 140, 143, 144, 146, 149, 150, 151, 152, 178, 185

Succubus, 201

Suicide, 38, 149, 151, 168, 192, 199, 225

Superstitions, 195

Swearing, blasphemies, obscenities, 84, 190

Symptoms of a family curse, 89

T

Tattoos, 197, 198

Trail of Tears, 168

Training the team, 39

Traits of a successful deliverance minister, 35

Transcendental meditation, 130, 194

Trauma prayer, 178, 234

Trauma, shock, 175, 177

Twisting scriptures, 125, 153

U

Unbelief, doubt, 183, 189, 196

Unforgiveness, 67, 68, 72, 73, 164, 175, 185, 242

Unrepentant sin, 219

V

Victim, victim spirit, 61, 127, 135, 156, 220

Vietnam veterans, 198

Violence, 90, 94, 133, 134, 184, 186, 187, 189, 194, 197, 198, 200

Vision Quest, 167

Voodoo, 197

W

Walking out deliverance, 56, 66, 228, 229, 236

Warring Spirits, 166, 169

Water witching, 119

Whoredoms, spirit of whoredoms, 112, 113, 115, 116, 117, 200

Wicca, 118, 156, 194, 226

Witchcraft, 43, 52, 54, 60, 100, 118, 120, 121, 122, 125, 156, 183, 193, 194, 195, 196, 197, 226, 234

Word Curse, 59, 66, 90, 124, 169, 170, 171, 176, 192, 193, 199, 206, 232

Word of Knowledge, 73

Worry, worrier, 83, 140, 152, 190, 213

Y

yoga, 195

Yoga, 129, 195